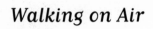

Walking on Air

Walking on Air

The Aerial Adventures of
PHOEBE OMLIE

Janann Sherman

University Press of Mississippi • Jackson

Willie Morris Books in Memoir and Biography

www.upress.state.ms.us

Designed by Peter D. Halverson

The University Press of Mississippi is a member of the Association of
American University Presses.

Photograph on page ii by P. W. Hamilton, photographer for the *Minneapolis
Tribune.* Phoebe Omlie Collection.

First printing 2011
∞
Library of Congress Cataloging-in-Publication Data

Sherman, Janann.
Walking on air : the aerial adventures of Phoebe Omlie / Janann Sherman.
p. cm. — (Willie Morris books in memoir and biography)
Includes bibliographical references and index.
ISBN 978-1-61703-124-3 (cloth : alk. paper) — ISBN 978-1-61703-125-0 (ebook)
1. Omlie, Phoebe Fairgrave, 1902–1975. 2. Women air pilots—United States—
Biography. 3. Air pilots—United States—Biography. 4. Aeronautics—United
States—History—20th century. I. Title.
TL540.O45S56 2011
629.13092—dc22 [B]   2010053401

British Library Cataloging-in-Publication Data available

To Charlie,
who taught me how to live

Contents

Acknowledgments

So many people have helped and guided me throughout this long journey. The following people have helped me find information, read my drafts, kept up my spirits, and most of all, never let me down.

I'm listing names alphabetically but, because I've spent my whole life as an "S," I'm doing so in reverse order: Pat Thaden Webb, Susan Ware, June Viviano, Steve Trimble, Heather Taylor, Michael Shenk, Matt Shearer, Janet Scott, Thelma Rudd, Cathie Rochau, Patrick Pidgeon, Shirley Oakley, Lisa Norling, Kim Nichols, Dee Navrkal, Vicki Murrell, Lynn Mirassou, Bob Minter, John McWhorter, Chriss Lyon, Marilyn Locke, Betsy Kidd, Jim Kacarides, Jim Johnson, Betty Huehls, Candice Hawkinson, Della May Hartley-Frazier, Ken and Jerry Guthrie, Andrea and Mattie Green, Velma Gillispie, Jim Fulbright, Harry Friedman, Delories Duncan, Patti du Toit, Charles Crawford, Lisa Cotham, Beverly Bond, Meg and Mike Bartlett, Paula Barnes.

I hope I haven't forgotten anyone. I am profoundly grateful to you all.

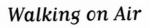

Walking on Air

Chapter One

Aviation pioneer Phoebe Fairgrave Omlie was once one of the most famous women in America. In the 1930s, her words and photographs were splashed across the front pages of newspapers across the nation. The press called her "second only to Amelia Earhart Putnam among America's women pilots," and First Lady Eleanor Roosevelt named her among the "eleven women whose achievements make it safe to say that the world is progressing."

Phoebe Fairgrave began her career in the early 1920s when aviation was unregulated and wide open to those daring enough to take it on, male or female. She bought a plane, established her own flying circus, and did stunts for the movies. She later earned the first commercial pilot's license issued to a woman and became a successful air racer. During the New Deal, she became the first woman to hold an executive position in federal aeronautics. For twenty years, she was centrally involved in the development of commercial and private aviation policy and production.

Yet somehow she got lost to history.

She was forgotten partly because of the long shadow of Amelia Earhart, which has obscured the achievements of many daring women pilots, and partly because of the sad circumstances of her decline and death. She died in poverty and obscurity. Personal papers, documents of her life and achievements, were scattered and gone.

She grew up rootless and perhaps that helped shape what she was to become, although one should be cautious about overdetermining a life. She was born into a troubled marriage between Madge Traister and Harry John "Jack" Park, a day laborer, in Des Moines, 21 November 1902, two years behind her only sibling, Paul. Named for her maternal grandmother, Phoebe Jane was six when her parents divorced in 1908.[1] Although Madge told her children that their father had died, Jack Park had a distressing way of turning up occasionally until his actual death in a car accident in Missouri in 1962.[2] At least twice in later years, Jack tried to make contact with his children: in 1943, he knocked on his son's door in Omaha, and he once tried to speak to Phoebe after an air meet in Cleveland, but she rebuffed him with the remark that he couldn't be her "real" father, her father was dead.[3]

Three years after the Parks divorced, Madge married Andrew E. Fairgrave, who was himself divorced from a childless marriage. In 1915, Andrew and Madge and her two children, Paul, aged fifteen, and thirteen-year-old Phoebe, moved to St. Paul, Minnesota. From 1916 to 1919, Andrew Fairgrave ran a saloon downtown. After that, though his business was still in the same spot, he changed to soft drinks and "near-beer" with the advent of Prohibition.[4]

Phoebe and her brother attended Mechanic Arts High School, which emphasized training in both the liberal arts and manual arts. The approximately 1,500 students were a diverse mix of children from families with modest incomes, including recent and second-generation immigrants from Ireland, Norway, Austria, Germany, Poland, and Sweden, with a handful of African American families.[5] Mechanic Arts self-consciously saw itself as "a working model of the melting pot," emphasizing equality of opportunity, regardless of ancestry, race, gender, or economic status. Any student could aspire to leadership in the school.[6]

Phoebe thrived in this environment. She enjoyed working with her hands as well as her mind. In her third year, despite her diminutive size and her gender, she was elected president of her junior class. Her classmates noted that she was "the first girl to hold office as president of a Mechanic Arts class, but we felt that Phoebe was competent and had enough executive ability to manage the class successfully."[7] Her friend, Hugh O'Neill, whom she replaced as junior class president when he moved away, included her in his final poem, "History of the Class of 1920." She appears in the eighth stanza:

I forgot to mention, you'll excuse it, I hope,
A feminine head of suffragette note—
Miss Phoebe J. Fairgrave who took up the stroke
When the masculine head disembarked from the boat.[8]

While at Mechanic Arts, Phoebe was active in the Cogwheel Club, which wrote for and edited the school newspaper, and the Mechanic Arts Literary Society, which compiled and published a periodical of students' stories and poems called *The M.* In addition to creative writing, Phoebe found drama a welcome vehicle to act out her fantasies and build her self-confidence.[9] She worked on school plays during her junior and senior years, and starred in her senior revue's playlet "When Love is Young," which her yearbook noted was "exceptionally well acted." She even briefly enrolled in the Guy Durrel Dramatic School, despite her parents' efforts to discourage her from pursuing drama. They were especially keen for her to go to the university in the fall; her brother Paul had disappointed them by opting out.[10] But she already had other, grander ideas about her future, formulated during a chance encounter with the greatest adventure she could imagine.

She was in physics class when the idea struck her. The year was 1919, her senior year at Mechanic Arts, and her head was filled with plans to become an actress. The sound that drove her to the window that spring day would change everything. She looked up to see three enormous biplanes, flown by veterans of the recent war, make a low salute to President Woodrow Wilson as his motorcade wound through the streets. The president had come to St. Paul on his tour to promote his League of Nations, determined to win support from the people when he found little in Washington. He received a tumultuous reception in St. Paul where they pulled out all the stops in making him welcome. Wilson arrived by special train and was greeted by "a seething, undulating, cheering mass of humanity." Some 45,000 people stormed the Kenwood Armory where the president was to speak, although he would be heard only by "the 10,000 vigorous" who got there first.[11] Among the disappointed were "Toiling and moiling, sweating and swearing, men ready to fight, women hysterical, children almost suffocating . . . like a great human whirlpool . . . . Some were there who had come hundreds of miles to listen to Mr. Wilson."[12] The president's parade, including "several hundred War Camp Community girls in costume, more than 1000 discharged soldiers in uniform [and] the government's reception committee," was serenaded by troops of singing schoolchildren along the route. Overhead thundered an aerial escort of military planes. As they followed the procession, the planes paused from time to time to do aerobatic stunts—steep climbs and rolls—in order to accommodate the speed of the planes to the pace of the parade.[13] This is what Phoebe saw outside her classroom window. She later described her response to the noise, the power, the sunlight flashing off the spinning propellers, the sheer grandeur of those airplanes.

> As the three planes zoomed across the capitol park, on upward against our fabled Minnesota sky-blue back-drop, my heart did a series of nip-ups which rocked me to depths I didn't know existed in human makeup. And out of the brief, violent inner tempest arose a vast yearning so intense that my very bones ached. Oh, how I wanted to fly! There was no gradual development or emergence, instead it was a vast compulsion such as makes butterflies burst from their cocoons and which defies description. I can only say that long before those airplanes had reached the top of their zooms, I was forever enthralled. Then, as the little clickers of sunlight on the upper surfaces of the top wings beckoned to me to come on up out of this world I recall distinctly saying to myself, "That's what I want to do . . . this is it!" And from that moment hence my eyes have never been out of the heavens.[14]

The show was life changing, though it is unlikely that it was her first introduction to the romance of flight. While military planes signaled the thrill of sheer power, young women like Phoebe also had female role models among these daring young fliers. The most prominent of these at this time was Ruth Law.[15] Law's spectacular flying circus made annual appearances in the Twin Cities during Phoebe's formative years, from 1915 (shortly after Phoebe's family moved to St. Paul) into the 1920s, when Phoebe was competing with Law for fair contracts.[16]

Aviatrix Ruth Law had been front-page news since she executed thirty-five consecutive loop-the-loops in her open Curtiss Headless Pusher aeroplane over Lake Michigan in September 1916. Law made this plane famous, and it became the most widely used exhibition plane between 1909 and World War I. The pilot sat on a seat in the open-air forward of the wings, feet planted on rudders and gripping two "sticks"; the engine was mounted behind the wings. Built of wood and bamboo with flight surfaces of varnished linen, the plane was stable and maneuverable but expensive: in 1911 a complete Pusher delivered from the factory in Hammondsport, New York, cost between $4,500 and $6,000 (the equivalent of over $100,000 today).[17]

In 1916, Law set distance and speed records in a flight from Chicago to New York, landing at Hornell, New York, 590 miles nonstop from Chicago. She took on minimal fuel to complete her journey to New York City. As her engine faltered from lack of gas over Harlem, she rocked the plane to splash fuel into the carburetor, and landed completely dry in a precision dead-stick landing on Governor's Island.[18] Her spectacular show in New York that December captured the front pages again. As President Wilson, aboard his yacht *Mayflower* in New York harbor, touched a button to light up the Statue of Liberty, Ruth Law flew out of the darkness carrying magnesium flares on her wingtips and an electric sign spelling "Liberty" on her plane's lower wing.[19] By 1917, she had established herself as America's premier female flier, holding records for flying continuous loops, cart-wheeling her plane wing over wing, flying upside down for a mile and a half, and flying to an altitude of 11,200 feet.[20]

Before the United States was officially involved in the war, Law went to Europe, flew with French aviators, reported back about the front, and demonstrated "the latest flying tactics in the great war" at county fairs.[21] She enlisted in the U.S. Aviation Corps, eager to fly combat missions; the military authorized her to wear a uniform but denied her permission to fly in combat. Instead she served as a recruiting officer, dressed in the smart khaki uniform they permitted: a visored cap, regulation breeches and put-tees, with her khaki collar ornamented with bronze eagles. She predicted that sooner or later Uncle Sam would come to his senses and make use of women in the army aviation service before the war ended.[22] Failing to go to battle, Law engaged in "bombing" the midwestern states with pleas to buy liberty bonds.[23] Her frustrated cry to "Let Women Fly!" was published in *Air Travel* and repeated in many newspapers. Her achievements reflected glory on all American women, noted an article entitled "Ruth Law, Hailed as New Superwoman, Destined to Lead Her Sex to Achievement." She was proving to all the world that "being a woman is not a handicap, that, after all, women can do anything."[24]

Before the war was over, Law had established a flying circus and began signing state fair contracts for shows throughout the Midwest. These featured all her tricks including automobile-to-plane transfers, aerobatic stunts, flying through fireworks, wing-walking, and illuminated night flying. Her shows were well-staged extravaganzas and enormously popular.[25] Indeed, on the very eve of President Wilson's visit, the *St. Paul Pioneer Press* described an event at nearby White Bear, where Lt. Ray Miller, flying a Curtiss Flying Boat called the "Sea Gull," took a number of young women, described as "embryo Ruth Laws . . . for trips in the clouds." Much to their apparent delight, Miller treated them to a full complement of stunts: loop-the-loop, the "falling leaf," and Immelman spirals. The falling leaf required the aircraft to be stalled and forced into a spin; as soon as the spin began, the controls were reversed to force the spin in the opposite direction. The Immelman, also known as roll-off-the-top, is an ascending half-loop followed by a half-roll. These maneuvers were almost certain to inspire nausea in inexperienced fliers. Although none of them as yet had attempted to follow Law's career path, wrote the reporter, many were hoping for an airplane in their future.[26]

Phoebe clearly had the same dreams. The Saturday following the president's visit, she determined to go have a closer look at these marvelous machines. She took the trolley to the end of the line, then hiked a mile along a gravel road to reach the fence at the Curtiss Northwest Flying Field. There she beheld two JN4D biplanes, affectionately called "Jennys." "What a joy they were to behold," she later recalled, "so beautiful, so magnificent and so utterly unafraid." Visiting this airfield became a ritual as the final year of her high school career unfolded. To her, "those two Jennys became living, breathing creatures, as animate as any pet I've ever owned."[27]

Throughout the summer after graduation, she worked at a series of unsatisfying jobs, trying to earn money so she could "break into flying." She worked as secretary at the Noiseless Typewriter Company, manager of the candy counter at the Emporium Department Store, stenographer at an insurance company. Daydreaming about flying was distracting so none of the jobs lasted very long. She lived for Sunday afternoons and her trips to the field. Every weekend she positioned herself closer and closer to the hangar, until by and by she stood by the gate, where she could see and hear the mechanics working. And once in a while, she would thrill to "the heavenly call from the office to 'roll her out.'" She stood there with her face pressed against the perimeter fence, watching pilots come out, trim the plane, twirl the prop, and take off. Despite her position close by, the men ignored her.[28]

After several months, Phoebe decided to venture inside. She had come to realize that the only way she could get the men to pay attention to her was to propose to buy an airplane.[29] She entered the hangar, asked to see the president, and said she wanted to buy a Jenny. She thought such a declaration would, at the least, earn her a test flight, much like someone buying a car would take it for a test drive. At the most, it might afford her an opportunity to learn to fly. The manager, William Kidder, told her that they did not teach flying, only sold airplanes. Their completely overhauled and refurbished war surplus Jennys cost $3,500 (the equivalent of $38,152 today).[30] When she didn't flinch at the price, Kidder introduced her to a salesman. He took her out on the line, walked her around the huge machine, even let her climb in the cockpit for a look at the instrument panel. But when she asked for a demonstration flight, he told her that if she was interested in buying, he would take her up for $15, which would be deducted from the purchase price if she bought the plane. She didn't have the $15 but vowed to return.[31]

After this close encounter with a Jenny, Phoebe was more determined than ever to find a way to own one. She had been reading all she could find about aviation. A few popular magazines carried stories about exhibition flying and the daring young men who did it. She followed the exploits of wing-walker Ormer Locklear, the first man to change planes in midair, who had been lured to Hollywood to perform the first car-to-plane transfer on film in *The Great Air Robbery* (1919).[32] She read about Ruth Law and her spectacular exhibitions, and she read about Charles Hardin, who had invented a new kind of parachute he called the "Lifepack."[33] It was this last story that particularly caught her attention. Hardin lived just across the river in Minneapolis, and she vowed to investigate his invention further.[34] Phoebe was a big fan of the Saturday serial, *The Perils of Pauline*, that featured a consistently victimized, but always triumphant, young woman.[35] Thinking about it, she believed that about the only escape from peril that Pearl White, who played Pauline, had not yet employed was by parachute. So Phoebe hatched a plan. She would go to the film company, sell them on the idea of using her as a double for Pearl White in a parachute stunt, and earn enough money to buy that Jenny.[36]

Fox produced *The Perils of Pauline*, and Fox Film Corporation had an office in Minneapolis.[37] Phoebe dropped by and proposed her bold plan for doing aviation stunts for the movies. What she did not know at the time was that the local manager, Mr. Weisfeldt, was simply a distributor and had neither clout nor contact with Hollywood. Nonetheless, apparently charmed by the young woman, he treated her kindly, asking if she could fly. No, but she was going to learn. Did she have a plane? No, but she was going to buy one. Had she ever jumped with a parachute? No, but she was going to. He told her that he thought she had a good idea and that when she was ready, she should come back and see him. To her, his remark was tantamount to a signed contract.[38]

Next she arranged to meet Charley Hardin at the airport. He arrived with a large canvas bag carrying what to her looked like soiled sheets. She helped him spread the parachute on the grass to air and then refold. She talked with Hardin and his wife, Kathryn, whom Phoebe was pleased to find was not much larger than she. Kathryn had made numerous jumps at local fairs and carnivals. The Hardins provided some rudimentary instructions about how to use the shroud lines to spill a little air out of the canopy in order to control the parachute's direction of drift, and warned that spilling too much air would cause the canopy to collapse sending her plummeting to earth. Nonetheless, the Hardins assured her that parachute jumping was not at all dangerous if she was careful about packing her own chute.[39]

Hot-air balloonists commonly carried parachutes but the contraption was not popular with pilots. Chutes were bulky affairs, packed into large duffle bags that were affixed to the landing brace. Those wishing to use one, then, had to climb out of the plane, crawl beneath the fuselage and hang with one arm on the running gear as they fastened the chute onto their harness, jump free of the plane, and hope the pull of their falling bodies would open the chute. Given this state of the art, most pilots preferred to trust their ability to land a crippled plane rather than rely upon "a hunk of rag."[40] But Phoebe was enchanted with the idea of jumping and convinced by the Hardins that it was safe and fun. They agreed to make her a special chute trimmed with blue ribbon to reflect the Mechanic Arts High School colors.[41]

Now, about the airplane. To date she had managed to save only $300. She needed $3,500 for the plane and $500 for the parachute. She tried to borrow money on the strength of her "contract" with Fox, despite the fact that it was, at best, a verbal expression of interest. Finally, she approached the bank of "Mom," extolling the wonders of flying and the potential for huge profits from movie work and exhibition flying. Her mother agreed to loan her the money, but suggested they keep the deal secret from Dad, who might not be so receptive to the idea. The money had been painstakingly saved in anticipation of opening a new saloon.[42] Mrs. Fairgrave's one stipulation, besides a strict repayment schedule, was that Phoebe interest her brother, Paul, in her endeavors. She would not allow her daughter to engage in such activity unchaperoned. This apparently was not an obstacle, as Paul immediately began learning to fly.[43]

On a cold January day in 1921, Phoebe took her stack of $20 and $50 travelers' checks to the Curtiss Northwest Company to purchase her plane. She was finally entitled to a ride. Excited and scared, bundled up in a borrowed fur-lined flying suit, sheepskin-lined boots, helmet, and goggles, she was boosted into "MY great big beautiful Jenny!" The pilot, Ray Miller, lifted his thumb to a man standing in front of the propeller, and called, "contact." "Contact," the man replied, giving the propeller a couple of turns, then pulling it through. The engine started with a loud roar, the plane vibrating fiercely, making the needles in the instruments in front of her dance. Now that her dream of flight was finally happening, Phoebe's stomach lurched. Anyone who says "that he or she flew for the first time without fiddle-taut nerves" is lying, she later wrote. But once she left the ground, her nerves gave way to wonder. "The tiny toy farm buildings, their roofs bare against the frosted earth, looked like decorations on a giant wedding cake . . . It was such an exalted experience that I felt a bit overcome and lay my head back against the cowling. As I did my eyes were raised into the blue infinity of heaven. The sublimity and grandeur of the sky as seen far above the earth's dust and haze remains overpowering to behold, and I still find it difficult to breathe in the rapture of it all."[44]

Her poetic reverie was soon shaken by Miller's aggressive, even sadistic, approach to flying. He startled her with a "quick, violent shake" of the controls, then signaled her with a circular motion of his hand. Not comprehending his message, she simply nodded and smiled to indicate that she was enjoying the ride. She soon learned what he meant. He dropped the nose into a steep power dive, then hauled back on the stick, going straight up. For a heart-stopping moment, the huge biplane hung in the air, then fell off to the left, spinning toward the earth. At the last moment, Miller pulled out of the spin, turned, and grinned at her. Then he suddenly flipped the plane upside down, flooding the carburetor and causing the engine to cough ominously. Once they were again right side up, Miller shouted to ask how she liked it. Not wanting to appear as frightened as she felt, she nodded vigorously, which he justly took as encouragement. He then proceeded to take her through a series of snap rolls, wingovers, and loops in rapid succession followed by a long tailspin. Her stomach pitched in time with the maneuvers, but she was determined not to show the slightest weakness. Once the plane was finally safely on the ground, Miller asked her how she liked the ride. She responded that it was great and that she'd be back for more.[45]

But, as it happened, it would be a long time before she got another ride. She took the trolley and walked to the airfield every weekend, but all the available men were simply too busy to bother with her. Yes, she was the proud owner of an airplane, but without someone to take her up in it, the plane had to remain parked in the hangar. It was not until a new pilot arrived on the scene that she got her chance.[46]

Vernon Omlie strode onto the airfield one day in early spring. Tall and ruggedly handsome, he was a twenty-five-year-old veteran of the Great War and an experienced flight instructor.[47] Like so many veteran fliers, he was searching for a way to make a living in aviation. At that time there were few opportunities beyond entertainment. He flew exhibitions and competed in stunts at the Minnesota State Fair in 1919, then joined Clarence Hinck and his Federated Fliers' barnstorming tour in 1920, flying exhibitions and "hopping" passengers.[48] Omlie flew the first forest fire patrols in the United States over the Minnesota woods. And he once flew a calf from the twin cities to South Dakota to demonstrate that cattle could be transported by air. After failing to establish his own company in Aberdeen, he ran a garage in Minneapolis during the winter, and worked for Curtiss Northwest ferrying planes to new owners during the summer.[49] He also served as pilot for Arthur C. Townley, head of the Non-Partisan League, an agrarian political organization.[50]

This day, he had come to the field to prepare the League's two Curtiss Orioles stored there for the coming summer tours. Phoebe joined the group gathered around the popular Omlie. "It was not one of those theatric moments when a young girl's heart is supposed to go pit-a-pat," Phoebe later recalled. "He looked more like a pilot than anyone I'd yet seen, and all my thoughts in those days were centered on aeronautics . . . . What I felt . . . was that maybe here was someone who would extend a helping hand."[51] She wasn't looking for romance; she was looking for a pilot. She was in business; she needed to make money right away to pay off her debt. Phoebe began a conversation with Vernon by referring to her classmate Bonita Townley, Arthur's daughter. She told him that she owned a plane and wanted to learn stunts, and complained that no one would work with her nor teach her to fly. She told him of her "contract" with the movies and insisted that she needed to get going in order to earn money to repay her loan for the plane. Unlike the other pilots at the field, he listened attentively. Apparently intrigued by this tiny young girl with the steely determination, he looked dubiously at her slight frame and told her that she would first have to build up her strength before he would consider helping her prepare stunts.[52] When she could chin herself twenty times from a hanging position, without touching the floor, they would start her training. That was just the incentive she needed. Within a few weeks, by the time the weather turned warm, she was ready.[53]

Vernon turned out to be the perfect foil for Phoebe. He took it upon himself to temper her youthful enthusiasm when that threatened to lead to dangerous recklessness. He spent time on the ground explaining the rudi-ments of aerodynamics, trying to familiarize her with how airplanes flew and how they responded in certain situations. The Jenny was an enormous biplane. Its fuselage was 27.5 feet long, with a 43.7-foot wingspan. Its two wings were supported by heavy struts, four between the wings on each side and four short ones beside and in front of the front cockpit. On top of the top wing was a short strut that supported guy wires leading to the fuselage. Guy wires laced back and forth between the wings, providing abundant handholds. "They used to say that after the mechanics had rigged the plane," wrote Charles Planck about the Jenny, "that is, adjusted the wires and struts for the best flying position, they would put a canary in between the wings. If he got out, the plane wasn't rigged right."[54] Phoebe was short enough that she could almost stand upright between the wings. Vernon showed her where she could step on the wing, where the ribs joined a spar. The rest of the wing was unsupported fabric covered with a hardening agent called "dope"; if she stepped there, her foot could easily go right through the wing. He suggested Phoebe wear close-fitting clothing that would not easily catch the wind, basketball shoes with suction cups attached to the soles to help her footing, and a harness with belts around her waist and thighs.[55]

Vernon rigged a safety line from the cockpit to her harness. He told her to be sure to stay in front of the rigging because if she slipped or lost her hold, the prop blast would glue her to the wires long enough to get another grip. When they reached 2,000 feet, he gave her the signal to climb out of the cockpit and walk along the wing to the end of her tether. Each day he lengthened the rope, allowing her to travel a bit further. By the time she was allowed to go the full length, she was familiar with every inch of the rigging and wing surface; she could have done the walking blindfolded. One day she forgot about using the safety rig until she was standing on the wing with her leg wound around the outer-bay strut. She felt free and confident, but Vernon was vigorously waving at her to come back. She ignored him, wanting to show what she could do, so she climbed onto the top of the wing and stood up, holding the upper mast. As she looked down into the cockpit at Vernon, he sharply waggled the controls to express his displeasure. She hastily climbed back down.[56]

Once they had landed, Vernon told her that they had to work together as a team, that each had to know what the other planned and was thinking, or they would court serious trouble and, he implied, he would work with her no more.[57] Still the safety line was clearly more of a psychological tether than a safety one since if she'd fallen while still attached to it, there was little either of them could do to rescue her. She would not be able to climb back up the rope to save herself, given the speed and strength of the relative wind of the prop. Vernon did not dare turn the Jenny loose in order to help since the plane would immediately slip into a spin, especially with the human drag dangling below. And, of course, landing with her in that position was out of the question.

As they worked together, Phoebe worried that Vernon would soon return to flying for Townley. But as it happened, the problem resolved itself. One day as they arrived at the field, they found the hangar containing the League's two Curtiss Orioles had burned to the ground. The organization could not afford to buy another ship, so Vernon was effectively released from that job. He was left only with a verbal contract with Curtiss Northwest for $25 a week, and much more free time to work with Phoebe.[58]

Once she felt comfortable wing-walking, Phoebe was eager to tackle the parachute jump. Charley Hardin brought her beribboned parachute to the field, and she spent long hours learning to pack and repack the chute. It was critically important that the chute be dry and freshly packed immediately before takeoff to minimize the possibility of the silk sticking together and tangling. The chute was packed into a duffle bag and tied to the strut of the landing gear.[59]

They planned the whole stunt very carefully. Vernon would climb the plane to 1,200 feet and pass over the field, flying into the wind while estimating the approximate wind drift of the chute. When he had the plane lined up properly, he would tap her on the shoulder as a signal for her to climb down. Phoebe first practiced on the ground the difficult and complex journey to reach the chute. She climbed out of the cockpit, down over the leading edge of the wing. She placed one foot on the shock absorber, being very careful not to step on the tire because once in the air, the wheel would turn. Then she had to slide herself through the landing gear struts into position next to the chute tied to the spreader-board of the axle. This was much more dangerous than walking among the struts on the wing. She had little to hang onto and this time the slipstream would be against her. If she slipped, the wind would blow her away. Once she felt stable on the axle, she would clip the chute to the harness around her waist. As soon as he saw her in position, Vernon would throttle back, the signal for her to cut loose. Make sure the snaps are good and secure, he instructed, and don't jump until you are certain you are ready. We can always go around again. Given the signal, Phoebe would slide off the strut until she was hanging by her harness. Then she was to pull the cord attached to the flaps that held the chute in the bag, and jump. As she fell clear of the plane, the folded silk should play out of the bag like a fire hose, first the shroud lines, then the canopy itself. To keep the whole thing from dropping out of the bag at the moment of the cut-away, the vent (or crown) of the chute was tied to the bag with a piece of light twine that was supposed to break after the chute was fully deployed.[60]

Finally it was time to try it in the air. They decided not to tell anyone because of the experimental nature of the jump. There would be ample time to alert the press later. Phoebe did tell her mother. She enlisted her brother to vouch that she was well trained for the jump, and that Vernon was such a careful pilot that he would never approve the jump until he was certain Phoebe could do it safely. Her mother promised to bring her dad to the field, although she would not tell him beforehand why they were there.[61]

It was a beautiful spring day, the seventeenth of April, and many people were milling around the airport enjoying the nice weather. Phoebe repacked her chute very carefully. Then she climbed aboard. All the practice and care paid off. She jumped free of the plane without a hitch. It felt like being in a "high, gossamer swing where the oscillation is as smooth as the silk above you. There is no noise, strain, or mechanical vibration and no feeling of descending speed." She looked up to see Vernon circling nearby; down below her brother Paul, and his passenger Charley Hardin, bounced across fields and through ditches trying to follow her in his car. Phoebe was so entranced with the view, "the dull light of the setting sun against the big white umbrellas which, set against the background of the blue sky . . . was so enchantingly beautiful" that she forgot to look where she was going until she was only a few hundred feet off the ground. Ahead was a small stand of trees, which from the air looked "soft and inviting." She slid through the branches until her chute caught on a tree top. Dangling several feet off the ground, she unsnapped her harness and dropped to her feet. People rushed toward her; among them were her mother and father. Her parents, perhaps grateful that she had survived, hugged her close and, apparently accepting the inevitable from their headstrong daughter, chose to be proud of her.[62]

Word about a young girl who jumped soon reached the press, and several members turned up at the field the next day to talk to her.[63] She told reporters that parachute jumping was even more exciting than doing stunts on the wings of speeding airplanes, and she intended to make it a regular practice from now on. "I find no trouble in climbing anywhere on a moving plane, but I was just a little scared when I began to sail through the air. And I almost lost my nerve before I made the jump. But after this I am sure I shall like it." Phoebe announced that she was planning a tour of county fairs with her brother, giving "dare-devil exhibitions."[64]

All that spring, Phoebe trained herself to do a host of standard stunts and some of her own invention. As it turned out, her brother did not become her pilot. Although he traveled with Phoebe on her exhibition circuit throughout the summer of 1921, it was Vernon who flew the plane.[65] A little over a month following that first jump, on 21 May, Vernon officially quit his job with Curtiss Northwest to work full time as Phoebe's pilot. Despite her lack of resources, Phoebe offered him $75 a week plus expenses, in addition to what they could make "hopping passengers" during the barnstorming season.[66] She also arranged to sell stunts to the movie companies, although it was not as lucrative as she had at first assumed. In the early years of the Hollywood stunt pilots, for example, the going rate for a midair transfer was about $25; crashing an airplane paid $100.[67]

After a couple of months of intensive practice, the Phoebe Fairgrave Flying Circus was ready for its debut. The thrill show featured the daring Phoebe, wearing riding breeches, a silk shirt, a goggled leather helmet, and basketball shoes with suction soles. Once airborne, Phoebe would climb out onto the wing, make her way to a vertical strut, then climb to the top of the upper wing. She told the press that wing-walking wasn't much different from climbing up on a table: "You shinny up the strut, grab hold of something on the top wing, throw your knee up there, and climb up."[68] Once on top, with the wind whipping her clothes, she would hook a toe beneath a guy wire, spread her arms wide and ride, and sometimes dance, while Vernon put the plane through loops, wingovers, and touch-and-go landings. She did headstands and handstands on the top wing and hung from the tail skid with one hand. Phoebe had a special leather mouthpiece attached to the end of a rope tied to the landing strut which she gripped between her teeth as she dangled and twirled in the plane's slipstream as Vernon made low passes over the crowd. The showstopper, though, was her own invention: a double parachute drop. "As no other woman in the world was doing a double parachute drop from an airplane, I made up my mind that I would be the first and only woman doing this stunt."[69] It started like a standard jump, but once she was free of the plane and apparently headed for a safe landing, she would cut loose from the canopy and free fall. With the crowd holding its breath—thinking her chute had failed—Phoebe would wait until the last possible moment, then pull the cord on a small drag chute just in time to slow her descent and prevent certain death. Because the double jump was both "more attractive for the people on the ground . . . . and more remunerative to the jumper," Phoebe did this jump almost exclusively.[70]

The hazards of a double drop were more than double because of having to depend upon two parachutes opening instead of one, and the second chute was necessarily smaller so that it could be worn. The drag chute had less lift and was less maneuverable than the main chute, and this had sometimes dangerous consequences. Her first double parachute jump (only her third jump and less than a month after the first), which she insisted on executing despite rain and wind, took her more than a mile from her intended landing place. Unable to control the drift of her drag chute, she floated into the middle of a small lake. Fortunately, the air trapped in the canopy acted as a sail and the wind carried her some 150 feet to the bank.[71] On her way down at an exhibition at Ottumwa, Iowa, she hit "an air pocket," the chute lost its lift, and she fell into a field of timothy. She tried to take the fall on the run but twisted her leg and sprained her ankle. As the crowd rushed to her aid, she got to her feet and walked to a waiting automobile. "That was the bravest thing I ever did in my life, I guess," she later told a reporter. "The ankle really hurt like blazes."[72] A few weeks later, while attempting a double drop in Des Moines during an American Legion air show, she had a much more serious accident. As she was coming down with the drag chute, she noticed a tangle of utility wires at the edge of the field. She managed to skid the small chute sideways but not enough. She struck high-tension lines hard enough to bounce away, but not before 2,300 volts went through her body. Some 3,000 people were watching as the current knocked her unconscious and she fell to the ground. She regained consciousness later in the hospital where she was treated for severe burns. The hot wires had seared her flesh to the bone in half a dozen places. The current had blown out the bottom of her foot.[73]

As she lay in the hospital, her main concern was not her own recovery, but whether her mother would find out how badly she was hurt. Phoebe tried to discourage the press from making this a big story. She told a reporter that she wasn't "hurt a bit," and begged him: "Don't put it in the papers. I don't want my mother to worry."[74] After he did so, she decided she needed to counter the accident coverage with coverage of her return to the sky. A cameraman from one of the motion picture studios was waiting for her to get back to work, so she told him she would go up. With her hands and legs wrapped in bandages and her arm strapped to her side, she climbed into the cockpit and asked a reluctant Vernon to take her aloft. Once she was in the air, she extricated her injured arm from the bandages and inched her way across the wing of the plane. She later described the incident:

> On my one hand I could use only two fingers, the others being burned. But really it didn't hurt—much. Everything went splendidly until the camera plane swooped up for a close shot. I got the full blast from its propeller and, taken without warning, I lost my grip entirely. I was falling backward, but the Lord and luck didn't desert me. I doubled a leg and it caught on one of the struts. The camera got it all.[75]

The local newspaper reported that she had returned to work, so apparently she had only been slightly injured. She mailed the news clipping to her mother. But "the truth is I didn't get back to work until two weeks later."[76]

Six months after her first plane ride and barely two months after her first jump, Phoebe decided to go for the world's record parachute jump for women. On 10 July, she climbed into a specially rigged high-performance Curtiss Oriole for the attempt. Even though the day was very hot, she dressed warmly in anticipation of the altitude, and because there were so many lakes in the vicinity, she wrapped a partially inflated inner tube around her body in case she should land in water. Aboard the plane with Phoebe and Vernon was the official recorder of the Minneapolis Aero Club to verify the record. As 15,000 people gazed into the sunlight trying to follow the Oriole, the big plane strained to climb into the thinning air and out of sight. It took an hour and ten minutes to get to their target altitude of 15,000 feet. The temperature dropped rapidly as the plane climbed; frost formed on her goggles and the motor started to miss in the thin air. At 15,200 feet, struggling for breath, she climbed out of the plane and began to make her way to the parachute. She was too short to climb down on the landing gear of the Oriole, so she had tied the chute to the wing strut. She had never before been out on the wing of such a fast airplane. The wind whipped her about as she inched along from handhold to handhold. She struggled to clip on her harness "with my hands numbed and my body shaking from the intense cold."

> On account of the rarefied atmosphere, I dropped like a bullet for about 5,000 feet, then the parachute started to quiver but did not open immediately. Finally the chute opened and I started a more gradual descent to the earth. After reaching about 10,000 feet, I hit an air pocket. My chute nearly collapsed and I fell for about 1,000 feet after which the chute opened again. I fell through several of these pockets in the course of my

descent . . . . It took 20 minutes from the time my chute opened until I reached the ground, this ending the biggest event in my career.[77]

She had gotten sick because of the violent tossing and swinging of the parachute on the way down, she told reporters, adding, "It was terrible; I never want to try it again."[78] But she had handily broken Mabel Cody's record of 11,000 feet, set in Chicago the previous summer.[79] After they all got back to the field, Vernon invited her to dinner at the elegant Radisson Hotel in Minneapolis to celebrate. It was their "first real date," she recalled, and the beginning of a blossoming romance.[80]

The Phoebe Fairgrave Fliers kept up an incredibly grueling schedule during the summer of 1921 with sixty performances in Iowa, eleven in Illinois, nine in Missouri, eight in Minnesota, eight in Mississippi, and seven in Tennessee.[81] These were sometimes associated with fairs or carnivals, but more often they simply flew over small towns dropping handbills to attract spectators and negotiated with farmers to use their pastures for temporary runways.[82] The stunts would attract attention and, with luck, induce folks to go up and see their world from the air. Income depended on "passenger hops." Few itinerant barnstormers did well financially. An oft-repeated anecdote has a barnstormer, when asked what he thought was most dangerous about barnstorming, reply, "The risk of starving to death." The Phoebe Fairgrave Fliers would often go many days without carrying enough passengers to meet expenses.[83]

Midway through the summer, they linked up with accomplished stunt flier Glenn Messer, who had managed his own flying circus for two years. Messer was widely known for his demonstrations of orthodontic prowess. He often hung by his teeth from various points on his airplane. To drum up publicity on the ground, he would demonstrate his strength by pulling, with his teeth, a two-ton truck loaded with forty children the length of a city block.[84] Although he had been relatively successful on his own, Messer knew that teaming up with this fearless young woman and her pilot had potential. Messer found himself charmed by the couple's "strong bond of good fellowship" and their playfulness with each other. Vernon would be "sitting around and she'd run up and push him over," he said. "He was very attentive to her and she hung around him all the time." Vernon, a skillful and cautious pilot, was "pleasant and good natured and hard to get excited," recalled Messer. Phoebe, on the other hand, was "very headstrong about her ideas . . . she was kind of like a man, rough and ready and scared of nothing." Shrewd and smart and sure of herself, Phoebe had high expectations for the success of the combined Messer-Fairgrave Flying Circus. Together they would perfect and perform more spectacular stunts for the movies and better compete with the larger circuses for lucrative fair contracts.[85]

One of the new stunts the team hoped to refine involved changing from plane to plane in the air. They found a barn in Iowa that had a central runway from end to end, and rigged a trapeze bar from the rafters. While Messer hung by his knees with his arms extended, Phoebe stood on the seat of an old buggy as Vernon piloted the team of horses. As Vernon drove the buggy through the barn, Phoebe would reach up to grasp Messer's hands and be pulled up alongside him on the trapeze. Gradually they increased the speed of the horses to a fast trot until she could connect with Messer on every pass. When they thought they had the stunt perfected, they alerted Fox to send a camera crew to film it. Three planes took off and jockeyed into position: the upper plane carrying Messer and the trapeze, the lower plane with Phoebe and Vernon, and the third supporting the movie cameraman.[86]

Messer was hanging from the axle of the upper plane, hands down, ready to grasp Phoebe, as the two pilots tried to get into a good position for the camera. Suddenly the lower plane hit an up-draft. Phoebe, standing near the right wingtip of the upper wing on the lower plane, with her toes hooked under two guy wires, saw the upper plane's propeller coming rapidly toward her. She dropped to her knees, reached under the leading edge of the wing and grabbed a strut. Then she flipped forward and over the edge, and shinnied down to the lower wing, safely out of the range of the whirling prop. The wing of Omlie's plane crashed into the landing gear holding Messer and locked there. They were charging across the sky at 80 miles per hour with both planes locked together. "More in desperation than anything else," Vernon later recounted, "I kicked hard right rudder and the wing tore loose. Just enough of the aileron [the control surface on the trailing edge of the wing] was left to let me manage the plane." After landing, he patched the aileron "with a couple of pieces of haywire" and, since the movie people were still eager for the footage, they went back up and did it all again, this time successfully. Folks watching from the ground praised the troupe for their marvelous showmanship, particularly in "that 'fake crash' in mid-air."[87] Talking it over later, the trio agreed to make the stunt a bit less dangerous. After that, Messer hung by his knees from the lowest rung of a twenty-foot rope ladder to grab Phoebe's hands, leaving a margin of unoccupied air between the planes.[88]

Phoebe also worked with Messer to perfect a car-to-plane transfer. This was particularly difficult because of the necessity for high speed on the part of the automobile and the extraordinary steadiness required of the plane at a very low and unstable altitude. She had not, she told a reporter, heard of any deaths from wing-walking, "but there were a few in the car-to-plane transfers—people would jump and miss—first law is never to let go of one grip until you have the other firm."[89] Despite her apparent confidence, the Messer-Fairgrave Circus never did quite perfect this stunt. Still, Phoebe thrived on the attempt. The very best thing about all this stunting was, she said, that "flying never gets monotonous. There's always a new thrill or a new risk that keeps you on your toes every minute you're in the air and makes your blood tingle to the tips of your toes."[90]

The Messer-Fairgrave troupe played fairs and air shows throughout the rest of the summer, while continuing to sell stunts to the movies.[91] Crowds estimated from 2,000 to 15,000 attended the meets. Featured air shows were such a strong draw that many times the whole town shut down to attend them. In October, in the town of Mexico, Missouri, students were released from school and downtown merchants closed their doors for the afternoon.[92] While the shows often attracted large crowds, many spectators did not pay. This was a continual problem for promoters. At Cedar Rapids, of the estimated crowd of 14,000, only about 1,000 paid the admission fee to the fairgrounds. Parked cars blocked the roads leading to the fairgrounds where spectators watched the show for free. At Phoebe's Baldwin Park show the newspaper reported, "Probably a thousand people lined the road banking their cars in the middle of the road rendering passing difficult for those who wished to attend. These people watched the show from their machines, refusing to pay admittance, and hundreds of others lined the fences at either side of the field, refusing to pay admission and watching the show."[93]

The stunts were dangerous and mishaps common, during the shows and in between. For example, when the circus arrived at Cedar Rapids, Vernon couldn't spot the field. He made a forced landing in a potato patch, broke the tip off his propeller, and seriously bruised himself and his passengers, Phoebe and Paul. The next day, show day, the wind was very strong. As Phoebe and her team of six men worked to open and refold her huge parachute, the wind caught it and dragged the team several feet before catching on the side of a truck and lifting it off the ground. Phoebe got a cut on her wrist from the friction of trying to hang onto the cord, and Vernon severely cut his hand. They decided not to jump that day.[94] At one big show at Swaney Field in Des Moines that featured twenty-three planes, Phoebe made four attempts to transfer plane-to-plane to Glenn hanging from the trapeze. The first three failed because unstable air prevented the planes from getting close enough together. Undaunted, they finally succeeded in the late afternoon. Phoebe's spectacular double parachute drop closed the show at twilight.[95]

In addition to the day-to-day hazards, barnstormers were frequently reminded about the dangers they faced every time they performed. So many of their numbers did not survive the season.[96] In July, Phoebe won a parachuting competition against Bud Bridgens. She pasted the clipping in her scrapbook. Just a few weeks later, Bridgens died when his parachute failed to open during a show in Rockport, Illinois. She clipped the notice and pasted it alongside the other in her scrapbook.[97] In early 1922, the *St. Paul Dispatch* composed an obituary for Phoebe and placed it in their files for retrieval in a hurry. Clearly they did not expect her to grow old in this profession.[98]

As the weather cooled and summer changed to autumn, the Messer-Fairgrave Flying Circus moved south. At the end of October, the troupe ended up broke in St. Louis. Messer split off and headed home to Alabama; Phoebe's brother, Paul, had left a few months earlier.[99] In early November, Phoebe was back in St. Paul in time to fly over Lexington Park to drop the football on the gridiron to open the Mechanic Arts–Central High game. What a thrill that must have been for the recent graduate.[100] Vernon and Phoebe carried on, now once again the Phoebe Fairgrave Fliers. They played to smaller and smaller crowds, battling bad weather and mounting debt. In Cairo, Illinois, in December, the weather was bitter cold and few tickets were sold. Phoebe did handstands on the upper wing, performed a trapeze act on a bar suspended from the landing gear, and double jumped, but they took only two passengers for rides.[101] They went on to Memphis after that to do a benefit at the Tri-State Fairgrounds. When bad weather grounded them, Phoebe supplemented their income with lectures and films of her work for the movies. She spoke at Fulton, Kentucky; Clarksdale, Mississippi; and in Memphis at the Princess Theater. Her posters called her "Miss Phoebe Fairgrave, Movie Actress and Aviatrix."[102]

The barnstormers secured permission to store their airplane in one of the hangars at the then-abandoned World War I training base at Park Field outside Memphis and took the train back to St. Paul.[103] Vernon and Phoebe were married in her parents' home on 18 February 1922. The next day, the headline on the local front page announced "Wedding to Pilot Vernon C. Omlie Comes as Surprise to St. Paul Friends." Phoebe sounded a bit defensive when interviewed by the press, but she was clear about her priorities: "Why shouldn't I marry him? Lt. Omlie was the only aviator who didn't tell me that I was a silly kid and that I ought to have some respect for my neck.

And he was the only one who would take me up to go after that record. Now I'm sure that I have a husband who won't interfere with my professional career—and I must jump."[104]

The couple left immediately for a honeymoon in Chicago where they attended the National Convention of State Fairs, hoping to obtain contracts for the coming season. They were competing against large multi-plane organizations like Ruth Law's, which could secure lucrative contracts with up-front money. Small-time operators like the Omlies obtained most of their income from taking rubes for rides. Phoebe was carrying in her pocket an urgent telegram that must have given her some considerable pleasure. It was from Ruth Law offering her a position with the Ruth Law Flying Circus. The message noted that she already had three "girl acrobats" but that she would give Phoebe preference; she asked her to name her price but included the admonition to "remember advertising you receive with us worth more than money to you."[105] The invitation was tempting, but the Omlies opted for their own show. They teamed up with Charley and Kathryn Hardin. The Fairgrave-Hardin Flying Circus specialized in parachute jumps; besides Phoebe's double parachute drop, Kathryn and Phoebe would do parallel jumps from either end of the wing. Charley would sometimes jump with five, even ten, parachutes strapped to him, opening one at a time with a free fall in between. His most spectacular stunt was to jump at night trailing burning torches.[106]

But 1922 turned out to be yet another summer spent trying to make ends meet. They flew exhibitions across the upper Midwest: St. Paul, La Crosse, Grand Forks, Litchfield, Minnesota. The Hardins dropped out in late summer and the Omlies gradually drifted south: Caruthersville, Steele, Kennett, and Hayti, Missouri; Stuttgart, Arkansas; Dyersburg, Union City, and Dresden, Tennessee. They finished up at the Mid-South Fair in Memphis in the fall, discouraged and broke.[107]

Chapter Two

*I*t was time to reassess their options. Two summers of barnstorming had failed to provide a viable income. The Omlies landed in Memphis in late fall, hoping the Mid-South Fair and local exhibitions would provide their last chance to make some money to see them through the winter, but bad weather kept them grounded as their meager funds trickled away. They had to hock their clothes and luggage to the Arlington Hotel where they were staying until they could resume flying and discharge their bill.[1]

They talked about settling down. Vernon wanted to make a living from aviation that didn't involve stunting and daredevil flying. Like many barnstormers, his ultimate goal was to establish aviation as a legitimate business. Vernon, who had been briefly stationed at Millington's Park Field during the war, recognized the potential for a warm weather base in the center of the country, and knew that the area's reputation for being "air-minded" could accommodate a business like he envisioned.[2]

Air-mindedness was a kind of "air intoxication" that gripped Americans during the golden age of aviation in the early twentieth century. This romance with the endless possibilities of aviation is difficult to appreciate today when aviation is simply a transportation system. Air-mindedness embodied a sense of awe and mysticism, which gave rise to utopian hopes for the dawn of a New Age of progress and prosperity. So great was aviation's impact on the national imagination that "Americans widely expected the airplane to foster democracy, equality and freedom," wrote aviation historian Joseph Corn, "to improve public taste and spread culture; to purge the world of war and violence; and even to give rise to a new kind of human being."[3] The idea that somehow flying was divine, and aviation could lift people to a realm fundamentally different from the one in which they lived, literally swept its enthusiasts to flights of fancy about its potential to elevate human life to a metaphorical heaven.[4] Almost since the advent of flight, certainly from the earliest days of exhibition flying, Memphis had been enthralled with aviation. Before the first decade of the twentieth century had passed, many of the most famous aviators in the world performed in the city.

Aviation in America was slow to get off the ground after the Wrights tested their flying machine on the dunes of North Carolina in 1903. Only five people witnessed their twelve-second flight, and the Wrights were secretive about what they were attempting to accomplish for fear that their ideas would be stolen before they could secure patents. As a consequence, the Wrights kept their developments shrouded in secrecy for five years, until 1908, when they demonstrated this amazing new technology to the military. Thus it was not until late in the decade that powered aircraft began to capture the public imagination.[5] The first great flying carnival ever held in America launched the era of air meets and exhibition fliers at a ten-day event in Los Angeles in January 1910.[6]

Four months later, the National Air Meet came to Memphis. When Glenn H. Curtiss, the most famous flier of his time, took off from the backstretch of the racetrack at the Tri-State Fairgrounds, few Memphians had seen powered flight. In Europe, by contrast, large crowds attended exhibitions and record-setting flights, particularly in France and Great Britain.[7] Curtiss had established an international reputation the year before, challenging some of the world's best fliers in a speed contest for the Coupe Internationale d'Aviation, a silver cup and cash prize of $5,000 awarded by James Gordon Bennett, publisher of the *Paris Herald*, during the world's first air meet in Rheims, France, in 1909.[8] Flying two laps around a 6.2-mile circuit, Curtiss beat France's Louis Bleriot (just one month after Bleriot became the first man to fly across the English Channel) by 5.8 seconds, averaging an astonishing 46.6 miles per hour.[9] Curtiss followed this with another win at the Grand Prix of Brescia, Italy, in September, easily winning the 50,000-lira prize.[10]

At Memphis, Curtiss roared off in *Miss Memphis*, his thirty-foot wide and thirty-foot long open pusher plane. The wings were held in place by a web of bracing struts and cross wires, the plane's single seat placed in front of the exposed motor with virtually nothing underneath. He made a circuit at thirty feet off the ground, then climbed to seventy-five feet, turned and headed for the grandstand. "As the airship sped down the 'homestretch,'" the newspaper reported, "the thousands leaped to their feet and cheered lustily." There were three crashes during the meet, caused by a combination of wind, fragile aircraft, and a racetrack infield too small for safe takeoffs and landings: Curtiss crashed near the bleachers knocking a spectator off his feet, Charles Willard tore off a tire as he tried to land and crashed into a fence, and J. C. Mars's plane caught a gust of wind and struck an automobile occupied by five spectators, one of whom was injured by the propeller.[11] Undaunted, on the second day of the meet, Curtiss took his wife, Lena, for a plane ride in which she became the third woman in America to go up in an aircraft. "Thousands in the grandstand were brought to their feet with a vociferous roar of applause when the biplane raced past with the plucky little woman as its passenger."[12] From Memphis, Curtiss went to New York where he flew his *Albany Flyer* down the Hudson River from Albany to New York City, winning a $10,000 prize put up by the New York *World*.[13]

The largest and most spectacular of all the flying exhibition companies in 1910 was the Moisant International Aviators, Inc.[14] The Moisant brothers, Johnny and Alfred, brought their flying circus to Memphis in December 1910, after being rained out in Chattanooga.[15] The company chartered seven railroad cars to carry their eight planes, a Fiat racer, two dozen mechanics, thirty roustabouts, and eight aviators: Johnny Moisant, famous for flying the English Channel one week after seeing his first plane, and fresh from winning $10,000 in the Statue of Liberty race at an average speed of 60.6 mph, two miles faster than was thought possible for his 50 hp Bleriot biplane; Roland Garros, who had recently set an altitude record of 1,500 feet in the tiny 35 hp bamboo and silk Santos-Dumont Demoiselle, the smallest flying machine in the world, earning him the nickname "the Cloud Kisser"; Rene Barrier, a tall rangy Frenchman with a law degree and nerves of steel; Rene Simon, known as the Fool Flyer, who did an inside loop purely by accident, then tried for a month before he managed to do another; and the tiny Swiss, Edmond Audemars, weighing in at less than one hundred pounds, who specialized in flying Demoiselle formations with Garros.[16] Three Americans rounded out the company: former stunt parachuter Charles K. Hamilton, scarred from head to toe from his various aviation misadventures; John J. Frisbee, an ex-balloonist and parachuter; and Joseph Seymour, who was both a flier and an auto racer whose stunt was to race his high-powered Fiat against the planes.[17]

Despite high winds and freezing temperatures, the fliers spared no effort to put on a good show. This indeed was "the kind of crowd pleasing that killed pilots." Exhibition aviators took enormous risks to keep flying despite the weather. Crowds that attended these aerial circuses often grew violent when aviators declined to fly in bad weather. As a consequence, pilots would take off when they shouldn't and many were killed. They knew that the crowds came to see them flirt with death. The Moisant International Aviators emphasized this point by featuring portraits on advertising posters of their pilots who had been killed performing.[18]

Johnny Moisant opened the show in the Bleroit with which he had won the Statue of Liberty race, taking off "flying straight into the teeth of a gale that at times held his 60 mph Bleriot at an absolute standstill, 1,500 feet above the earth, and in a temperature below the freezing point." He made twelve circuits of the one-mile track at the fairgrounds while the "spectators went wild with enthusiasm."[19]

Three days of rain, sleet, and snow followed the opening, but once the skies cleared, the show resumed. On 7 December, Rene Barrier broke the world's speed record at Memphis. Barrier and Moisant flew head-to-head around a 16-mile course from the Tri-State Fairgrounds to and around a mark on Hen and Chickens Island, twice around a mark on Presidents Island, and back. "Business in Memphis was practically at a standstill," as tens of thousands of Memphians watched from roofs of houses and downtown buildings and along the riverbank. Moisant's choice to climb to 7,000 feet apparently cost him the race, as Barrier chose to stay at 3,000 feet despite fog that obscured the tops of some of Memphis's taller buildings. Barrier completed the circuit in ten minutes fifty-five seconds with an average speed of 87.93 mph. Moisant took forty-three seconds longer. The flamboyant Moisant, though, had the big finish: he held his altitude until he was directly over the fairgrounds, then put his plane in a steep dive to the landing.[20]

Day after day, the newspaper carried the circus's exploits on the front page with giant headlines, proclaiming "INTERNATIONAL AVIATORS FULFILL EVERY PROMISE MADE TO MEMPHIS."[21] The large crowds and enthusiasm encouraged local businessmen to raise $10,000 to prolong their stay.[22] Held over by popular demand, the show remained in Memphis for sixteen days, "the longest continuing flight exhibition ever held in the United States."[23]

After the great success of these popular exhibitions, the infield of the former harness-racing track north of town, the North Memphis Driving Park, became the focus of a variety of aviation activities as local entrepreneurs and visiting fliers used the long flat surface of the former infield golf course as a makeshift landing field.[24] Built before the turn of the century, the North Memphis Driving Park had hosted huge crowds as part of the Grand Circuit of harness racing, but such activities came to an abrupt halt in 1906 when the Tennessee General Assembly made it unlawful to bet on "any trial or contest of speed or power of endurance of man or beast."[25] Without the gambling incentive, harness racing quickly lost its popularity and cache.[26]

When America sent troops to France in 1917, the Army Signal Corps began teaching men to fly at the landing strip at the Memphis Driving Park until the facilities at Millington's Park Field were completed.[27] The winter of 1917 was among the worst in Memphis history. The Mississippi River froze over as temperatures dropped below zero for several days. Some area residents believed that somehow the airplanes had stirred up the terrible winter weather.[28] With the spring thaw, the sod fields at the airbase turned to deep mud, forcing the Air Service to once again use the Driving Park for pilot training.[29] In 1919, the Memphis Aerial Company flew from the Driving Park.[30]

In the fall of 1922, when the Omlies arrived in Memphis, their airplane was parked in the middle of the track at the old Memphis Driving Park, from which they did their flying for the fair. Given its history and long association with aviation, the park seemed like the perfect venue for them to build a business. The landing field was in good shape, the steel grandstands could accommodate 3,500 people, and it was a ten-minute streetcar ride from downtown Court Square. Vernon and Phoebe struck a deal with the Memphis Business Men's Club, which managed the park, and began to host exhibitions and offer rides and flight training. Vernon taught his wife to fly and to master the rudiments of airplane mechanics, making her a full partner in his enterprise.[31] Gradually the Omlies gathered together a clique of air-minded Memphians, many of them World War I veteran fliers like Vernon, to talk about the future of aviation in Memphis.

By 1924, the activities at the Driving Park had clearly outgrown the facilities. After that year's Armistice Day parade, the group of fliers gathered in front of the Hotel Chisca at the end of the march and discussed the need for a real airport. The following year, Armistice Day 1925, the group met in a luncheon to finalize the organization of the Memphis Aero Club and elect Everett Cook as their first president. Their first effort was petitioning the government for the abandoned Park Field at Millington. Cook enlisted the aid of Senator Kenneth D. McKellar, but to no avail; the government refused to relinquish the land.[32] When efforts to interest city fathers in funding a municipal airport also failed, the Aero Club pooled their resources and leased seventy acres of cow pasture at Woodstock, on the old Millington Pike north of Memphis, not far from the Driving Park.[33] With the help of the Shelby County Commissioners, they graded the field. The street car company furnished cinders for the runway, and the Illinois Central Railroad hauled them to a siding next to the field for free.[34] The first plane to land there, 26 June 1926, was piloted by Vernon Omlie, described in the press as "for five years the torch-bearer for aviation in Memphis."[35]

This first official Memphis airport was dedicated the following Armistice Day, 11 November 1926, and named for Lt. Guion Armstrong, a Memphis pilot killed in France during the war. More than "three score of airships" flew in for the ceremony from as far away as Chicago. A special train departing from the Poplar Street Station was available for a sixty-cent fare. Nonetheless, "the roads out of Memphis were jammed with traffic from one end to the other" as some 12,000 spectators attended this grand "coming out party" for the Memphis Aero Club. The paper reported "thrills galore and hair-raising emotions" as over one hundred aviators competed in two closed-course races, and the U.S. Army pilots and National Guard Squadron demonstrated formation and combat flying. Phoebe was the star of the show:

> Taking the olive branch for the most daring and thrilling stunt was Phoebe Fairgrave, in private life Mrs. Vernon C. Omlie, wife of the manager of the port. Phoebe did some stunts which to hire certain newspaper men [to] do would make the war debt look like a postage stamp. She walked the planes [wings] of her husband's ship, hung from them by her toes, at one time hung from one end of the ship by her teeth and wound up her day by leaping from the plane in a parachute.[36]

Only two days later, the great Fokker Trimotor airplane, *Josephine Ford*, landed at Armstrong Field, just six months after making the first successful journey over the North Pole, thus, as a reporter gushed, "establishing contact between this city and the Artic regions."[37] After Richard E. Byrd and his pilot Floyd Bennett flew over the North Pole on 9 May 1926, the Guggenheim Fund for the Promotion of Aeronautics sent the plane around the United States to demonstrate the possibilities of commercial flying.[38]

Bennett and his passengers, representatives from the U.S. Commerce Department and the Guggenheim Fund, were greeted by the Omlies and feted by the Memphis Aero Club with a lunch at the Peabody Hotel, a tour of the city, and dinner at the Lions Club.[39] With the opening of her first airport, and the hosting of this celebrity of the air, Memphis became an important hub for aviation routes across the nation.[40]

The Omlies established Mid-South Airways at Armstrong Field, offering flying lessons, aerial photography, air-taxi charters, cargo transport, crop-dusting (pioneering the practice of combating the boll weevil from the air), and aerial mapping of the river, power lines, and various commercial developments.[41] Phoebe eagerly took on the duties of secretary, office manager, flight instructor, transport pilot, and mechanic for their new business.[42] Vernon began active lobbying for a municipal airport, taking local dignitaries, including former mayor E. H. Crump, for free rides to see Memphis from the air.[43] After Mid-South Airways secured the Waco agency, to sell and maintain Waco airplanes, Phoebe added sales manager to her duties.[44]

In 1927, the Mississippi River Valley was inundated by one of the nation's most destructive natural disasters. Abnormally high amounts of rain had fallen throughout the Midwest during the fall of 1926. This was followed by record-setting snowstorms in the north and heavy rains in Tennessee and Kentucky that winter. The rain and snow melt saturated the earth and overflowed creeks and tributaries along the Ohio and Mississippi, setting the stage for a massive flood in the spring of 1927. Floodwaters began to break through the levees built to contain the river, eventually breaching them in 145 places, flooding farmers' fields and numerous towns and villages from Missouri to Louisiana, some to depths of thirty feet. The city of Memphis became an emergency depot, struggling to care for thousands of refugees pouring in from all directions.[45]

Responding to the disaster, President Coolidge appointed his secretary of commerce, Herbert Hoover, to coordinate rescue and relief efforts from a headquarters in Memphis. Hoover put the Red Cross in charge of responding to the emergency. They faced immense problems with communication and distribution of supplies and services throughout the flooded region. There was a complete paralysis of ordinary communication: no mail, telegraph, or telephone service. As the scope of the disaster became clearer, the agency rapidly outgrew its offices downtown and relocated into the enormous Ford Motor Company assembly plant with its huge warehouse space served by a railroad spur.[46] On the twentieth of April, "a great concentration camp for refugees" was set up at the Tri-State Fairgrounds. More than five hundred people arrived the first day. "Many were half-clad, caked with mud and in a dazed condition from the sudden loss of all their worldly possessions."⁴⁷

During the emergency, the airplane became an indispensable means of fast communication and distribution of vital commodities to the stricken area. Aviators of the U.S. Navy and the National Guard assisted the Red Cross with information on levee breaks and flood depths. The Omlies, as well as other members of the Memphis Aero Club and anyone else with available aircraft, took to the air to do what they could. "The Omlies were everywhere, flying above the ugly, yellow torrents, carrying photographers and newsmen, doctors, nurses, medicines, antitoxins and food."⁴⁸ When the bridge washed out at Memphis, the Omlies hauled the mail from Memphis to Little Rock. They dropped food to people marooned on rooftops, in trees, along levees. They transported messages from rescue headquarters to inundated areas and back again. They patrolled the levees to spot "sand boils," indications of ruptures. They flew news reporters and photographers to document the disaster, Phoebe's aerial photographs supplementing those of the professionals.⁴⁹ Every day for nearly eight weeks the front pages of the Memphis newspapers, the *Commercial Appeal* and the *Press-Scimitar*, carried accounts and photographs of the flooded areas, along with wrenching stories of tragedy and heroism. The flying itself was heroic, without the option of a safe landing in case of a flight emergency. Phoebe later recalled, "At three thousand feet altitude you couldn't see dry land half the time, and we were flying tiny land planes." Several people were killed in airplane accidents during the emergency, including the general reconstruction officer of Mississippi Valley Flood Relief for the Red Cross Earl Kilpatrick, who died when his plane plunged into the water while flying between Vicksburg and New Orleans.⁵⁰

The Omlies had one Waco fitted with pontoons so that they could land passengers, rescue the marooned, and deliver nurses and medicines. One day Phoebe flew down to Mississippi to rescue a boy who had been bitten by a rabid dog and was stranded in the second story of his home. She had to land the plane on the water such that the current would drift her past the house and allow the boy to climb from the window to the plane. Her skill saved that boy and likely countless others.⁵¹

In the flood of 1927, twenty-six thousand square miles were inundated, an area roughly equal to Massachusetts, Connecticut, New Hampshire, and Vermont combined. Along the lower Mississippi, the flood put as much as thirty feet of water over lands where 931,159 people had lived; flooded homes numbered 162,017. An estimated 330,000 people were rescued from treetops, roofs, chimneys, telegraph poles, railroad cars, levees, and patches of high ground. Not until mid-August, more than four months after the first break, did all the water leave the land.[52] The Red Cross built 154 tent cities in seven states and a total of 325,554 people, the majority of them African American, lived in these camps for as long as four months. An additional 311,922 people outside the camps were fed and clothed by the Red Cross. Direct losses to the seven affected states (Illinois, Missouri, Kentucky, Tennessee, Arkansas, Mississippi, and Louisiana) were calculated to be $236,334,414, with indirect losses estimated at $200 million more. Officially, the Red Cross reported 246 people drowned, but the death toll was almost certainly higher because it was impossible to know how many bodies were buried under tons of mud or washed out into the Gulf.[53]

For the Memphis aviators who flew in the rescue efforts, the disaster had one positive benefit: it clearly demonstrated the critical function of the airplane as a transport vehicle. "It was eight weeks of tough work, with mighty little sleep," Phoebe recalled, "but it helped a lot to prove the usefulness of airplanes in disaster relief."[54] And it helped to transform public perceptions of the pilots who flew them from thrill-seeking performers to purveyors of a legitimate business with real utility in the community.

In the midst of the disaster, Vernon and Phoebe were also preparing to apply for United States pilots' licenses. In 1927, the federal government began formally regulating commercial and civil aviation. Until this time, anyone who could obtain an airplane, or build one in his backyard, could fly it. Pilots had no licenses, no rules or regulations; there were no restrictions on aircraft. In the air he could do as he pleased, perform outrageous stunts over populated areas, land and take off wherever he chose. Flying was for the reckless, often with tragic results. Responding to a clamor to assume control of "the chaos of laissez faire in the air," the federal government finally set up a regulatory apparatus under the Air Commerce Act of 1926.[55] The Aeronautic Bureau of the Department of Commerce was charged with fostering air commerce, establishing airways, and licensing aircraft, engines, pilots, and mechanics. Having heard about the coming regulations, Phoebe submitted her application for a transport license and an aircraft and power-plant (mechanics) license on 16 February 1927. She requested and obtained a Letter of Authority from the chief of the Air Regulation Division, authorizing her to act in those capacities pending examination. Phoebe, along with her husband, took the written and flight tests on 22 April 1927, in between flood rescue missions.[56]

Since soloing in 1923, Phoebe's accumulated flying time far exceeded the necessary minimum of 200 hours. A transport license permitted her to fly interstate, in any type of airplane, carry passengers for money, and teach others to fly. To qualify for an aircraft mechanics license, she needed a minimum of two years experience in shop practice, including work on internal combustion engines, one year of which must include actual practice of maintenance on aircraft engines and actual experience building, maintaining, or repairing aircraft. She had to pass a written examination and satisfy her inspector that she could overhaul an aircraft engine and adjust the ignition system.[57]

On 28 June 1927, she received Transport Pilot's license No. 199 (Vernon applied the same day and got license No. 200) and her Aircraft and Engine Mechanics License No. 422, becoming the first woman to obtain a pilot license from a civilian agency of the U.S. Government and the first woman issued an aircraft and engine mechanic's license.[58]

In July, while floodwaters remained over many areas along the Mississippi River, the National Air Tour landed at Armstrong Field. The National Air Tour for the Edsel B. Ford Reliability Trophy was an annual event, a kind of traveling industrial show designed to promote aviation advancements and to demonstrate the safety and reliability of air travel.[59] The tour also had the effect of spurring municipalities to improve landing fields in order to be chosen as hosts. These facilities gradually established a nationwide airway system.[60] The first tour, in 1925, visited twelve cities in the Midwest, and covered 1,775 air miles over six days.[61] In 1926, pilots flew a 2,585-mile circuit over fourteen days. In 1927, the tour was extended to sixteen days and 4,121 miles.[62]

Like much of America, Memphians had been avidly following news of the tour. In May of that year, Charles Lindbergh had become the first person to fly solo across the Atlantic Ocean. Coming on the heels of Lindbergh's magnificent achievement, fascination with aviation was at a fever pitch. Thousands turned out to greet the arrival at Armstrong Field of biplanes and monoplanes, single engines and huge Ford Tri-Motors, open cockpit and closed, fourteen pilots, thirty-nine passengers, and one monkey named "Honko." Along with the excitement of the tour itself, the local newspapers freighted the visit with introducing commercial aviation to the region and assured readers that Memphis had taken her place in the grand sweep of the air age in recognizing "the value of commercial aviation on the broad scale that it is practiced in the east and north."[63]

With so much interest in aviation, business boomed at Mid-South Airways, particularly in flying lessons and aircraft sales. Vernon was increasingly occupied with commercial work like crop-dusting and aerial surveys; Phoebe devoted much of her time to working with students, flight instruction, and check rides. On 28 August 1927, she had her first serious crack-up since blowing out her foot on the high-tension line in 1921. She had taken a passenger, Leo Speltz, for a ride in a Waco biplane from Armstrong Field. As Phoebe banked the plane, at an altitude of 800 feet, to turn into the field for a landing, Speltz braced himself, unwittingly pressing his feet against the rudder pedals and throwing the ship out of control. Because she could not manipulate the rudder, and could not dislodge Speltz, Phoebe could not bring the ship out of the turn. It spun into the ground demolishing the front of the fuselage and both wings.[64] Vernon rushed to his wife's side and spirited the two to the hospital. Phoebe had a severe gash on her forehead, a fractured skull, a broken left arm, and two broken legs; Speltz had broken his foot.[65]

Phoebe was laid up for some weeks, but still found ways to keep working. She and Vernon had a big job doing aerial mapping for a pipeline from Monroe, Louisiana, to Memphis, Tennessee, and West Memphis, Arkansas. She rode along, took photographs and spent many hours developing film while on crutches.[66]

Phoebe was still hobbling with a cane when America's most famous aviator arrived. Charles A. Lindbergh landed at Armstrong on 5 October 1927, just five months after his epic nonstop solo flight from New York to Paris. Lindbergh's visit to Memphis was the sixty-second stop in his eighty-two-city tour promoting public acceptance of the airplane as reliable transportation.[67]

"To the blast of whistles and the chiming of bells, the first flier to conquer the Atlantic" circled the city several times.[68] Some 10,000 spectators at Armstrong Field gazed skyward, cheering as Lindbergh

> pulled back his stick and the *Spirit of St. Louis* reared like a thoroughbred horse. Around the field he circled, the sunlight glinting on the silver sheen like a sparkling jewel in a sea of blue . . . . A couple of zigzags of the rudder and the silver ship with its heroic cargo dropped to the ground as lightly as a dead leaf in an autumn breeze. It was a masterful demonstration of the flyer's absolute control over his ship.[69]

Lindbergh was rushed to Overton Park where some 30,000 Memphians, many of whom had been waiting in the hot sun for two hours or more, jostled to see their hero. The ceremony began with the mayor of Memphis presenting a fifty-seven-piece silver service to Capt. H. B. Lackey, commanding officer of the U.S. Navy Cruiser *Memphis*, which had been sent by President Calvin Coolidge to fetch Lindbergh and his plane, the *Spirit of St. Louis*, back to the United States after his epochal flight. As Lindbergh stepped forward, thunderous bursts of applause, accompanied by auto horns, and chants of "Lindy! Lindy!" produced a cacophony that stalled the aviator's speech for some time. "All Memphis fawned at his feet, but the boyish conqueror of the Atlantic [showed] a distinct dislike for pomp and pageantry," wrote one reporter. Lindbergh made it clear that he was there solely to promote aviation. Declining to exalt his recent achievement, "he tried to convey the impression that his epochal flight was merely a trip which can be accomplished by any healthy flier properly equipped."[70]

Lindbergh gave a short outline of the history of aviation and its progress in the previous two years, saying that he believed the next two years would witness even greater advancement. But he cautioned that "aviation cannot be developed without support from the public. And aviation cannot be developed without airports, so it is important that the country awake to the necessity of constructing more airports. The nation, Tennessee, and the city of Memphis need your cooperation."[71]

After his speech, the parade began. Seated on the folded top of a flag-draped convertible, Lindbergh led the parade to the Peabody Hotel where a dinner and reception hosted by the Memphis Aero Club were held in his honor. The newspaper reported that "One hundred thousand people cheered him as he rode through Memphis streets."[72] At the dinner that evening, "fully 500 men and women broke bread with the noted aviator" who reiterated his basic message calling for support for civil aviation. He announced that he would not be visiting Nashville the next day as planned, in deference to the sorrow occasioned by the recent death of Governor Austin Peay. Instead, Lindbergh enjoyed an unaccustomed day of privacy and rest while his ship, *The Spirit of St. Louis*, posed in majestic display at Armstrong Field. The newspaper summed up the success of Lindbergh's visit: "He had a message and he delivered it. And with that deed accomplished, his work in Memphis was over. But his mere presence brought more stimulus to aviation interest in this city than all the work done in that direction heretofore."[73]

The clamor that accompanied Lindbergh's visit apparently had its desired effect of convincing city fathers of the importance of ushering in the air age with a new municipal airport. Memphis boss E. H. Crump's hand-picked candidate, Watkins Overton, made the construction of a Memphis airport a major issue in his mayoral campaign.[74] Once in office, Overton quickly appointed five men to the Airport Planning Commission, at least three of whom were Aero Club members: Col. J. Walter Canada, chairman; Edmund Williams, secretary; W. Percy McDonald, Memphis attorney and later head of the Tennessee Aeronautics Commission; R. Brinkley Snowden; and Claude J. Tulley.[75]

In the meantime, Omlie expanded his business. On 7 May 1928, Mid-South Airways began regular passenger service to Chicago, three round trips per week with Captain Omlie flying a six-place Stinson Detroiter. The first ticket was sold to W. Percy McDonald. Depending on the winds, it sometimes took five hours to reach Chicago (a flight distance of 488 miles); the fare was $60.[76]

Phoebe, too, looked for ways to expand Mid-South Airways. After hearing about an exciting new small aircraft being manufactured in Iowa, Phoebe flew up to check it out. The mid-1920s were a time of great experimentation in design and manufacture of postwar planes for civilian use. The war-surplus Jennys then dominating the air were unsuited for the development of aviation as a personal transportation system. They required two men to move them in and out of hangars; controls were sluggish and they were slow and drafty with their cockpits open to the elements. The goal was to build a cheap, reliable, easy-to-fly personal-type airplane that people would enjoy owning and flying. When Henry Ford, builder of the original "flivver" (his Model-T), came up with a prototype "Ford flying flivver" in the summer of 1926, the public was entranced. People said that private planes would one day replace cars, but would clearly be more heavenly to "drive." A columnist for the *New York Evening Sun* described flivver ownership this way:

> *I dreamed I was an angel*
> *And with the angels soared*
> *But I was simply touring*
> *The heavens in a Ford.*[77]

In the fall of 1926, Don Luscombe, a promoter and advertising man who fell in love with flying during the war and spent many hours tinkering with aircraft design, and Clayton Folkerts, a mechanic who had been designing and building airplanes in his basement since 1918, teamed up to begin building their "aerial coupe" in an old clapboard tabernacle built by evangelist Billy Sunday in Bettendorf, Iowa. They called themselves the Central States Aero Company and their plane the Monocoupe.[78]

The Monocoupe was a two-place, high-wing monoplane fitted with side-by-side dual controls in a velour-upholstered, fully enclosed cabin. It cruised at eighty-five miles per hour and sold for $2,285.[79] As word spread about the Monocoupe's closed-cabin comfort, responsive controls, speed, and economy, the company could not build them fast enough, largely owing to the difficulty of obtaining reliable engines. Don Luscombe contacted Moline automaker Willard L. Velie as a potential source of engines. Velie, maternal grandson of farm implements maker John Deere, owned the Velie Carriage Company, an innovator in engine design, which built the first six-cylinder valve-in-head motor in 1908.[80] Velie subsequently bought out Luscombe's Central States Aero Company to form Mono Aircraft, Inc., a subsidiary of the Velie Motor Corporation in January 1928, providing the new 55 hp Velie M5 radial engine and much-needed capital for the company.[81]

The Velie Monocoupe was enormously successful. The company produced 275 planes during 1928, and by 1929, fully 10 percent of all registered aircraft in the United States were Velie Monocoupes.[82] This was attributable in no small measure to the amount of positive publicity Phoebe Omlie would attract for the company.

Chapter Three

Phoebe had gone to Bettendorf hoping to convince the company to allow her to market the Monocoupe in Memphis. She got the franchise and a lot more. Phoebe became a consultant for the company and ultimately the plane's "ambassadoress," as she demonstrated the Monocoupe in a variety of activities over the next few years.[1] Monocoupes had a "pixie-like" quality, described in ad copy as "pert . . . an airplane [with] wholesome charm . . . a jolly, friendly sort of airplane," not unlike that of Phoebe herself.[2] Although Phoebe was a highly skilled pilot with at least 1,000 hours of accumulated flight time in a host of different aircraft by the time she joined the company, she built her career with the company on proving that "the Monocoupe is made so well and is so easy to fly that a girl can pilot it."[3]

In the summer of 1928, Phoebe, flying her black and orange Monocoupe 70, affectionately dubbed *Chiggers*, joined the fourth annual Ford Reliability Air Tour. Her "flivver" had just barely enough power to compete; rules indicated that entries must be capable of speeds in excess of 80 miles per hour.[4] She was the only woman competitor in the race and she flew alone. Given the uncertain reliability of many of the planes and their engines, there was no question that mechanical problems would arise along the way. Indeed, the tour featured a litany of broken wing-bracing wires, punctured oil pans and fuel lines, overheated engines, and broken propellers. One participant,

Dan Beard, in anticipation of difficulties, shipped eleven propellers around the country ahead of time.[5] While many of her fellow competitors carried mechanics to help keep their planes flying, Phoebe resolutely declined. "Why would I need a mechanic? I have an aircraft mechanic's license. Besides if I did take one, people would say he flew the ship over the worst parts. No, I'll go it alone."[6]

The 1928 National Air Tour was the third annual tour and the longest one yet: thirty-two cities in nineteen states and 6,304 miles over desert, plain, and mountain range. The circuit headed south out of Dearborn, to Indianapolis, St. Louis, Wichita, Tulsa, down into Texas, turning west at San Antonio, through New Mexico, Arizona, north at San Diego, up the west coast all the way to Tacoma, Washington, then headed east across Idaho, Montana, North Dakota, Minnesota, Wisconsin, and back to Dearborn.[7] The circuit was demanding enough to test the planes and the pilots in every kind of condition. Though the planes departed at one-minute intervals, they soon dispersed across the sky and each was essentially alone.

Navigation along the route was a challenge. Over familiar territory in nice weather, plotting a course was simple. Pilots used road maps and depended upon visual references like highways, rivers, and railroad tracks (sometimes referred to as the iron compass). Unfortunately, often several sets of rail-road tracks radiate out from a town making it all too easy to choose the wrong set. This method (known as pilotage) has some obvious disadvantages in remote areas with few landmarks or in inclement weather when limited visibility could be disorienting. In the days before the widespread use of radio or other navigational aids, pilots used "dead reckoning," an unfortunate term for mathematical calculations based on airspeed, compass heading, elapsed time, and distance, to plot their course to a destination. If the route was flown at the planned airspeed, when the elapsed time was up, the destination should be visible. Wind is the critical element in the calculation; its speed and direction directly affect the aircraft and its progress over the ground. So if wind velocity and direction are unknown, the plane could be blown off course. Weather reporting was rudimentary at best along the route, so it was very easy to get lost, particularly in areas where landmarks were few.[8]

Takeoffs and landings were very demanding. Most airfields were called fields, and that is mostly what they were: a relatively level pasture with the grass cut to demark the "runway." A windsock, a tube of bright-colored fabric at the top of a tall pole, indicated wind direction. Most had no facilities for fueling or servicing airplanes. Pilots and tour coordinators had to make prior arrangements to be certain fuel, parts, and mechanics would be available to them. Short fields at high elevations or on hot days were hazardous, much easier to get into than out of. Municipal airports were sometimes in a bit better shape, some having cinder runways or access to water with which to periodically settle the dust. But since airports were often located in or near urban areas, countless obstacles encircled the fields—buildings, trees, chimneys, power lines. Pilot and humorist Will Rogers described the best way a pilot could find an unfamiliar field:

> Locate a high tension line, follow it till it crosses another higher tension one. There is almost sure to be a field there. If not, follow it till it comes to an intersection of three or more lines and there will be located the city's municipal field.[9]

A crowd estimated at an astonishing 175,000 people watched as Phoebe took off at 10:15 AM on 30 June.[10] She was allowed to take off first ahead of her twenty-four competitors out of deference to her sex and perhaps to her plane.[11] Most of the other planes were equipped with motors four to ten times more powerful than hers. Her tiny Monocoupe was small enough to hide under the wings of the giant tri-motors. Like her larger competitors, her plane was equipped with the basic instruments: tachometer, altimeter, compass, oil temperature gauge, and clock. Phoebe wore a blue enameled ring with a tiny compass set in it, in case she made an emergency landing and had to find her way across alien terrain on foot.[12]

Flying the slowest plane, Phoebe was the last to arrive at the first stop in St. Louis.[13] The tour resumed, crossing Missouri into Kansas. A patchwork of farms stitched together with hedgerows gave way to prairie, vast as an ocean. Wichita to Tulsa, then down into Fort Worth and San Antonio, the terrain gradually turned more barren and brown, covered with sagebrush and scrub pine. In the scorching heat, the planes became more sluggish and unruly. The hot air had less density, thus less lift, so planes required longer runways in order to get airborne. For a low performance plane like Phoebe's, summer temperatures severely impaired its ability to clear obstacles at the end of short runways.

Phoebe was thrilled when Estelle (Mrs. Eddie) Stinson climbed into her Monocoupe at Fort Worth for the next two legs of the tour. Eddie Stinson, pioneer pilot and manufacturer, had won the 1927 National Air Tour and was a competitor in this one. Phoebe wired her hometown newspaper, the *Press-Scimitar*, to relay the news: "Think Eddie told her to go. That is one of the greatest compliments I've had on the tour."[14] Off they went, across the open Texas hill country to San Antonio. Low clouds forced them to fly sometimes only 50 feet above the ground as they skirted the west Texas mountains, following the railroad tracks to Marfa.[15] Located on a Chihuahuan Desert plateau, Marfa was the highest city in Texas at nearly 5,000 feet. At such a high altitude the planes would land fast. Phoebe, coming in hot, overshot the runway and ground looped (a sudden sideways rotation of the aircraft on the ground caused by excessive speed and/or side winds). A wheel collapsed, the wing went down, and the airplane nosed over.[16]

Beginning with her initial takeoff, Phoebe's tour was extensively covered by an eager press who found the diminutive female pilot fascinating. Following her accident, the *New York Times* reported that she had "escaped death, but was forced out" of the tour and that her "plane was completely demolished."[17] This was not quite true. She and her passenger were shaken up but uninjured. The same could not be said for *Chiggers.* One wing and the landing gear were smashed. Jack Atkinson, a Monocoupe dealer from Gary, Indiana, who had joined the circuit at the last moment, offered her the use of his plane while he remained behind to get hers repaired. She hurriedly wired Vernon that she was unhurt: "Damage not serious. I am all right and am going on as pilot of other Monocoupe."[18] Phoebe and Estelle swapped ships with Atkinson and headed on to El Paso where Estelle rejoined her husband, Eddie, for the next leg. Atkinson was later able to catch up with the tour at San Francisco by flying 1,100 miles in fifteen hours so they could swap back.[19]

Phoebe took off alone from El Paso, headed across the desert southwest to Tucson. Scorching hot in July, the air shimmered as if aflame. Dust devils—vertical columns of hot air that rotate and travel along the ground like miniature tornadoes made visible by dust sucked into the vortex—danced across the flat barren earth. This was alien terrain to a midwestern flier: no landmarks, no water towers, all dry creek beds, canyons and ravines, cactus and chaparral. It was unforgiving country if one went down very far from a road. As she made scheduled stops in Tucson, Yuma, then San Diego, in her tiny plane, Phoebe was often the last to arrive but grateful for another successful leg. To the press, she reiterated what she had said from the first: that she did not join the race to win it, but to finish. "To finish and prove that the light plane is practicable and that the average man or woman can operate one the same as an automobile."[20]

Estelle rejoined Phoebe at San Diego for their trip up the Pacific Coast to Los Angeles. The view was spectacular as the curvy white beach, nipped and tucked with inlets and sloughs, met the vivid blue Pacific. Near Laguna, Phoebe ran out of gas and had to set down on a strip of beach. By the time the wheels stopped rolling, the women had to climb out and wade in shallow water to the shore. While a team of horses towed the Monocoupe back to solid sand, Phoebe and Estelle were whisked away dripping wet to a formal banquet at the Ambassador Hotel.[21]

At every stop, capacity crowds greeted the tour, hundreds of planes joined the competitors, including military squadrons and stunt pilots, gliders, auto-gyros (early helicopters), and balloons, to put on exhibitions and take locals for rides. Some estimated as many as a million Americans witnessed some phase of the tour.[22] Aero clubs, chambers of commerce, and events coordinators planned myriad opportunities to meet and honor the pilots: luncheons, banquets, receptions with dignitaries, tours of the local area.[23] The pilots and their passengers gamely attended air rodeos in Texas, a Fourth of July extravaganza at Tulsa. They crossed the border at Juarez for a glimpse of Mexico, attended a fish fry in Montana, and toured the Metro Goldwyn Mayer Studios in Los Angeles.[24] One of the more unusual events they attended was in St. Paul, where air tour participants were invited to the all-Minnesota dance marathon, which had already been going on for 134 hours by the time they arrived. Tour guests occupied special boxes to witness "makeup applied to every girl in the marathon during the evening. Since the dance began, the dancers had been given 389 marcels (finger waves), 191 hair washes, and 64 trims, all using the 15-minute rest periods allowed." Another feature was "a fishing party, in which contestants [fished] on the floor for ice cream molded in the form of fish."[25] All the activities along the route meant that the pilots had little time to rest, plan the next day's journey, or spend maintaining their aircraft. It was party until late, then up at dawn and take off.

At Los Angeles, perhaps believing she was the cause of Phoebe's bad luck, Estelle ended her stint as Phoebe's passenger. Phoebe went on alone to San Francisco, with a dogleg over the verdant Imperial Valley for a luncheon stop at Fresno. Getting into San Francisco was uneventful, but getting out was another story. Fog in the bay, always worst in the summer months, had begun rolling in as the pilots rolled out. By the time Phoebe lifted off, after being reunited with the repaired *Chiggers*, she was in thick soup at 100 feet. All she could do was maintain her controls in the same position, scanning her brain for any obstructions in her way. Holding steady, she climbed to nearly 900 feet before she broke out in the clear and began to breathe again.[26]

More poor visibility greeted the pilots on the way to Portland. Dense smoke from burning forests obscured their vision as they made their way up the Pacific Coast. Several pilots altered their course to fly out over the ocean to escape the smoke and to be certain that they cleared the mountains. Then on to Tacoma, Washington, with its picturesque setting on Commencement Bay in Puget Sound for more banquets and receptions. The monotony of the menus and entertainment for these soirees was reflected in the wild applause that greeted the host at the closing banquet in Detroit when he promised the menu would not include chicken. "Not hot nor cold, nor roasted, boiled, fried or fricasseed. Nor in soup or salad or sandwiches. Furthermore, you will not be forced to listen to any rendition, in any form: orchestra or trio, solo or chorus or quartet, of that familiar song, 'Romona.'"[27]

The tour turned back south so that it could cross the Cascade Range, one of the most beautiful mountain barriers in the United States, through the Columbia River Gorge, a spectacular river canyon that forms the boundary between Washington and Oregon. The silver thread of the river wound between black basalt cliffs and mountains rising steeply on both sides punctuated by Mount Hood, and off in the distance the majestic Mount Rainer and Mount St. Helens.

After a brief stop at Spokane, the planes crossed over the Rockies, range after range broken by sunless valleys and topped with snow, heading for a big trout fry on the banks of the Blackfoot River at Missoula. Then on 21 July, the air tour crossed the Continental Divide and landed at Great Falls, Montana. Back in the flatlands of the Great Plains, the terrain was beginning to look like home. Across the wheat belt of North Dakota to St. Paul, where Phoebe got even more than her share of press attention because of her history in that city. The paper reported approvingly that one race participant called her "a game little girl and not a cry-baby," one who had earned the respect of the men on the trip. She told the press, "I'm not in the race to win, but I want this buggy to finish."[28]

After Milwaukee and Chicago, it was finally time to turn home to Dearborn, four weeks and six thousand miles after they departed.[29]

Phoebe was hoisted on the shoulders of Edsel Ford and Michigan governor Fred W. Green at the finish line.[30] The *Detroit Press* extolled her accomplishment and its impact on the aviation industry:

The contest has revealed an unparalleled development in the small plane for individuals of modest means through the performance of Mrs. Phoebe Fairgrave Omlie and her little 47-hp Monocoupe . . . . Mrs. Omlie's little plane carried her through the contest at an average speed of seventy miles an hour, weathered sweltering heat over the desert in the southwest, soared over some of the highest peaks in the Rocky Mountains, maintained a more precise schedule than some of the higher powered and more expensive planes and completed the flight with an average of about fifteen miles on a gallon of gasoline.[31]

John Wood, in his 225 hp Waco Ten, was declared the winner; Phoebe finished last but with a perfect score for navigation. Mono Aircraft was so pleased with her performance that they presented her with *Chiggers*, which she proudly flew back to Memphis.[32]

A large crowd was waiting for her as she circled the field twice in salute before touching down on her home field. The tour had been a success, she said, and had clearly "helped to make many more people air-minded . . . . When 23 out of 24 airplanes carrying 85 people can travel over the most hazardous parts of the United States in all kinds of weather without serious mishap, it is proof air transportation is here to stay."[33]

Yet, on the heels of her triumph came a devastating crash, one that nearly proved fatal.[34] It was a lovely autumn day in October; Phoebe was the star attraction at the air circus for the dedication of the new airport at Paragould, Arkansas, a tiny town about ninety miles northwest of Memphis. It was midmorning, before her scheduled afternoon performance. Aboard *Chiggers*, her passenger, E. Z. Newsom Jr., was a pilot for West-Nash Airlines of Paragould. As they made a pass over the airport, the plane suddenly veered right, flipped over, then righted again as Phoebe struggled for control. It seemed as though she would succeed in bringing it in for an emergency landing, but then, at about 250 feet off the ground, *Chiggers* dived nose first into a fence. Both aboard were severely injured. First reports indicated that Mr. Newsom had internal injuries and was not expected to live and that Phoebe had broken both her legs so severely that amputation might be necessary to save her life.[35] When Vernon came for her, he'd rigged the Stinson like an ambulance. This was the second time in as many years that he had rushed to the side of his seriously injured wife. If he had words with her about it, no record survives. Likely as not he knew Phoebe lived to fly and that was that.

After both pilots had been transferred to Memphis' Baptist Hospital, the extent of their injuries was clearer. Newsom had a broken leg as well as internal injuries of an unspecified nature. Phoebe had broken her left leg near the ankle and the right near the knee. She had also reopened the long scar over her left eye from her crash at Armstrong the previous year. *Chiggers* did not survive.[36]

Five months later, Phoebe appeared in the newspaper again, wearing braces and smiling after landing from her first flight since the accident. She reported that she was "almost thankful" for the crash. She explained that she hated to see any sort of aviation accident because it retarded the whole industry, but in this case, there was a benefit. Careful analysis of the accident revealed that a wing control cable had slipped off a pulley, causing the controls to lock and hurling the plane to the ground. As a result, the company modified the pulley on all subsequent Monocoupes.[37] Still depending on a cane to help her walk on her damaged legs, Phoebe headed back to Moline to pick up a new ship to replace *Chiggers*. The Monocoupe 113 was powered by a new seven-cylinder Warner Scarab 110 hp motor and dubbed *Miss Moline*.[38] Phoebe began making plans to break a record. First she considered attempting to shatter the women's endurance flight record of twenty-two hours.[39] For unknown reasons, this quest was abandoned in favor of setting a new altitude record. The standing altitude record for women was set by Louise Thaden at 20,200 feet; the record for light planes was 24,000 made by Barney Zimmerling.[40] Phoebe made arrangements to do the attempt during the Memorial Day program at the airport in St. Louis.[41] Unfortunately the official sealed barograph sent from the National Aeronautical Association, which was necessary in order to substantiate a new record, was inadvertently given to another flier. So no attempt was made. Phoebe considered trying it again at the grand opening of the new Memphis Municipal Airport, but there was not enough time to get the necessary equipment in place since she was already committed to participate in the Michigan Air Tour, Indiana Air Tour, and a race in Iowa that summer.[42] But she did not abandon the idea.

The new municipal airport opened in Memphis with appropriate fanfare that June. Pressed by Universal Aviation of Chicago, which wanted a route from Cincinnati to New Orleans to go through Memphis, and the increasing demand for passenger service demonstrated by Mid-South Airways, the airport commission finally responded. They leased about 200 acres of land at Winchester and Hollyford Road (now Airways) seven miles from downtown. The commission contracted with Standard Oil Company to construct a hangar and administration building in return for exclusive sales of aviation fuel. The result was a two-story filling station with airport offices on the second floor.[43] Mid-South Airways, Curtiss-Wright, and Universal Aviation all bid for exclusive rights for a fixed base operation at the new airport.

The giant Curtiss-Wright won easily. They bought out Omlie's Mid-South Airways and employed Vernon Omlie, "one of the safest and most practical pilots in the South," as chief pilot and operations manager.[44]

"Memphis is a full-fledged flying city now," proclaimed the newspaper at the new Memphis Municipal Airport's official dedication on 15 June 1929. By midafternoon, Hollyfield Road was blocked for over a mile by cars trying to get to the celebration. "A wriggling mass of humanity . . . estimated at 25,000, moved about the sidelines under a blistering sun" to see the new facilities—three hangars and a sod-field runway—and the more than 200 airplanes that flew in for the opening.[45] A military squadron from Pensacola Naval Base flew over in a perfect "V" formation, and a stunt flier named Freddie Lund, billed as the "Bronco Buster of the Skies," was "responsible for many a sun-burned tonsil" as he thrilled the crowd with his aerial prowess. Summing it all up, the *Commercial Appeal* proclaimed, "A new era dawns which knows no boundaries, no roads, no limitations."[46] The stock market crashed four months later.

After the celebration, Phoebe flew back up to Moline to make one last attempt at an altitude record. Her ship was fitted with oxygen tanks and officials from the National Aeronautical Association tucked the sealed barograph into the small cabin. Dressed in a fur-lined flying suit and heavy gloves, she took off into the clear blue sky over the quad cities. For two hours, several thousand spectators anxiously scanned the sky. As she came in sight, she was flying a bit erratically and as she spiraled to earth, spectators could see that the front glass on her plane was covered with oil and frost. She stumbled from the cockpit, pale and bleeding from her nose, and collapsed.[47] Once she got her bearings again, she told the press what had happened.

> It began to get pretty cold. At 15,000 feet it was winter and the atmosphere began to thin out. I put on the oxygen mask and turned the oxygen tanks on. I thought the oxygen would run out and cut down the flow and right there I made a mistake. I had it too thin and it began to tell on me . . . . When the altimeter reached 25,400 feet my motor blew a spark plug. Almost at once the main oil line went bad and the oil began to spray back in my face. It blinded me and I was half dizzy from lack of sufficient oxygen. I nosed the ship down and started for earth. I guess I was pretty dizzy when I finally got down low enough to breathe well and peek out a little hole in the side of the cabin to see where I was heading. I managed to swing the plane around the field a couple of times and start side-slipping and fish-tailing in. The ship landed all right but I was groggy.[48]

Her altimeter topped at 25,400, smashing Thaden's record by 5,200 feet and Zimmerling's altitude record for light planes by nearly 1,500 feet. This was, said the newspaper, "a personal triumph and a convincing demonstration of the ruggedness and power of the Monocoupe."[49] The sealed barograph was lifted out of her plane and sent to Washington to be verified.

The press talked with Vernon that night. He expressed pleasure that his wife had been successful. "But I wasn't worried about it," he said, "I knew she would make it."[50] Phoebe told her husband on the phone that she was "pretty thrilled and happy . . . . I'm coming home in about two weeks—just as soon as I can complete my plans for the Cleveland race."[51] She announced to the press that she would enter the Cleveland transcontinental race to be held in August "provided event officials permit feminine pilots to compete. It was announced recently that a special race would be arranged for women if five entries in each of the two classes could be secured."[52]

Three weeks later, the Bureau of Standards announced that its calibration of the barograph carried by Phoebe Omlie did not substantiate the establishment of a new record. The calibration indicated she reached a maximum altitude of 17,467 feet. Bitterly disappointed, Phoebe said that she could not believe that her altimeter could vary by as much as 8,000 feet.[53] She said she hoped to make another attempt and that when she did, two barographs would be carried along with a new altimeter for her Monocoupe.[54]

But first she had other obligations. She was booked to compete in an air race sponsored by the Iowa Aeronautical Association in connection with the state aviation show at Des Moines. The unusual format for the race provided that the pilot must start from some point outside the state of Iowa and arrive at Des Moines between 8 AM and noon on 19 July. Prizes were awarded on the basis of speed, distance covered, and the combined weight of the pilot, plane, and baggage.[55]

Four Monocoupes entered the race, one starting from Hasting, Nebraska, another from Manhattan, Kansas, a third began in Dodge City, Kansas. Phoebe elected to make the longest flight of the race, beginning at Albany, New York.[56] She flew nonstop from Albany to Moline, then continued on to Des Moines the following morning. Despite encountering two severe thunderstorms en route, she made excellent time and, given her great distance, was the clear winner. She was barred from the free-for-all light plane race at the meet, but handily defeated "all other feminine entries in the 30-mile race for women," and shone "in various types of exhibition flying."[57] By this time it was the end of July and Phoebe was keen to join the

Cleveland air races, which had finally decided to let "the girls" have a trans-continental race of their own.

The National Air Races were a combination of major public spectacle and industrial fair. Calling itself the "Air Classic of the Century," the ten-day extravaganza featured nine cross-country derbies, thirty-five closed-course race events, stunt flying in a wide variety of airplane sizes and capabilities, army and navy maneuvers, gliders, dirigibles, and parachute jumping. A new $10 million public hall in downtown Cleveland housed some 250 exhib-its of aircraft, motors, and accessories. The "most expensive airplane ever placed on exhibition" was a jewel-encrusted model tri-motor airplane val-ued at $400,000. Boeing's newest tri-motor transport was on display out-side Cleveland City Hall. Reflective of the ballyhoo of 1920s air-mindedness, the events and races had a kind of split personality. On the one hand, the stunts and daredevil aspects dazzled the crowd, but on the other, organizers were committed to winning public acceptance for commercial aviation by emphasizing safety, economy, comfort, and reliability.[58]

It was this second aspect that the organizers had in mind in sponsoring a women's derby. Having women participate would surely demonstrate that aviation was safe and easy. Marketing director for the derby, Frank Copeland, asserted that "If the . . . weaker sex accomplishes the art of flying, it is posi-tive proof of the simplicity and universal practicality of individual flying."[59] Or, as Louise Thaden once put it, "Nothing impresses the safety of aviation on the public quite so much as to see a woman fly a plane." If a woman can handle it, she said, "the public thinks it must be duck soup for men."[60] For their part, the women wanted to compete for the same reasons men did: to experience adventure, to make history, to demonstrate their abilities, "to show the world that we could do it."[61] German pilot Thea Rasche remarked, "Flying is more thrilling than love for a man and far less dangerous."[62]

Since the announcement, race coordinators had been debating the ground rules, mostly designed to protect the women from potential haz-ards. Suggestions included requiring the women to carry (male) navigators so they wouldn't get lost, male mechanics to keep their planes running, and to begin the race somewhere east of the Rockies to spare them the danger-ous mountains. These ideas were met with stiff protests from the women pilots who argued that should male navigators or mechanics accompany the women, any Hollywood starlet could enter and have her mechanic do the flying. Further, with a man along, women pilots would be assumed to have had the men do the flying. Amelia Earhart told the *New York Times*, "I for one and some of the other women fliers . . . think it is ridiculous to advertise this as an important race and then set us down at Omaha for a level flight to Cleveland. As for suggesting that we carry a man to navigate our own course through the Rockies I, for one, won't enter. None of us will enter unless it is going to be a real sporting contest."[63]

The suggestions were dropped. This first National Women's Air Derby, Santa Monica to Cleveland, would cover 2,700 miles over eight days, with seventeen stops in as many cities. It would be a real test of their navigational and piloting prowess and include tangible rewards. The Santa Monica Exchange Club, which sponsored the race, put up $8,000 in prize money and sponsors at the various overnight stops put up lap prizes for each leg of the race.[64] The women's race was one of three cross-country races set to converge at the 1929 National Air Races and Aeronautical Exposition at Cleveland. The other two cross-country races for men began at Portland, Oregon, and Miami Beach, Florida.[65] The Graf Zeppelin, in the course of its around-the-world flight, was also heading for the rendezvous in Cleveland.[66]

Seventy women held U.S. Department of Commerce licenses in the summer of 1929 (compared to over 9,500 men), but only forty met the Women's Derby requirements: one hundred hours of solo flight including twenty-five hours of solo cross-country flights of more than forty miles from the starting point. In addition to a Department of Commerce pilot's license, competitors had to hold a license issued by the Federation Aeronautique Internationale (FAI) and an annual sporting license from the National Aeronautic Association, the American representative of the FAI.[67]

Twenty women signed up to participate. They came from across the United States and included Thea Rasche, Germany's first female stunt flier, and New Zealander Jessie "Chubby" Keith-Miller, the first woman to fly from England to Australia.[68] More than half were experienced pilots like Phoebe and Ruth Nichols, who had both been flying since 1922.[69] Phoebe had accumulated over 2,000 hours of flying time, making her the most experienced pilot in the race. Though she was still wearing braces on her legs and hobbled with a cane in each hand, that didn't seem to affect her flying. She had even come up with a method to reduce her fatigue in the air by rigging up a door spring on the stick to act as a stabilizer.[70] Her most important asset was her experience in the Ford Reliability Air Tour. As a result, she was intimately familiar with what she and her machine were capable of as well as many of the challenges a cross-continental race entailed.

Seven women held transport licenses in 1929, and six of them were in the race.[71] Some of the women flew for a living, like Phoebe, Louise Thaden, and Ruth Nichols, who demonstrated airplanes for their manufacturers, and Marvel Crosson, who was an experienced bush pilot in Alaska. Many had gone after records for endurance and altitude, but Louise Thaden held the trifecta: she had set a woman's altitude record at 20,200 feet in December 1928; a women's endurance record at 22 hours, 3 minutes, 28 seconds in March 1929; and a women's speed record at 156 miles per hour in April 1929.[72] Ruth Elder had just made an unsuccessful attempt to be the first female to replicate Lindbergh's achievement of a solo transatlantic flight.[73] More than half of the entrants were relative newcomers to flying, having acquired their licenses within the past year. And a few, like Opal Kunz, Gladys O'Donnell, and Mary Von Mach, had barely achieved the minimum flying hours in time for the race.[74] Amelia Earhart, the most famous of the women competing, was better known for her writing and speaking tours following her famous transatlantic flight—as a passenger—the previous June. She was flying the derby to prepare herself to fly the Atlantic, this time as the pilot.[75] G. P. Putnam, Amelia's sponsor and later husband, offered Elinor Smith, a highly experienced pilot, a guaranteed two-year income if she would consent to be Amelia's pilot and mechanic during the derby. Smith would fly the plane while Amelia would appear to be doing it. Putnam indicated that Amelia was not "physically sturdy" nor experienced enough to fly herself. Smith refused. As a consequence, Smith was unable to secure a ship to fly in the derby, although she did compete in closed-course races in Cleveland at the end.[76]

The women flew a variety of machines, from light sport planes to high-performance aircraft, from Phoebe's 110 hp Monocoupe to Amelia's giant six-passenger 450 hp Lockheed Vega. Six of the competitors flew 225 hp Travel Airs. Most of the planes had open cockpits, subjecting their occupants to high winds, relentless sun, and needles of rain.[77] The planes were divided into two classes based on cubic-inch piston displacement (the sum total volume of all of the engine's cylinders). In the CW class were the lighter sport planes with 510 cubic inches or less.[78] The DW class covered planes with up to 800-cubic-inch displacement engines.[79] Pilots could either fly alone or carry one other woman who had never soloed in an airplane to act as her mechanic. No male person would be allowed to ride in any ship in the derby.[80]

They gathered at Clover Field in Santa Monica on 18 August 1929 for the eight-day race that would land them in Cleveland on the twenty-sixth. Phoebe almost didn't make it on time for takeoff. She'd gotten a late start and encountered a headwind on the way west. It was dark when she arrived in the Los Angeles area, and she couldn't find the airport. They either had no lights or had shut them off. She was low on gas so she picked out a dark spot she hoped was a hayfield and landed. She taxied to a house on the edge of the field where the farmer and his boys helped her stake her plane down. As they were walking to the house, a car arrived with two men who demanded to know who she was and what she was doing there. She explained she had arrived for the Women's Derby set to start the next day, but had been unable to spot the unlighted airport. Being low on gasoline, she had landed in the field. The men, from the sheriff's office, suspected she was "running dope." They finally consented to drive her to the airport where people there could identify her and verify her story. Mollified, they released her. It turned out she was only about six miles from the airport; she flew in the next morning for the start of the race.[81]

A crowd estimated at 200,000 and hordes of press greeted the women pilots at Clover Field, many of them enchanted with the very idea of a woman setting off alone across the sky.[82] Among them was pilot and humorist Will Rogers, who had been invited to provide commentary. He joined with the many others engaged in trivializing the women's skills and achievements. The women were entering a world reserved for men, rejecting roles women were expected to play. The men regarded them with a mixture of dread and derision and this was reflected in Rogers's remarks. Though he avoided some of the more common sobriquets of the day like Petticoat Pilots and Flying Flappers, as he looked over the field of female pilots, he remarked that it looked like a "powder puff derby" to him. The name stuck.[83]

Far more interest was shown in the pilots' clothing than the displacement of their engines. Most wore coveralls or jodhpurs, but they would need more feminine garb for the many banquets and public events they would have to attend along the way. Having very little room on board, some of the women sent clothes on ahead. Marvel Crosson told reporters that she would not be sending clothes but would wear a dress beneath her aviation coat and "take a toothbrush. That's all." Gladys O'Donnell impatiently told reporters that "flying fast will be hard work." She would wear coveralls "and nothing else," pointedly adding, "This is no tea party."[84]

The race was serious business. Planes were often unreliable and much of the terrain they would cover was remote and potentially hazardous. Limited navigational aids—a road map and a compass—made them vulnerable to losing their way, and poor wind information might force them to use more fuel than they anticipated. It was so risky that all the pilots were required to carry a gallon of water, enough food for three days, and a parachute.[85]

Nineteen planes lined up at the field. Mary Haizlip's plane had failed to arrive; she would join the race later. The deafening growl of aircraft engines vibrated the air. Louise Thaden described waiting for takeoff with "dry mouths, wild pumping hearts, sweating hands fumbling over maps, controls, adjusting goggles . . . . [The pilots experienced] hope, determination, a feeling of history in the making . . . adventure, youth soaring carefree on wings of romance."[86]

A pistol shot fired at Cleveland and radioed to Clover Field was the signal for the takeoff. The winner would be the one who completed the race in the shortest elapsed time. This meant that the women in the CW class had little chance against the higher-powered and thus faster planes, but there would be a trophy for the winner in the light planes and lap prizes along the way.

The six CW entries went out first, at one-minute intervals. Then after a ten-minute pause, the DW planes left at one-minute intervals. Their first leg was deliberately short, a sixty-six-mile hop to San Bernardino, a chance to shake down the planes before the longer laps and to enjoy the first of many chicken dinners. The flight path followed the pass between the San Bernardino Mountains to the north and the San Jacinto Mountains to the south. Here the cool, moist coastal air met the hot dry desert air, fueling violent updrafts and downdrafts that tested the strength of the planes and the resolve of the pilots.[87] This first stop set the stage for the others to follow. Three things were immediately clear: the pilots could count on mechanical failures, challenging landing fields choked with dust, and over-scheduling of their time. Engine trouble and forced landings began immediately; crackups they called them, as though they were minor inconveniences: broken propellers, shattered undercarriages, smashed landing gear. Repair crews on the ground and accompanying the race in chase planes usually had the planes back in the air overnight. Dust was a major hazard at every airport along the route. Runways were graded dirt. Most planes did not have brakes. Instead they had tail skids, flat metal shoes that dug into the ground to slow their speed upon landing. These were perfect for grass landings but a big problem when dozens of planes were landing on a dirt runway. The tail skids stirred up dust that rose dozens of feet into the air, as impenetrable as thick fog, obscuring vision and camouflaging the runway.

With their schedules at the whim of dignitaries, chambers of commerce, exchange club coordinators, and aggressive reporters, the women had little choice but to be available and gracious for an endless stream of events, speeches, luncheons, banquets, autographs, and interviews, many of which lasted late into the night. All this activity left the women with little time to take care of their planes, plan for the next day's flight, or sleep.

Phoebe, first out, was the first to arrive in San Bernardino, thirty-two minutes and fifteen seconds later.[88] Amelia Earhart and Mary Von Mach arrived late, having turned back to Santa Monica with engine trouble, before resuming the race. Thousands of spectators, eager to see the women, had parked along the graded runway, narrowing the field and allowing no margin for error. This was particularly treacherous for the large planes. The landing gear consisted of two wheels in front and a small wheel or skid on the tail; this nose-high posture meant that visibility was blocked during takeoff and landing. The pilot had to lean out the side to see the runway, plan the landing, then land essentially blind.

The women were landing dangerously close together in the swirling dust. Von Mack, upon seeing how crowded the field was, elected to land elsewhere and try to catch up the next day. Amelia came in hot, overshot the runway, and scattered the crowd. Opal Kunz ground-looped off the short landing strip and collapsed one side of her landing gear.[89] At San Bernardino, a mechanic mistakenly poured oil in "Chubby" Keith-Miller's gas tank; the same thing had happened to Ruth Elder in Santa Monica. Fortunately, the mistakes were caught in time.[90]

The race almost halted at San Bernardino when a protest developed over the next stop. The women balked at continuing the flight because of their objections to a recent change in the route that required them to land at Calexico on the Mexican border. The field, they argued, was too small to permit fast planes to land safely. After long and contentious debate, a compromise was reached at midnight: the pilots would fly low over Calexico to permit checkers to register their numbers. The next landing would be at Yuma.[91] Because of the distance, the morning takeoff time was changed from 8 AM to 6 AM. To bed by 2, up at 4, ready to take off at 6.[92]

Coming across the trackless desert of southern California, Mary Haizlip got lost and wandered into Mexico. Haizlip, who had started the race a day late while awaiting a new plane after having mechanical problems with the first one, approached Calexico after dark. After landing where she saw lights, Haizlip learned she was on the wrong side of the border. It took her several hours to work her way through the red tape to get clearance from Mexican authorities and get out of there.[93] Three women were forced down in the desert with mechanical difficulties. Bobbi Trout ran out of fuel just short of Yuma, landed in a plowed field, cart-wheeling her Golden Eagle and doing serious damage. She was out of the race for three days while her plane was repaired.[94] Thea Rasche damaged her landing gear in a forced landing in the desert after a clogged carburetor stopped her motor; her fuel line was full of contaminants, including scraps of fiber and rubber. Rasche had been handed a telegram while still in Santa Monica warning her to watch out for sabotage. This, she said, was proof.[95] Further proof seemed to come from Claire Fahy, who had been forced down at Calexico with broken wing struts on her Travel Air. She claimed foul play; she charged that someone had deliberately poured acid over her wire wing braces. Following a hastily called press conference, Fahy withdrew from the race.[96]

Yuma was "ten degrees hotter than blazes."[97] Wind had drifted sand over the runway, making it difficult to distinguish the landing strip from the surrounding desert. Phoebe landed okay, leading the way in the small plane class. Amelia ran off the edge, nosed over, and broke her propeller. She immediately called to have a propeller flown in from Los Angeles. The other pilots elected to delay the race long enough for Amelia to get back in the race.[98] As a consequence of their late start for Phoenix, they took off in the hot afternoon. One-hundred-twenty-degree temperatures bred heat thermals, violent updrafts followed by equally violent downdrafts that pitched the pilots about in their seats. The struggle to maintain control and the desolation of the terrain stirred their fevered imaginations. Thaden described her experience:

> Surreptitiously you strain to the side, searching out possible spots where a landing might be made, analyzing swiftly, working out a plan of possible procedure. Would it be better to pancake in, or go in on a wing to absorb shock? Through your mind's eye flashes a picture of a twisted mass of tangled wreckage, lying in a small crumpled heap far off the beaten track. You see yourself painfully crawling from between broken logerons and telescoped cowling, to lie gasping under the pitiless glare of the desert sun, helpless and alone.[99]

Phoenix was like an oasis, a big well-maintained airport with experienced mechanics, hot showers, and another chicken dinner. Pancho Barnes was late into Phoenix. She had apparently followed the wrong set of railroad tracks coming out of Yuma and wandered over the border. She realized her mistake when locals told her "hola" instead of "hello." Pancho hurriedly took off, avoiding a confrontation with authorities that had delayed Haizlip. Upon arrival, Pancho painted "Mexico or Bust" on the side of her plane.[100]

Phoebe was still leading in the light plane division, running about two hours behind Thaden, who had been consistently ahead in the heavy plane class.

Everyone arrived safely at Phoenix except Marvel Crosson. She had not been seen since the group took off from Yuma. Rumor had it that she had crashed in the desert, but search parties had found nothing. The women met to comfort one another and reassure one another that Marvel, no matter what happened, would want them to go on. Thaden was philosophical.

If your time has come to go, it is a glorious way in which to pass over. Smell of burning oil, the feel of strength and power beneath our hands. So quick has been the transition from life to death there must still linger in your mind's eye the everlasting beauty and joy of flight . . . . We women pilots were blazing a new trail. Each pioneering effort must bow to death. There has never been nor will there ever be progress without sacrifice of human life. . . . To us the successful completion of the derby was of more import than life or death.[101]

The women took off for Douglas, Arizona, the next day. The news of Crosson waited for them. Following the directions of witnesses who said they had seen the plane go into a tailspin, diving earthward from about 1,000 feet, and plunge into heavy cottonwood growth along the Gila River, searchers found Marvel's body in a boulder-strewn ravine at daybreak. They carried the body out of the remote area north of Wellton, Arizona, on horseback. The badly broken body was found about 300 feet from her smashed plane, around her was draped a parachute that had not opened.[102]

The news of Crosson's death, along with charges of sabotage by Fahy and Rasche, and the two incidents of oil being put in fuel tanks early in the race, prompted a series of investigations, focused mainly on the security of the planes at San Bernardino and to a lesser extent, Clover Field. The report issued by the district attorney at San Bernardino two days later said that the investigations failed to disclose any foundation for the sabotage charges. They found that the planes had been adequately guarded from suspicious characters or overly curious crowds and that Rasche's telegram had been proven spurious. Someone from Moth Aircraft, the maker of Rasche's ship, found no evidence of tampering and attributed the contaminants to a recently replaced fuel line.[103] J. W. Noel, an inspector for the Federal Department of Commerce who investigated Crosson's crash, also found no evidence of tampering. It was his opinion that she fell ill due to the desert heat and lost control of her ship. She may have tried to jump but had insufficient altitude to open her parachute.[104]

Calls for stopping the race bounced around in the media following the death of Marvel Crosson. Women should not be allowed to risk their lives, cried the headlines. "Airplane Races Too Hazardous an Adventure for Women Pilots," said an editorial in *The New York American*;[105] "Women Have Conclusively Proven They Can't Fly"; "Women's Derby Should Be Terminated."[106] But as Amelia later wrote, "A fatal accident to a woman pilot is not a greater disaster than one to a man of equal worth. Feminine fliers have never subscribed to the super-sentimental valuation placed upon their necks."[107] A Texas oilman named Halliburton stated categorically that "Women have been dependent on man for guidance for so long that when they are put on their own resources they are handicapped." Derby manager Frank Copeland responded that "We wish officially to thumb our collective nose at Halliburton. There will be no stopping this race."[108] The women pressed on to El Paso.

Chubby Keith-Miller ran out of gas and had to set down in the desert. She walked eighteen miles for fuel only to return and find that cactus had ripped her fuselage. Some assistance from a farmer armed with duct tape got her going long enough to get to El Paso.[109] At El Paso, fierce winds and swirling sands made landing treacherous. Phoebe was still leading the CW class with an elapsed time of 8:35:24, and still about two hours behind Louise (6:48:31).[110] Reports of dangerous thunderstorms at Pecos, their next stop, held the women in El Paso overnight.[111] Fatigued from long days of flying, long evenings of festivities, and the endless fixing and patching of their planes, the pilots looked forward to a brief respite at El Paso since it had not been intended to be an overnight stop. Word quickly spread, however, and hundreds rushed to the field. Derby participants spent some three hours signing autographs. The women were "marooned at our crates by mobs who demanded signatures. Books, scrap paper, backs of envelopes, fine writing paper and everything else . . . . Without doubt, every man, woman, and child in Texas has our autographs," wrote Louise.[112]

The next day dawned bright and clear, perfect weather as they climbed to 6,000 feet to get over the mountains, but the trip to Pecos was yet another test of the women's abilities. The runway at Pecos was a narrow strip hastily cleared out of mesquite and sage brush, lined with automobiles on both sides. To avoid hitting them, Edith Foltz ground looped and Gladys O'Donnell overshot the field, both mishaps causing minor damage to landing gear. But this was a very bad day for Pancho. She had been forced to turn back to El Paso shortly after takeoff when one cylinder stopped functioning. She was on her way in an hour after the repair of her broken exhaust valve. But coming into land at Pecos, she smashed her plane into an automobile parked too close to the runway. She was unhurt, but both wings had been irreparably damaged. She had to withdraw from the race.[113]

Blanche Noyes landed shortly afterward, wobbling down the runway on one wheel. She emerged from the cockpit covered with black soot. She told a harrowing tale of having fought a fire in her baggage compartment. The terrifying smell of smoke forced her to land quickly in the desert, side-slipping her plane to take the airflow away from the direction of the smoke. She could not budge her fire extinguisher from its holder, so she ripped it and part of the wooden flooring out of the plane, severely burning her hand. Then she used sand to put out the rest of the fire. She had lost a wheel taking off from the soft sand. Her burns were treated and her plane repaired in Pecos.[114] Chubby arrived to tell of being caught in a dust-devil, a miniature twister common in the desert. Helplessly, she hung on while her plane flipped several times in the air, losing altitude fast. Deciding against using her parachute, she rode through the ordeal, managing to retake control of her plane a few hundred feet from the ground.[115]

The fliers pressed on through three stops in Texas, Midland, Abilene, and then Fort Worth for an overnight stop. Phoebe, with an elapsed time of 13:28:50, and Louise at 11:04:30, maintained their leads in their respective classes. By this time, the pilots were exhausted. Several of them had made multiple unplanned landings, multiple repairs, and this day was one of their longest for having to make up for the unexpected overnight stop in El Paso. Margaret Perry, who had been battling illness for several days, checked herself into the hospital. She told physicians that she barely remembered landing her plane in Fort Worth. They found she had typhoid fever. Perry was out of the race.[116]

There was a three-hour stop in Tulsa, then on to Wichita, Kansas, Louise's home, for a tumultuous welcome. The pilots finally left the desert behind, but they danced in between thunderstorms all the way to Kansas. Upon arrival, they dutifully cleaned up and dressed up as best they could for the banquet and festivities, but they could not disguise the white pattern of their goggles across their brown sun- and wind-burned faces. Coming out of Wichita, Gladys O'Donnell upended her plane, damaging the propeller. Her mechanic quickly filed off the tip and she was on her way.[117]

From Wichita the fliers turned eastward for their next overnight stop at Parks Airport in East St. Louis. The field was very short with obstructions at either end. Blanche Noyes landed first but, in her second Women's Derby accident, she damaged a wheel. Neva Paris came in too fast, overshot the field, and cracked her undercarriage. Ruth Nichols also had trouble landing and damaged one wheel. Thea Rasche was still struggling with contaminated fuel; she reported a forced landing between Kansas City and St. Louis to clean a clogged fuel line. Mary Haizlip was also forced down fourteen miles west of St. Louis with a broken gasoline line. And Bobbi Trout, a full day behind because of engine trouble at Pecos, still had not caught up.[118] Louise Thaden maintained her lead with an elapsed time of 16:27:57, although Gladys and Amelia were gaining a bit on her. Phoebe, at 20:23:33, was almost two hours ahead of her nearest CW challenger, Edith Foltz.[119]

In Cleveland, the big party had already started without them. On 24 August, the day the derby landed in East St. Louis, the 1929 National Air Races and Aeronautical Exposition opened at Cleveland for a ten-day run. An estimated 300,000 spectators lined the streets for a massive parade: four miles of floats, most of them covered with fresh flowers, depicted the advance of transportation from the horse-drawn skids of native Americans to the chariots of the Persians to the locomotive and automobile and culminating in the airplane. Twenty-one bands and 1,500 marchers accompanied the floats while an armada of military and civilian aircraft, including three blimps, flew overhead. Every evening featured a musical extravaganza with a cast of 120 called "Wings of Love," capped by night-flying exhibitions and pyrotechnic displays. Over 100,000 spectators paid admission to the first day of the races, the largest gathering in the city's history, overflowing the 30,000-seat capacity grandstands and the 38,000 parking spaces. Roads leading into Cleveland were blocked for hours.[120]

The daily flying schedule included "dead-stick" landing contests with pilots coming in with the engine off, glider demonstrations, balloon-bursting contests, lighter-than-air craft, homing pigeon races, endurance contests, aerobatics exhibitions, parachute jumping contests, and military demonstrations. The Navy High Hat precision flying Squadron of nine planes performed intricate aerobatics while roped together with twelve-yard ropes in units of three. They took off together, rolled together, looped together, never losing their formation and never breaking the ropes that connected them.[121]

As the women left East St. Louis, there remained only two intermediate stops—Terre Haute and Cincinnati—and one more overnight stop at Columbus. Then a short hop into Cleveland on the final day. Chubby Keith-Miller was forced down near Xenia, Ohio, with engine trouble. She decided to stay the night with the farm family nearby.[122] Bobbi Trout landed in a farmer's field outside Cincinnati with engine trouble, then further damaged her plane when the fence ripped a large hole in her aileron. She patched it with a piece of tin can and some bailing wire, then limped back into the race.[123] Thea Rasche and Ruth Elder also made emergency dead-stick landings. Rasche discovered her oil case was almost empty; Elder's motor failed on final approach and she skillfully threw her ship into a sharp bank to avoid a smashup.[124] Louise and Phoebe were still leading their respective classes, due largely, it seems, to the fact that they had not had mechanical problems. Louise suspected sabotage at St. Louis: "I was still in the lead which may account for someone filing the breaker points on both magnetos during the night." Fortunately, her mechanic discovered them before takeoff.[125]

The final day of the race, owing to a late takeoff for the short hop into Cleveland, the women were able to rest in the morning. Ruth Nichols, who'd had some work done on her plane, took it up for a shakedown before the race resumed. As she came in for a landing, she failed to see a steamroller parked at the end of the runway and smashed into it head on, somersaulting the plane and landing upside down in the dirt. Nichols crawled out of the wreckage, but her plane was totally destroyed and she was out of the race.[126]

As the women took off for the 126 miles to Cleveland, Phoebe was comfortably in the lead in the CW class, and Thaden was an hour ahead of O'Donnell and almost two hours ahead of Earhart. A huge crowd awaited the arrival of the Women's Derby and when Louise Thaden's Travel Air came into view, the crowd went wild. She barely got her prop stopped before the crowd surged around her. A dozen men picked up Thaden and her plane and carried them to a spot in front of the grandstand.[127] Into the microphone thrust in her face, Thaden said, "I'm glad to be here. All the girls flew a splendid race, much better than I. Each one deserves first place, because each one *is* a winner. Mine is a faster ship. Thank you."[128] Thaden later told reporters that she won only because she had the fastest ship. Since the Women's Derby was a speed race, "the heavyweight rates the honors."[129]

Thirteen women came in behind her. Gladys O'Donnell was the second to arrive, Amelia Earhart third, and Blanche Noyes fourth.[130] Phoebe was the fifth plane to land, hardly noticed in the tumult that gathered around Louise and Amelia. Nonetheless, she had handily won the trophy for the CW class and the $600 prize money.[131] Altogether the women had traveled 2,759 miles, averaging just over 300 miles and two chicken dinners a day.[132]

The finish generated considerable excitement, but it was the closed-course races that provided the most thrills for the fans in the stands. These head-to-head races were ten laps around a five-mile circuit marked by prominent towers called pylons. This kind of flying requires a great deal of skill and control. The contesting planes line up abreast of each other. At the drop of the starter's flag, they all begin their takeoffs simultaneously and head for the first pylon. Any plane passing another must keep at least 150 feet to the right of, or 50 feet above, the plane being overtaken, and must never attempt to pass between that plane and the pylon. The plane being overtaken must hold its altitude and course so as not to interfere with the faster plane. The trick is to fly as fast as one can and as close to the pylons as possible, tipping the plane up on its wingtip at an alarming 40–50 degrees of bank, sweeping around the pylon with just a few feet to spare.[133]

The Ladies CW Class Race was the first appearance of women pilots in closed-course racing.[134] Adding to the danger were other events taking place simultaneously. Due to the direction of the wind, the U.S. Navy exhibition team took off directly in front of the stands, sending up a cloud of dust near the home pylon and making the women's race temporarily invisible to the crowd and extremely dangerous for the women making the turn.[135] Despite the difficulties, "Phoebe Omilie [*sic*] in particular seemed to be gifted in her ability to get around the pylon in a matter of a few seconds in her diminutive Warner-powered Monocoupe."[136] She clocked the race at 112.37 mph, easily defeating her opponents. Chubby Keith-Miller finished at 98.73, Lady Mary Heath 96.17, Blanche Noyes 85.12.[137] Upon landing, Phoebe learned that she was disqualified for missing a pylon. Adding injury to insult, as Phoebe climbed out of *Miss Moline* at the end of the pylon race, she stepped from her plane into a hole in the field and once again broke her ankle.[138] She filed a protest against her disqualification arguing that when she had realized she had flown inside a pylon she had doubled back and circled it, so her win should count. Her claim was substantiated by Chubby Keith-Miller and Lady Heath.[139] The Contest Committee ultimately reversed their decision; Phoebe added $500 and another trophy to her winnings.[140]

Best of all, Phoebe took the Aerol Efficiency Trophy. The Cleveland Pneumatic Tool Company, maker of Aerol (air and oil, the first oleo-pneumatic landing-gear shock absorber) struts, donated the perpetual trophy called "Symbol of Flight" and $5,000 prize money to the Women's Derby.[141] Their aim was "to equalize the chances of the small and large planes to win this trophy."[142] In the contest for efficiency, it was not the fastest, highest-powered plane that won but the pilot who demonstrated ingenuity, navigation, and endurance. The $3,000 solid silver trophy of a woman flier standing atop of a globe was awarded based upon a computed formula: average mph times 2.5 divided by the cubic-inch piston displacement. This would yield the figure of merit. Phoebe's figure of merit was 289.3; the derby winner, Louise, had a figure of merit of 273.2. Though Phoebe's average speed was 108.19 mph while Louise's was 135.97, when that was divided by the cubic-inch displacement of their respective planes, Phoebe won for efficiency or the best miles per hour per engine size.[143]

The competition had been tough, and the women had certainly proven themselves capable. Newspapers across the nation carried the Cleveland story extolling "the rise of women pilots to the status of men . . . . Official results of the national air races here reveal the feminine fliers have established themselves firmly in the field of aviation. The skill they displayed generally during the races earned them the right to compete with men in future air meets."[144]

As the games continued with men-only competitions, a group of women fliers met under the grandstand to talk about the future. Now that women had arrived as aviators, they felt a need to form an organization that would formalize their comradely bond with one another and promote women in aviation. Where the idea originated is unclear—some say it was Amelia's idea, others assert it was Phoebe's.[145] The group decided to include all women licensed pilots, not just those who had participated in the race. Amelia offered her secretary in New York to "get the ball rolling."[146] Ultimately, it was a group of women pilots who worked for the Curtiss Flying Service at Valley Stream, Long Island, who sent out the invitations to the 117 licensed women pilots in the United States asking them to join the as-yet unnamed organization.[147] Recipients were assured that the group would not be "a tremendously official sort of organization, just a way to get acquainted, to discuss the prospects for women pilots from both a sports and breadwinning point of view, and to tip each other off on what's going on in the industry."[148]

Twenty-six women pilots attended the formative meeting in Long Island on 2 November. Choosing a name proved one of the most difficult decisions. It was easier to reject inappropriate ones than to settle on a favorite. Among the rejected were The Climbing Vines, Homing Pigeons, Gad Flies, Angel's Club, Cloud Chasers, and Bird Women.[149] Ultimately the decision was made to base the name on the number of charter members. After eighty-six replies arrived in short order, the group was dubbed the Eighty-Sixes.[150] Within a few weeks, a few more responses arrived and the name was revised to the Ninety-Nines. The organization maintained a loose organizational structure, with Louise Thaden acting as general secretary, until the Ninety-Nines elected Amelia Earhart as their first president in 1931.[151] The Ninety-Nines eventually went international, and while their membership currently numbers into the thousands, the name remains as a testament to the original pioneers in women's aviation.

Chapter Four

Phoebe loved the challenge and adventure of competitive flying. It was also a business for her, one she was good at and one that offered large purses to skillful pilots. "My aviation career started early in 1921 when I entered the game to make money," she told the press. "There was no commercial aviation in those days to speak of and we got what we could doing exhibition work."[1] During the spring of 1930, she continued her work as a liaison between the Monocoupe factory and its distributors around the country. She flew *Miss Moline* in several state aviation tours, where she easily captured first place in the races they allowed her to enter. She spoke on behalf of the company and encouraged airport development before civic clubs throughout the United States and Canada.[2]

In August, she took delivery of a new, more powerful Monocoupe, which she immediately christened *Miss Memphis*, and headed for Chicago, the site of the 1930 National Air Races.[3] From there, she and Blanche Noyes "piloted their boudoir-like little aerial coupes" to Hoover Field in Washington, D.C., to meet the president. Given the "comfort of speedy, modern, enclosed planes," the press noted, "the need for heavy breeches and leather leggings for women" had vanished. "Only a whiff of their powder puffs was necessary to prepare" the pilots for their reception by the president. The article featured a fetching photo of Phoebe, wearing her helmet and goggles despite her plane's closed cabin, powdering her nose.[4] Phoebe showed off her new scarlet and black Monocoupe to the press. "Proudly she called attention to the red leather cushions, the colored enamel control knobs and the little blue skylight curtain which keeps the sun from burning a pilot's neck. She took off her helmet, passed a powder puff over her nose and smilingly said she was ready to meet the president as soon as she changed her stockings, which were a bit grease spattered. She wore a green and white silk suit."[5]

Reporters were certain that readers would want to know the pilots' fashion choices, so they also reported that Mrs. Noyes wore a leather coat over a light blue knitted suit. Nancy Hopkins flew in from New York to meet them wearing "a smart blue and white linen costume under her coat." The group of women pilots presented President Hoover with a giant floral invitation to the races, covered with "Herbert Hoover Roses." Afterward, they dined with the president and first lady at the White House.[6]

For the 1930 National Air Races, rather than competing head-to-head, the women's derbies were divided between the lighter and heavier horse-powered planes. The Pacific Derby for heavier planes departed from Long Beach; lighter planes flew in the Dixie Derby starting in Washington, D.C. Both races were set to converge at the Chicago Curtiss-Wright-Reynolds Airport for the opening of the air races in August.[7] Phoebe signed up for the Dixie Derby, a 1,575-mile course from Washington's Hoover Field through Virginia, North Carolina, South Carolina, Georgia, Alabama, Mississippi, Arkansas, Missouri, and back to Chicago.[8]

As the most accomplished pilot in the race, Phoebe was expected to lead the pack, and she did. The other competitors were Vera Dawn Walker, Martie Bowman, Nancy Hopkins, Laura Ingalls, and Charity Langdon. The group took off into low-hanging clouds and a steady rain. Accompanied only by a silver rabbit's foot, Phoebe beat her five competitors into Richmond in thirty-eight minutes flat at an average speed of 163 mph.[9] The weather the next day was no better: thunderstorms, lots of rain, the ceiling at about a hundred feet. The weather was so bad that airmail pilots stayed grounded.[10] Nonetheless, the women took off. The weather began to break at Raleigh, but bad luck dogged Phoebe's competitors as they flew over the Carolinas. Vera Dawn Walker, who had been at Phoebe's heels the previous day, was forced down near Darlington, South Carolina, approximately seventy-five miles off her course, by a faulty fuel line. She was not injured, but a service plane had to be sent from Columbia to repair her ship. She headed for Atlanta an hour and a half late, only to be forced down once again at Athens, Georgia. Walker abandoned the race.[11]

Guided only by highway maps covered with a confusing blizzard of railroad lines, roads, and county boundaries, Martie Bowman and Laura Ingalls both wandered over the two Carolinas in confusion. Martie landed far from her course in Charlotte, North Carolina, to get her bearings; Laura Ingalls landed at Spartanburg, South Carolina, for the same reason.[12] Phoebe moved far out in front, landing at Atlanta with a commanding two-hour lead over Bowman and nearly three hours over Ingalls.[13]

Despite her lead, Phoebe was in trouble. Dust blown into her eyes at the Washington airport soon developed into a serious eye infection. By the time she landed in Atlanta, her right eye was swollen completely closed. Martie insisted on taking her to the doctor. Initially the doctor suggested Phoebe abandon the race. Under intense pressure to come up with an alternative, he offered to prescribe drops that would need to be administered every hour all night long if she was to continue in the race. Martie left a call at the hotel desk to be awakened each hour so that she could administer the drops to Phoebe. The next day her eye was much better, thanks to the selfless assistance of her friend. When the women arrived at Memphis, with Phoebe in the lead, she refused to take the lap money, insisting that the $300 go to Martie Bowman.[14]

As the other women pilots jockeyed for position behind her, Phoebe arrived first at East St. Louis, thirty minutes ahead of the pack and setting a record on her leg from Memphis to St. Louis for flying 245 miles in one hour forty-eight minutes.[15] When she landed in Chicago she had averaged 127.5 mph for the race, finishing well ahead of Martie Bowman, who came in second fully three hours behind her. Laura Ingalls was third. Phoebe won the first-place prize of $2,000, an undetermined amount of lap money, and the Washington City Club Trophy.[16]

Spectators crowded onto the field, overflowing grandstands built for one hundred thousand, to see the arrivals of the seven air derbies, part of a program of forty-four scheduled events and over one thousand airplanes on display.[17] The U.S. Navy's High Hat and Red Ripper Squadrons staged sham battles and stunts, including the spectacular "formation barrel roll," where a trio of pursuit planes, wing to wing, flipped over as one plane. Balloon bursting contests, dead-stick landing contests, demonstration flights by auto-gyros and gliders, pylon races, and the spectacular free-for-all Thompson Trophy Race, all competed for the crowd's attention.[18]

Phoebe's wheels had hardly stopped rolling before she was lifted out of her plane and carried to a battery of microphones. She was dressed to match her plane "in a yellow crepe sport dress and crimson beret, a silver wishbone from a fine chain about her neck and wearing neat white and brown oxfords and white silk hose." Her cabin plane, the newspaper reported, made her choice of fashion possible. "I'm glad I won," Phoebe shouted to the crowd. "Right now Chicago looks almost as good to me as Memphis." When a reporter asked what message she wanted to send to the folks back home, she replied, "Just tell 'em *Miss Memphis* came in first."[19] Vernon had driven all night to be there for the finish. He greeted his exhausted wife, who collapsed in his arms. The strain of the race had stripped fifteen pounds off her tiny frame and her right eye was again swollen nearly shut. Phoebe vowed later that night that she was through with cross-country racing. "I'm quitting," she told reporters. "I've had enough."[20]

She wasn't quite finished, though. Despite her swollen eye and its impact on her depth perception, Phoebe competed in two closed-course races (five times around a five-mile circuit) the following day. Phoebe took first place in both of them, with a top speed of 135.20 mph and 139.97 mph respectively, winning another $1,250. In all, Phoebe collected $3,250 plus an estimated $300 per lap for four of five laps, or approximately $4,450.[21] She headed home to Memphis to buy back her husband's business.

Business at Memphis Municipal Airport was struggling as the Depression deepened. When the airport opened in the spring of 1929, Curtiss-Wright and Universal Aviation had optimistically set up flying schools, invested heavily in large aircraft sales, and supported expensive airport improvements. When the new lighting system was installed in March 1930, an estimated crowd of 15,000 turned out to watch demonstrations of night take-offs and landings. For a finale, Vernon and Phoebe released fireworks from their planes high in the air and lit flares attached to their aircraft to trace a series of graceful silver arcs as they looped and twirled across the sky.[22]

Universal Aviation and Transcontinental Air Transport offered cross-country passenger service from Memphis through an innovative but short-lived program of air-rail service.[23] Passengers traveled by airplane during the daylight hours, then transferred to railroad sleeper cars for the overnight portion. By the end of 1929, several airline-railroad agreements had been established. Transcontinental Air Transport (T.A.T.) was the best known of these ventures, largely because of the direct involvement of Charles Lindbergh, who surveyed the route and flew the inaugural flight, and Amelia Earhart, who invested in the airline, christened the first plane, and made the inaugural trip. Universal indicated that their linking system made it possible to cross the continent in only sixty-seven hours. T.A.T.

countered with an advertising blitz claiming a coast-to-coast time of an astonishing forty-eight hours.

> Patrons of the T.A.T. can now board the "American," a de luxe [sic] limited train of the Pennsylvania railroad, in New York in the early evening, spending the night in a sleeping car. In the morning they are transferred to a waiting airplane in Columbus, Ohio, and a daylight flight is made to Dodge City, Kansas. Stops are planned en route at Indianapolis, St. Louis, Kansas City and Wichita. After dinner at Dodge City an Atchison, Topeka & Santa Fe trail [sic] takes the passengers on another night journey in a sleeper. At Las Vegas, N. M., the final lap by air either to Los Angeles or San Francisco, arriving late that afternoon.[24]

Memphians wishing to visit the west coast, for example, could rendezvous with either system at St. Louis. The trip was comfortable and safe, but also expensive and cut only a day off the regular train trip. Moreover, planes were frequently grounded by bad weather. The worsening economy and the increasing potential for night flying soon doomed these ventures.[25]

By early 1930, Universal had suspended operations at Memphis, and Vernon was able to reacquire Mid-South Airways from Curtiss-Wright the following year. The formal reopening of "the South's oldest flying service" was celebrated on 19 October 1930 with a special program of stunt and glider flying and a parachute jump (though not by Phoebe). Vernon's operation, "capitalized at $75,000," took over the abandoned Universal hangar. The company would be distributors for four popular makes of airplanes: Stinson, Waco, Monocoupe, and Aeronca, and offer flying lessons, cross-country trips in open and closed airplanes, and local passenger hops.[26] The next few years would be lean ones for aviation nationwide, but Vernon's smaller-scale operation continued to hang on, sustained at least in part by his wife's earnings.

Despite her vow at the end of the Dixie Derby to quit cross-country racing, Phoebe still had one more major race to go. The 1931 Sweepstakes race from Santa Monica to Cleveland, under the auspices of the National Air Races, was too tempting to resist. Unlike the preceding years, this one was a mixed event with both men and women—the first time that men and women pilots would be in direct competition in the air races. The National Sweepstakes Derby offered three distinct prizes for the fliers. The three winners in the men's division would divide $6,000, the three women winners would divide $6,000, and a special prize of a Cord Cabriolet automobile valued at $2,500 would be awarded to the high point scorer, regardless of sex.[27]

All the planes would be handicapped by speed. In practical terms what this meant was that, unlike preceding races where the fastest plane won (provided it didn't fall apart and/or the pilot made no major errors), all planes would be given a handicap speed based on the various configurations of the airplanes. Rather than racing against one another, pilots would race against their own handicapped speed, with the goal of making the actual ground speed as far over the handicap speed as possible. Provided the system of handicapping was accurate, all entrants would have an equal chance of winning the Sweepstakes. Press releases emphasized that "the winner will be the man or woman who exercises the best race generalship and performs the most accurate navigation."[28]

Phoebe was keen to take up the challenge. She had covered the route in competition twice before; she intimately understood her machine and its capabilities; she had confidence in her skill as a pilot. What's more, this would be a real competition, one that would not marginalize her for her small plane or for her gender, but allow her to push her machine and herself to their maximum capability against all other competitors. She explained her eagerness to participate this way:

> In the two preceding derbies, which we won, we were fortunate in having the fastest airplane in the race. This made it possible for us to ease down on the throttle and cruise most of the way. But here, with a handicap derby, there was an opportunity to try and show the aviation and lay world that the equipment could be pushed to the utmost, and because of its efficiency, along with its speed and endurance, have a chance to win the Sweepstakes.[29]

The handicapping runs to establish the target speeds were conducted by U.S. Army officers at March Field in Riverside, California. Handicapping was based on a schedule of the average speed made by each contestant in four dashes over a one-mile course.[30] Gladys O'Donnell had the fastest plane in the race; she registered 171 mph over the speed course.[31]

Sixty-three pilots, seventeen women and forty-six men, took off from Santa Monica on 23 August on the first leg of the Transcontinental Handicap Sweepstakes Air Derby. The eight-day flight would carry the pilots over eight states, with overnight stops in Calexico, Tucson, El Paso, Amarillo,

Bartlesville, St. Louis, and Dayton.[32] The first thousand miles of the route were deemed to be the most dangerous; pilots were required to wear parachutes and carry food and water in case they were forced to land in the inhospitable western mountains and desert.[33]

Phoebe's was the third plane to take off. She made a required turn around a pylon at the southwest corner of the field, then pulled the Monocoupe into a steep climb to clear the Coastal Range thirty-five miles east of Santa Monica. In order to cut straight across the mountains and save mileage, she climbed to 9,000 feet. There she was pleased and surprised to capture a slight tailwind that brought her a greater speed than her handicap, so that her score for the first day was greater than 100 percent.[34]

Crossing the hot desert the next day, Phoebe eased back on the throttle to avoid overheating her engine as she bounced around in the convection currents on her way to Tucson. Gladys O'Donnell landed first in Tucson, but Phoebe was only twelve minutes and one second later.[35] Still, she didn't like second place, so she decided that for the next leg into El Paso, she would apply full power.[36] Already eight planes had foundered on the early legs, dropping the field to fifty-five. Three more entrants were forced down with mechanical problems on the lap from Tucson to El Paso. None of them was injured. Blanche Noyes turned back at Tucson; Earl Rowland landed in the soft desert sand east of Douglas, Arizona, damaging his landing gear; and Barney Rawson also slightly damaged his undercarriage when he landed in the desert eight miles west of El Paso.[37]

Gladys O'Donnell again led the pack of fifty-two into El Paso, with Phoebe nineteen minutes behind her. Officials made certain to announce repeatedly that arrival time meant little. Under the handicapping system, O'Donnell, who landed first, ranked fourth in the race; Phoebe landed second and was ranked second to Eldon Cessna at the fifth checkpoint.[38] On the way to Amarillo, another plane was forced down with engine trouble. Ruth Stewart made a skillful landing in rough country crossed by ditches and arroyos near Roswell, New Mexico. After repairs, Stewart proceeded on to Amarillo.[39] Handicapped tallies at the overnight stop showed Phoebe had moved ahead of Cessna and was now the leader.[40]

The greatest challenge of the race was a fierce thunderstorm with very strong winds that threatened the fliers as they headed toward Enid, Oklahoma. "My little Monocoupe tossed about like a leaf and the rain came down so hard I could scarcely see ahead of me," Phoebe later noted.[41] A fellow pilot witnessed Phoebe's arrival as she fought the gusty sixty-mile-per-hour gale:

Phoebe Omlie has just landed—and what a thrill she gave us. She put the plane's wheels on the ground five times before she got down, and then rolled first on one wheel and then the other. The wind nearly turned her plane over after she stopped rolling. Several local committeemen rushed out to the field to help her taxi in. This wind is especially treacherous for landing a high-winged monoplane.[42]

All the pilots struggled to land safely in the strong crosswind. As soon as they touched down and slowed, men grabbed wingtips to keep the planes grounded until they reached their parking places and could be tied down.[43] O'Donnell managed to turn the wind to her advantage as a tailwind; she was said to have averaged 210 miles per hour for the rest of the leg into Bartlesville. Phoebe landed second.[44] The following day, landing in East St. Louis, the two women maintained their respective leads, Phoebe landing within sixteen minutes of Gladys.[45]

The weather remained treacherous. A series of thunderstorms generated a 60 mph tailwind, pushing average speeds well beyond handicap targets. As she had at every stop, Gladys O'Donnell landed first in Dayton, but the handicap point system had Phoebe as the leader. Again, between Dayton and Akron, Ohio, the pilots ran into converging storms filled with lightning that danced from cloud to cloud. Phoebe was, she wrote, "tossed like a salad" in her tiny plane, wondering "whether the airplane was right side up or standing on end." But she held on, anxiously scanning the horizon until she finally spotted the big dirigible hangar at Akron, and landed in a drizzling rain.[46] At least two other pilots, Jean La Rene and Pancho Barnes, had been forced to land in open fields to wait out the storm.[47]

Phoebe Omlie flashed across the finish line at Cleveland, first of the contesting men and women fliers in the Transcontinental Handicap Derby. Eldon Cessna was the first man to land at Cleveland; he finished third overall. O'Donnell landed next. Although she had consistently posted faster speeds than the other competitors, O'Donnell finished sixth. "The smaller, slower planes had the advantage all the way," she complained sourly. "If I ever fly a handicap Derby again, I'll fly an old war-time Jenny."[48]

Phoebe's official first-place finish would not be announced until the following morning after hours of handicap computation by race officials. Nonetheless, the crowd saw a winner. As her plane rolled to a stop in front of the grandstand, a mob rushed forward to drape a horseshoe of roses and sweet peas over the front of *Miss Memphis.* Then, as Phoebe hopped to the ground, the wreath was snatched from the plane and draped around her shoulders for photographs.[49]

Phoebe and her handicapped competitors arrived in the middle of a ten-day extravaganza dedicated to the "grandest spectacle that peace time aviation [could] offer."[50] "With speed and more speed, thrills and more thrills, the pageantry of the air" opened the day before with an estimated 400,000 lining the streets and perched on street lamp posts and trees to watch a five-mile procession of marching bands, flower-decked floats, "living flags," "floating gardens," and military regalia.

The 1931 air races had more events and more spectacular aerial demonstrations than ever before: stunt flying by both men and women in planes of many shapes and sizes, hair-raising acrobatics by an international stunt team, precision flying by naval and marine squadrons, and one feature demonstration of dazzling new radio technology. Al Williams, flying his Flaming Hawk biplane, took his stunting orders from his audience. The "voice of the people" talked to Al through the announcer and a radio transmitting and receiving set. This set was a seventeen-pound affair built for this demonstration by Western Electric Company. The transmitter came with a special helmet with headphones attached. All Al had to do was flip a switch and he could hear the announcer giving him flying instructions from the audience, which he would then execute. The communications were broadcast over the public address system as the crowd watched in astonishment.[51] The afternoon show featured "the greatest exhibition of daredevil flying ever staged in this air-thrill-wise city." German World War I ace, Maj. Ernst Udet, pitted "his flying skill against the laws of gravity," piloting his plane "in positions never intended by the Wright brothers . . . . Like a crazily bouncing ball, the little craft went hopping here and there, now bouncing on one wheel, now dragging a wing tip in the turf, now jumping a line of parked airplanes."[52]

Udet picked up a handkerchief off the ground with his wingtip, then ended his show with a loop and a landing on a dead motor.[53] Following his thrill show, Udet wanted to settle some unfinished business. During the war, he had shot down an American pilot named Walter Wanamaker. Udet had landed next to the crash and offered a cigarette to Wanamaker as they awaited German medics. The German ace cut the tail fabric containing the number of Wanamaker's plane as a prize of war. When Udet arrived in Cleveland some ten years later, he bore that souvenir fabric in a frame which he presented to Wanamaker, then the mayor of Akron, Ohio, who was in the stands.[54] Then, in one of the more moving events at the races, two World War enemies reached a separate peace when America's "ace of aces," Maj. Eddie V. Rickenbacker, shook hands with his German counter-part, Maj. Ernst Udet.[55]

The following day, 31 August , Phoebe Omlie, "[t]he stocky little woman from Memphis, who in her career in the air has won more victories in com-petition than any other woman flier in the country," was named the winner of women's division of the handicap transcontinental derby, more than ten points ahead of Martie Bowman, adding the $3,000 prize to a comparable amount in lap prizes.[56] But she wasn't finished. That afternoon she com-peted in two closed-course events for small planes. The first race was a free-for-all restricted to women flying planes powered by engines of not more than 510-cubic-inch displacement. The three women entered—Phoebe, Mary Haizlip, and Maude Tait—took off in a race-horse start, with the planes lined up and leaving the ground together.[57]

> The course lay over hilly and tree-covered country productive of extreme-ly bumpy air, but the women had their planes down over the tree tops for the whole six laps of the five-mile course . . . . Mrs. Omlie's Monocoupe took the lead at the take-off. She wasted no power climbing but flew along, her wheels just clear of the ground, until she approached the forest at the first turn. Mrs. Haizlip . . . rounded the first turn within ten feet of the Omlie plane, and Miss Tait . . . was close behind. In this fashion al-most flying formation, the three pilots made the six laps, and at the finish Mrs. Omlie was only three seconds ahead of Mrs. Haizlip.[58]

Phoebe averaged 129.885 mph, taking the $500 prize. "A few minutes later Mrs. Omlie, flying the same machine but at a faster clip took the women's race for commercial planes with engines of 650-cubic-inch displacement. The Monocoupe averaged 132.481 mph. over the thirty miles."[59] This time the prize was $750.[60] She also put in a respectable speed of 149.049 mph in the race for the Aerol Trophy, which she had won in 1929. The criteria for the race had changed from rewarding a cross-country handicap winner to a free-for-all speed race for women pilots.[61] Phoebe finished fifth, a full five minutes behind the winner, Maud Tait, who clocked 187.57 mph in her 215 hp Gee Bee Y racer.[62]

That night, at a huge banquet for the fifty-two finishers, Phoebe Omlie was officially declared the winner of the Sweepstakes Derby and presented with the keys to the long, low, rakish Cabriolet convertible.[63] During the rest of the festivities at the National Air Races, Phoebe and her husband,

Vernon, were frequently spotted riding proudly in their new Cord automobile around the grounds.[64] She had won the Sweepstakes against thirty-six men and sixteen women with a handicap score of 109.19 points. The winner of the men's division, D. C. Warren, finished second with 103.5 points. Altogether, Phoebe collected over $7,000, an extraordinary amount of money in the midst of the Great Depression.[65]

The National Sweepstakes would be Phoebe's last race. Her sponsor, Mono Aircraft, had been struggling for survival following the death of founder Willard Velie in October 1928, and the death five months later of his son and heir, Willard Velie Jr. The Velie family sold out to Allied Aviation Industries, which moved its operations to St. Louis in 1931.[66] Phoebe severed her relationship with the company, although she continued to fly her personal Monocoupe.

When she came home, the city of Memphis threw their famous aviator a big party at the Peabody Hotel. After she regaled the crowd with stories of the dangers encountered during the derby, the chamber of commerce presented her with a scroll "in formal recognition of nationally pre-eminent attainment in the field of aeronautics, through which has been furthered the objective of the 10-Year Program of Progress to advertise Memphis to the nation." The text of the scroll paid tribute to her as "victor over a host of rivals in the National Air Races of 1931 and a leader in the work of building a greater future for aviation in Memphis, the South and the nation."[67]

During the Depression, the key to survival for the aviation business was a contract to fly the mail; these funds sustained commercial aviation and served to underwrite passenger service. The airmail had finally come to Memphis in June 1931 after a five-year struggle. The first ship was christened the *Cotton States Mail* by Mary Hill Overton, the mayor's daughter, who dented the starboard wing motor cowling as she smashed the beribboned bottle against it.[68] Universal Aviation, which had been folded into American Airways, began operating a regular airmail service throughout the Midwest, with a stop at Memphis. Another airmail contract for a route from Chicago to New Orleans via Memphis brought a second airline, Pacific Seaboard, to the city. The airline soon changed its name to Chicago and Southern Air Lines and began offering passenger service.[69]

The regular airmail schedule and the support it required sustained the airport and Mid-South Airways through the challenging decade, and eventually led to significant improvements. After mail disruptions during the winter caused by the inability for heavy planes to land safely at Memphis, the airport improved its grass airfield with hard-surfaced runways. August

1932 also saw the introduction of air express, "the airline making an arrangement whereby packages can be picked up at the sender's door, transported by air and delivered direct to the consignee." The airport commission reported that 675 planes, exclusive of regularly scheduled airlines, had visited the municipal airport in the first six months of that year.[70]

Passenger service followed the airmail. A total of 5,391 passengers traveled to and from the airport in 1932. Chicago was now just six hours away, New York could be reached in fifteen hours, Los Angeles within seventeen hours. Memphis also proudly boasted a passenger connection to Europe, although the trip would require some patience. Passengers traveled by American Airways to Atlanta, the Southern Railroad to Miami, Pan-American Airways to Rio de Janeiro, and the Graf Zeppelin to Spain. "Memphians leaving here May 2 on the first trip would be in Spain within 13 days, allowing an afternoon and night in both Miami and another in Rio."[71]

Phoebe settled down to work as the secretary-treasurer for her husband's business, Mid-South Airways, Inc. She assisted her husband in training students, servicing airplanes, storing and repairing airplanes, making local passenger hops, and doing photographic work.[72] The local newspaper described the couple as former barnstormers who were "in white collar jobs now."[73] It seemed apparent that this would be their future together.

Then, a year after Phoebe's triumph in Cleveland, came a message that would change her life. A telegram arrived from the wife of the governor of New York, Mrs. Franklin D. Roosevelt. It read:

AS ONE OF THE LEADING WOMEN FLYERS IN THE COUNTRY AND A SOUTHERNER WOULD YOU BE WILLING TO HELP US ON THE DEMOCRATIC CAMPAIGN STOP OUR IDEA WAS THAT IF YOU COULD POSSIBLY ARRANGE IT WE SHOULD LIKE TO HAVE YOU FLY TO NEW YORK MEET DEMOCRATIC OFFICIALS AS OUR GUEST RECEIVE DEMOCRATIC CAMPAIGN LITERATURE FROM THE NATIONAL COMMITTEE HERE AND FLY BACK WITH IT TO MEMPHIS WHERE YOU WOULD AGAIN BE MET BY A NATIONAL COMMITTEE WOMAN STOP NEEDLESS TO SAY IT WOULD BE SPLENDID PUBLICITY FOR THE DEMOCRATS AND WE SHOULD GREATLY APPRECIATE IT IF YOU COULD GET IN TOUCH WITH ME BY RETURN WIRE COLLECT ON THE MATTER I SHOULD BE GREATLY OBLIGED[74]

Recruiting America's most successful woman pilot for the campaign was fitting for the air-minded Roosevelts. Mrs. Roosevelt took her first airplane ride in 1930 and loved it; she made it a point to say that her only chance to fulfill her crowded schedule was to travel by air.[75] Franklin had been a strong advocate for naval aviation while he served as assistant secretary of the navy. He would later become the first presidential candidate to fly when he chartered a Ford Tri-Motor from Albany to Chicago to address the Democratic National Convention in 1932. Their son, Elliott, was a licensed pilot.[76] This promised to be an administration receptive to aviation development, and Phoebe was thrilled to be asked to participate. In October, she flew to New York to meet with Mrs. Roosevelt and the Democratic National Executive Committee and key Democratic national committeewomen.[77]

Phoebe joined an extraordinarily well-planned, woman-centered campaign staff led by Mary W. "Molly" Dewson, director of the Women's Division of the Democratic National Committee. The group included Lavinia Engle, a member of the Maryland legislature and head of the women's speakers' bureau; Emily Newell Blair, vice chair of the national committee; and Tennessee attorney Sue Shelton White, executive secretary of the Women's Division.[78] They organized a precinct-level, door-to-door, woman-to-woman strategy for the 1932 presidential campaign. The Women's Division printed millions of leaflets (called "rainbow fliers" because they were printed in many different colors) to be distributed by women "grass trampers" directly to other women. Their strategy was to reject the conventional approach to going after "the woman's vote" by emphasizing their candidate's personality and charm. Instead, Dewson valued women's serious approach to politics. Her strategy was to appeal "to the intelligence of the country's women, to all those thousands feeling the pinch of hard times. Our[s] were economic issues, and we found the women ready to listen. They had been thinking hard about such things."[79]

Phoebe agreed to undertake a flying campaign tour for the Democratic presidential ticket using her winning Monocoupe, *Miss Memphis*, which was repainted with the slogan: The Victory Pilots—Win With Roosevelt.[80] Barely three weeks before the election, Phoebe took off with Sarah Lee Fain, one of the first two women to serve in the Virginia General Assembly, on a 5,000-mile campaign trip, the first air tour of its kind on behalf of a presidential candidate.[81] The pair stopped in numerous places in twelve states— Missouri, Kansas, Wyoming, Colorado, Nebraska, South Dakota, North Dakota, Minnesota, Iowa, Indiana, Kentucky, Tennessee.[82]

The women kept to the tight schedule worked out by the DNC, although severe snowstorms canceled them out of Bismarck and Carrington, North Dakota. In Watertown, South Dakota, they landed in six inches of snow. Because there was no heat in the plane, they wore multiple layers of stockings and sweaters.[83] While Phoebe was perfectly comfortable flying Ms. Fain and herself in her tiny plane, public speaking was another matter. Nonetheless, she tackled the problem with her usual can-do attitude and reportedly delivered an adequate if not eloquent effort, stating that she believed it to be the policy of Mr. Roosevelt to "bring stability from chaos" in all segments of the economy, including the aviation industry.[84]

By all accounts, the tour was a success, as, of course, was the campaign. Molly Dewson told the press, "We were proud of our women fliers because they carried through their schedules successfully, while the Hoover women fliers all came to grief."[85] As it turned out, Roosevelt flier Phoebe Omlie had herself come to grief. Sue Shelton White reported to Molly Dewson that Phoebe not only deserved but needed a job. She wrote:

Phoebe Omlie is a real casualty of the campaign. While she was out with her plane one of her creditors threw her in bankruptcy. The petition was filed with a federal judge who was appointed by Harding or Coolidge . . . Phoebe is very reticent about her personal affairs and had never told me this and does not know that I know it. It came to me yesterday through a mutual friend. I asked that friend if she didn't think you should know it and she said Phoebe asked her not to tell you, after she had wormed the information out of her. But hell, I am telling you now any how.[86]

Since before the election, Dewson had been preparing to secure patronage appointments for a host of Democratic women in the New Deal government, and White wanted to be certain that Phoebe was included. When President Roosevelt indicated he wished to have a woman in his cabinet, Dewson was ready to make a strong case for Frances Perkins for secretary of labor.[87] She mobilized her network to press Perkins's nomination, including asking Phoebe to write to the president at Warm Springs to lobby on Perkins's behalf.[88]

Instead, Phoebe flew down to Warm Springs to visit with the president in person. They talked for some thirty minutes "principally discussing the possibility of a woman in the new cabinet," Omlie told the press. She expressed surprise to find that "the Roosevelts are 'just folks'—and Mr.

Roosevelt himself is just like a Southerner in speech and manner and hospitality." She was gratified that he spoke of his own and Mrs. Roosevelt's interest in aviation.[89]

Though the newspaper didn't say so, Phoebe was also giving an impromptu job interview.[90] She clearly had a New Deal appointment in mind. Right after the election, Phoebe approached her flying sisters to lobby Eleanor Roosevelt and James Farley (Roosevelt's campaign manager, close personal advisor, and manager of New Deal patronage) on her behalf. She wrote to her friend, Pancho Barnes, founding director of the Women's Air Reserve (a quasi-military search and rescue organization), about her ambition to be assistant secretary of the Department of Commerce in charge of aeronautics, adding, "I do not care to do this unless the different organizations with which I have worked, and who are in a position to know the work that I have been doing in the past six or seven years in the development of aviation, will sponsor the appointment."[91] A few months later, Phoebe announced to the press that she was angling for the post of assistant secretary of commerce in charge of aeronautics.[92] Phoebe tried to rally support among the Tennessee congressional delegation, but the response was tepid at best. When she contacted her congressman, recently elected E. H. Crump, to intercede on her behalf, he discouraged her from approaching Secretary of Commerce Daniel C. Roper as "unwise," and took her to see Farley for an inconsequential two-minute anteroom visit.[93]

Letters between the women in the Women's Division reveal an abundance of political maneuvering on the part of many players in the fight to secure important New Deal posts. Rumors indicated that a friend of Elliott Roosevelt's was being considered for the post Phoebe sought until he was exposed as a Republican. Another story said Amelia Earhart was approached about the position but that she had refused the appointment.[94] "I am convinced that he is just stringing Phoebie [*sic*] along," noted Lavinia Engle after visiting with Crump on Phoebe's behalf. "If she is to get anything someone will have to go to [Commerce Secretary Daniel C.] Roper and to some of the men in the committee and go to the mat about it." Sue White told Engle that she thought Crump was simply using the "matter to bait [Tennessee senator Kenneth] McKellar . . . Sue thinks it is too late to do much about it. I sort of feel that I owe it to Phoebie [*sic*] to make a fight."[95] In September, both of her senators, Kenneth McKellar and Nathan Bachman, went with Phoebe to meet with Jim Farley to plead for a position in aviation policy.[96]

At the same time, Dewson lobbied hard for a significant role for Phoebe in the new administration. She sent FDR a list of fifteen women paired with appropriate appointments, noting such action would "mean a NEW DEAL for the women workers." Phoebe was number seven on her list. Dewson was nominating her for "Division Chief in Aeronautics Branch." Her qualifications: "Good flier. Won the Air Derby over men. One of the half dozen qualified airplane mechanics. Has been in one branch or another of the business for years, and wide aeronautics acquaintance. Has real horse sense. Is modest. Very easy to work with."[97]

The position of assistant secretary of commerce for Aeronautics was too large a plum to go to a woman. Indeed, the position itself would soon no longer exist. After Roosevelt appointed Daniel Roper to secretary of commerce, the president consolidated several positions under an assistant secretary of transportation. The new aviation position would report to the assistant secretary of transportation as the director of Aeronautics. There was a mad scramble for this prize. By May 1943, no fewer than forty-three people, each backed by some faction of Democratic Party supporters, had made a bid for the post. It ultimately went to Eugene L. Vidal, former Army Air Corps pilot, air line founder and manager, friend of Elliot Roosevelt and close acquaintance of Amelia Earhart, and son-in-law to the influential blind senator from Oklahoma, Senator Thomas P. Gore.[98] Phoebe finally obtained an audience with Vidal at the end of October 1933, due to the apparent intercession of the first lady.[99] Shortly afterward, Phoebe Omlie was officially appointed to a cobbled-together, loosely defined but impressive-sounding position of special assistant for Air Intelligence of the National Advisory Committee for Aeronautics (NACA) with additional duties as liaison officer between the committee and the Aeronautics Branch of the Department of Commerce.[100]

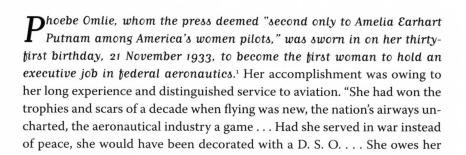

Chapter Five

*P*hoebe Omlie, whom the press deemed "second only to Amelia Earhart Putnam among America's women pilots," was sworn in on her thirty-first birthday, 21 November 1933, to become the first woman to hold an executive job in federal aeronautics.[1] Her accomplishment was owing to her long experience and distinguished service to aviation. "She had won the trophies and scars of a decade when flying was new, the nation's airways uncharted, the aeronautical industry a game . . . Had she served in war instead of peace, she would have been decorated with a D. S. O. . . . She owes her position not to politics but to a single-track ardor for commercial aviation such as few possess."[2]

Her job straddled the two primary agencies responsible for aviation in the New Deal administration, the National Advisory Committee for Aeronautics (NACA) and the Aeronautics Branch of the Department of Commerce. Their shared responsibilities set the standards and practices for the growth of private and commercial aviation in the United States. The NACA was established by Congress in 1915 with a $5,000 appropriation "to supervise and direct the scientific study of the problems of flight, with a view to their practical solution." By the time Phoebe joined the staff in 1933, NACA's Langley Memorial Aeronautical Laboratory at Hampton, Virginia, was the premier aeronautical research organization; its scientists

and engineers engaged in intense research into virtually every character-
istic of flight.[3] The government's role in aeronautical research was sometimes regarded with suspicion by aircraft manufacturers who were invited
to submit proposals for research but seldom allowed to participate directly.
As a practical matter and a political one, the NACA's director of research,
George Lewis, came to recognize the importance of positive publicity for
their engineering work, and so he sought ways to enhance communication
with aircraft manufacturers and the general public.[4] Phoebe was hired to
work in "a program to encourage the use of airplanes by making known the
results of research to improve safety and efficiency in civil aviation," acting
as spokesperson for the agency and liaison between manufacturers and the
NACA.[5] She saw it as a perfect fit, doing what she had "longed for years to
do—to preach, promote and popularize commercial flying in a big way."[6]

The Air Commerce Act of 1926 created the Aeronautics Branch of the
Department of Commerce. Passed during the barnstorming era in large part
in reaction to its dangerous and uninhibited practices, the act established
for the first time official government control and support for civil aviation.
The goal was to shift aviation from the purview of stunt fliers to that of
business and government officials charged with developing standards and
regulations that would allow aviation to flourish as a transportation system.
The Aeronautics Branch held fundamental regulatory powers to test and
license pilots, issue airworthiness certificates for aircraft, establish airways,
and investigate accidents.[7]

Early in her new job, Phoebe was loaned to the Bureau of Air Commerce
to make a three-month nationwide survey of the Federal Airways System,
"to obtain information as to the adequacy of fields and the effectiveness of
airways lighting, radio directional, radio communication, and radio weather
service."[8] The Federal Airways System, a sort of highway system in the sky,
included all airports, navigational aids and the straight-line pathways in the
sky between them. This information was critical for developing plans to for-
tify and strengthen this system. She inspected and cataloged airports and
navigational systems, consulted with pilots, fixed base operators, mechanics, airline managers, New Deal agency officials, and airplane manufacturers on aircraft design, safety issues, and regulations.[9]

In the fall of 1933, the New Deal, through the Civil Works Administration,
instituted a massive program of airport improvements. During the winter of 1933-1934, these agencies employed 70,000 men in 700 locations to
build new airports and improve existing ones, including lighting 2,681 miles
of airways with beacons placed on towers.[10] Phoebe's assignment on the

project was to see what was being done, help determine what needed to be done, and to aid municipalities wishing to acquire landing fields in applying for them. She reported to her superiors that "everyone of them are solidly behind the people in Washington who are working on Aeronautics."[11] She continued her survey until midsummer, logging at least 20,000 miles.[12]

Almost as soon as she returned from surveying the airways system, Phoebe was ordered to leave again in order to make "a general survey of the possibilities, plans and designs for the development of low-cost airplanes, and in particular to visit the shops of those who have recently submitted designs to the Government. You are expressly authorized to visit such places in Cleveland, Detroit, Chicago, Indianapolis, St. Louis, Omaha, Kansas City, Dallas, San Francisco, Los Angeles, San Diego, and also intermediate and adjacent cities and towns where plans or designs of low-cost airplanes may be inspected."[13]

The scope of her work can be seen in the handful of letters between herself and her superiors that have survived. In fulfilling both assignments, she did extensive inspections of airports and facilities from December 1933 at least until autumn 1934. She talked with pilots about issues of safety and design of aircraft which she reported back to the bureau. She reported on the design and safety work NACA engineers were doing at Langley Laboratory to pilots and manufacturers in the field and sent their concerns and comments back to the committee. She made numerous speeches promoting private aviation, especially to women's groups. She inspected facilities to determine if they were appropriate for new runways, new navigational equipment, lighting systems or installation of "blind landing equipment."[14]

The novelty of her gender paired with her official position as representative of the New Deal for aviation in the federal government ensured abundant media attention. She took every opportunity to repeat her consistent message that "President Roosevelt has saved and stabilized our industry, putting it on a businesslike basis . . . The individual operators thruout [sic] the nation are the ones who have made airports possible and created airmindedness so the airlines could exist . . . the little base-operator is the unsung hero of the aviation industry and, until this administration, he has never in any way received help from our government."[15]

While Phoebe was traveling around the country, bureau director Eugene Vidal enlarged the bureau's mandate, which had been limited to advising and assisting other agencies in carrying out research connected with airway and airport lighting, radio communication, and other air navigation systems, with an amendment to the Air Commerce Act to enable his agency to "encourage and participate in such research and development as tends to create improved aircraft, aircraft power plant, and accessories."[16] The Bureau of Air Commerce announced the creation of a Development Section in July 1934 and, with a commitment of half a million dollars from the WPA, Vidal began his project to encourage production of a safe, affordable, easy-to-fly plane—the aerial equivalent of the Model-T—for the "average American citizen." His idea was to stimulate the aircraft industry while at the same time "democratizing" aviation.[17]

Vidal's specifications called for an all-metal, low-wing, two-place mono-plane with a maximum speed of 100 mph. It was to be as easy to fly and as easy to pay for as an automobile. In an era when the average private aircraft cost $1,800–$2,500 and the average automobile cost $500–$1,000, Vidal's proposal was for a $700 airplane. Citing extensive surveys of licensed pilots, Vidal demonstrated "that an airplane for that price, sold on the installment plan, would have a popular appeal."[18] Vidal's task would be to encourage the industry to design and begin volume production of such an airplane. WPA money would be awarded to help manufacturers retool and guarantee a market of 10,000 units.[19]

Almost immediately, the aircraft industry responded "with a shower of dead cats and brickbats."[20] Manufacturers had several criticisms of the plan: (1) it wasn't feasible to build a plane with those specifications for only $700; (2) they weren't willing to gamble on such a departure from their standard designs; and (3) all the publicity about a future low-cost airplane was retarding sales for their current models. Who wanted to buy a $3,000 airplane with a $700 one on the horizon? Airplane builders expressed their wish to handle their own business while suggesting that the Department of Commerce tend to its own business of developing airports and airways.[21] In the midst of the brouhaha, the Works Progress Administration pulled the funding on the apparent justification that since aviation development benefited private industry, it did not meet the definition of public works.[22]

Determined to keep the dream alive, Vidal shifted from trying to encourage hostile manufacturers to build a cheap, safe airplane, to using his agency's fleet money to launch a competitive purchase program for planes to be used by his field inspectors. He abandoned the focus on the price tag in favor of setting performance and safety standards, asking manufacturers to design and build prototypes, and promising to buy twenty-five units from the winner, in the hopes that consumer demand and mass production would ultimately lead to lower prices.[23]

As the news came out of Washington, Phoebe was frequently called upon to discuss and defend plans for the low-cost airplane. What aviation needed most, she told reporters, was "a light, inexpensive plane, as near 'fool-proof' as possible."[24] She confessed that, "we deplore that we once made flying a show business and stressed dangerous stunts. The aim of our department now is to make flying safer and cheaper and give the little fellow a break. Lack of money for experiments is all that is delaying the production of safe, fast planes for around $700. My chief job is to travel around the country and give all the light aircraft makers the benefit of all government research free of charge."[25] While the large manufacturers had always, as a matter of course, turned to the Bureau of Air Commerce for information and aid, she said, "the little man striving to put new ideas of wings and engines together had thought of the bureau only as a policy agency. He has been suspicious and afraid of it." Her job was to change that perception.

> I found men working in garages, in back of drug stores, inventing, de-
> signing and modeling. At first they were incredulous—refused to believe
> that the Bureau of Air Commerce in Washington was earnestly inter-
> ested in what they were trying to do. When I finally convinced them, they
> brought out their plans and their blue prints. We studied them together.
> We changed a line here and there. When I left there was an added zest in
> their work and a new hope. It is impossible to predict what may evolve
> from this lone wolf experimentation. But whatever it may be, we want
> to encourage every man who is trying to further the development of the
> airplane in any way whatsoever.[26]

She encouraged private innovators, who she called the Bolsheviks of design, to take up the challenge. Bolsheviks, she said, were not afraid to test daring innovations and would give America its air flivver.[27]

Back in Washington, aeronautical research director George Lewis as-signed her to work in cooperation with the Aeronautics Branch of the Department of Commerce directly on development of the low-cost airplane. Phoebe was to consult with the Langley Memorial Aeronautical Laboratory "for the purpose of ascertaining the progress being made in the construc-tion and testing of the Weick airplane, and in other work being conducted by the laboratory in connection with the general problem." She would serve as liaison between the two agencies, acquaint herself thoroughly with the activities of both, and file weekly reports about Langley Laboratory research to the Bureau of Air Commerce and weekly reports to NACA "on the general project of the light airplane [including] your recommendations as to further studies which the Committee can conduct to assist in this important development."[28]

Much innovative research in terms of performance and safety in new small aircraft design was going on at Langley, led by NACA engineer Fred E. Weick. Weick and a group of nine other Langley engineers designed and built a small experimental airplane, the W-1A, to study the special needs of the private flier. The W-1A design had a pusher engine (the engine and propeller were behind the fuselage and faced the tail) located between twin rear fuselage booms, with twin vertical tails. The Weick design featured two key innovations: flaps to control speed for landing and tricycle landing gear, that is, two wheels on either side of the fuselage and a steerable nose wheel. Tricycle gear had been used on a 1908 Curtiss model, but since that early innovation, traditional landing gear had evolved to a configuration of two wheels forward of the center of gravity, with a skid (later a wheel) supporting the tail. This caused poor visibility on the ground, forcing the pilot to lean out the side window to see what was in front of the plane. The most serious problem with this "tail-dragger" configuration, however, was the plane's susceptibility to ground-looping, particularly in crosswind landings, the avoidance of which required a good deal of pilot training and more than a little luck. Ground-looping occurred when the pilot could not maintain directional control on the ground and the tail of the aircraft swung around to pass the nose. The sudden whipping of the plane resulted in damage to the undercarriage, tires, propellers, and wingtips. Some builders had tried to make planes more maneuverable on the ground by incorporating brakes in the two front wheels, with limited success. Despite its potential for eliminating ground-looping, Weick's adoption of tricycle gear was controversial, considered a throwback to earlier developments in aircraft design.[29]

Like all pilots of the era, Phoebe was intimately familiar with the problem of ground-looping. During her first competitive race in 1928, her plane ground-looped during a crosswind landing at Marfa, Texas. Her own research into the problem involved a toy model of her Monocoupe. She found that when she pushed it forward across a table the model ground-looped; when she pushed it backward, it did not. In other words, because of the location of the plane's center of gravity relative to its wheels, during forward motion the plane's tail, not its nose, tended to lead the way down the runway. At the lab, she worked with Weick in developing the performance and safety specifications for Vidal's competition, and constructed a scale model of the W-1 for testing and demonstration purposes. Working with the model, she became even more convinced that tricycle gear was the most stable, with the added benefit of vastly improving visibility on the ground.[30]

Since Vidal's goal was to make flying as easy and safe as driving the family automobile, Phoebe and the engineers looked for ways to simplify the traditional control system, which used three components: the elevator (control surfaces on the horizontal tail that control nose up or nose down), ailerons (control surfaces attached to the trailing edge of the wings, the movement of which causes the plane to bank in one direction or the other), and rudders (foot pedals attached to the vertical stabilizer of the airplane which when pressed move the nose of the airplane to right or left). Coordinating the ailerons and rudders in turns was one of the more difficult skills a pilot had to master. To make flying as simple as driving, one goal was to eliminate the rudders.

When Phoebe had a chance to fly Weick's prototype, she was eager to find out if the flaps could be made to act as rudimentary rudders, eliminating the need to fly with both feet. Flaps, an innovation on the W-1, were control surfaces on the trailing edge of the wings, next to the ailerons, that were used to increase lift at low speeds. While the plane wallowed a bit, she thought it would be possible, with some modifications, to link the left pedal to the flaps to act in place of rudders, the right pedal to act as a brake on the ground, and the throttle linked to a steering wheel to make the plane more like an automobile. Her suggestions, though, fell on deaf ears. Though she had an abundance of flying experience, and the self-confidence that went with it, her ideas were often dismissed by her colleagues for two reasons: she was not an aeronautical engineer and she was not a man. She would have to figure out her own way to test her theory.[31]

Once the specifications for the low-cost prototype had been developed by the NACA engineers at Langley, Gene Vidal announced the opening of bids. The new planes had to be simple and safe with low maintenance and operating costs, with greater visibility and ease of control. Among the requirements were a landing speed of thirty-five and top speed of not less than 110 miles per hour, a cruising range of at least 300 miles at twenty to twenty-five miles per gallon of fuel. Winning designs would feature an all-metal fuselage, dual controls, be capable of clearing an obstacle thirty-five feet high from a standing start 800 feet away and stopping within 400 feet upon landing, and be easily controlled on the ground.[32] While the award was ostensibly to replace flying equipment for the bureau's field personnel, the unusually detailed specifications required were clearly "part of the program on behalf of a safer, easily operated, low-priced airplane for private use."[33]

Fourteen manufacturers submitted bids with prices ranging from $750 to $6,670. The low bid of $750 "created astonishment" until it turned out that the bid had come from a tavern owner in Indianapolis with no manufacturing experience. The remaining bids began at $1,650.[34] There were two major impediments to a lower cost, bureau spokesman John H. Geisse indicated: the high cost of engines and the impact of volume production. A contract for fifteen to twenty airplanes at $3,190 each was awarded to the Hammond Aircraft Corporation of Ypsilanti, Michigan, whose design came closest to meeting the NACA specifications. The Hammond was remarkably similar to the W-1, a low-wing pusher-type monoplane, capable of 110 miles per hour, with tricycle landing gear featuring a steerable nose wheel with brakes.[35]

When the first Hammond arrived in Washington, Phoebe was one of three individuals from the Bureau of Air Commerce permitted to fly it.[36] One Saturday, after demonstrating the airplane to an influential congressman, she enlisted one of the mechanics to help her block the rudder on the Hammond. She took it up for a test flight and found, with a few minor adjustments, that it worked perfectly. Monday morning, she reported to her boss, Gene Vidal, what she had done. Vidal checked it out for himself. Then he invited the press to Bolling Field the following Sunday.[37] Vidal met the press with his young son, Gore, by his side, telling them that he wanted to prove that a ten-year-old child could fly the Hammond. Vidal told his son that he "was to take off, circle the field once, and land." After landing, father and son climbed out and Vidal asked, "How was it?" Gore responded, "It's easier than learning how to ride a bicycle."[38]

Vidal asked Phoebe to share her ideas for the rudder-less Hammond with a visitor she later learned had bought the company. In 1936, Lloyd Stearman teamed up with Dean Hammond, moved the company to San Francisco and developed an improved version of the Hammond Y, the Y-1-S, which featured a two-control flight system that relied upon differential aileron movement and eliminated the need for rudders.[39]

While enjoying her high profile as a participant in exciting aviation innovations, Phoebe had to proceed cautiously. She was fighting a rear-guard action against an issue as old as time: the limitations of her gender. Besides her marginalization by the engineers, she also had to contend with a press determined to emphasize her gender over her competence. Despite her repeated insistence in the press that "there is no prejudice whatever against women in aviation," she confronted almost daily instances of discrimination in her work and in media coverage. Many stories gave more space to her physical appearance and assurances of her femininity than what she had to say about aviation policy. Despite her position as a spokesperson for a male-dominated industry in a male-defined governmental position, or more likely because of it, newspaper copy persisted in reassuring their readers that Phoebe Omlie was hardly different from the typical American housewife. "[T]his plump, fresh-complexioned little person with her unaffected simplicity and frank indifference to clothes and cosmetics . . . looks like the kind of woman that a hard-working husband could expect to find waiting home evenings in a ruffled pink apron." Lest they find a woman in such a position to be too independent, readers were assured of her happy marriage to "good looking Capt. Vernon C. Omlie."[40]

Maneuvering within these limitations, Phoebe used her public voice to encourage women's involvement in aviation while at the same time employing gender conventions of the day to insist that women accept a sex-limited place. Women would never be suitable for flying heavy commercial transport aircraft, she insisted. Instead, they should seek futures in more gender-friendly areas like airplane design.

> I do not believe that there is a future in aviation for women flying U.S. air mail planes for the same reason that we do not see women at the throttle of express train engines, at the helms of our ocean liners or driving our big transportation busses. But I do believe there is a great future for women in aeronautics in the field of aircraft design and in the executive angle of manufacturing. If you stop to think of it, most of the present day air comforts have been inaugurated because women have demanded them, just as they did in the automotive world.[41]

Helen Richey's experience was certainly a lesson in limitations for women in aviation. Richey had over 1,000 hours of accident-free flying experience and a women's endurance record of nine days and twenty-two hours in the air, set with Frances Marsalis in 1933. The following year she won the featured event in the Women's National Air Meet, held in Dayton, Ohio, after women had been excluded from the National Air Races in 1934.[42] In December 1934, Richey was hired by Central Airlines, a new airmail and passenger line serving Detroit, Cleveland, Pittsburgh, and Washington, D.C. With her first flight as copilot of a Ford Trimotor flying from Washinton, D.C., to Detroit, Richey achieved a place in what she called "the last masculine stronghold of aviation, the cockpit of a passenger airliner."[43] She became the first woman to fly the mail and the first woman to hold a regular flying job with an airline. "I think this is the beginning of a number of girl co-pilots," Richey optimistically told the press, but "only time can tell if women will be accepted as first-string pilots."[44] She was not long in finding out. The Airline Pilots' Association rejected her application for union membership and threatened to strike if Helen continued to fly. Putting pressure on the Regulations division of the Department of Commerce, the pilots association contended that a woman did not have the physical strength to handle an airliner in rough weather. The department dutifully issued an order limiting Richey to daytime flying in clear weather. After that, Richey spent most of her time making speeches to luncheon groups, giving press interviews, and posing for photographs. She found herself doing too much public relations and not enough flying. After making only about a dozen flights in ten months in the face of constant hostility from the male pilots, Richey resigned in November 1935.[45]

A month later, thirty members of the Bureau of Air Commerce's medical division declared unanimously that women were "not physically or psychologically suited for flying a regular run." Moreover, for parts of each month, women were not suited to fly at all.[46] Their conclusions were based upon an article in the *Journal of Aviation Medicine*, which stated that, out of ten women who had been killed while flying, eight were menstruating.[47] Carroll Cone, assistant director of the Bureau of Air Commerce in charge of Air Regulations called Phoebe into his office to announce that women must be grounded during those nine-day periods. It would be her job to write the appropriate regulations. Phoebe immediately raised two problems with such a move: there was only sketchy and inadequate information about the issue (all Cone had was the article) and the enforcement of such regulations would be extremely difficult. Hoping to stave off hasty action, she proposed research to gather more information upon which to base such a weighty decision.[48]

During a subsequent trip to California on NACA business, Phoebe met with the Los Angeles chapter of the Ninety-Nines to try to plan strategy for responding to the threat. After Ninety-Nines vice president Gladys O'Donnell, who presided at the meeting, said her organization wanted nothing to do with the issue, Phoebe turned to Pancho Barnes, who offered her organization, the Women's Air Reserve (WAR). The plan hatched with the WAR was to arrange for their medical officer, Dr. Emma Kittridge, to be appointed as a Department of Commerce examining doctor and help to gather the data needed. Phoebe used a similar strategy when she returned east. After she encountered similar resistance from the Ninety-Nines in New York, she located Dr. Clara Gross of New York, who was associated with the Women's Medical College in Philadelphia and had expressed interest in being involved in the research project.[49]

In August, Pancho headed for Washington, D.C., with six of her WAR fliers in three open-cockpit biplanes in what they billed as the "first cross-country formation flight of women pilots" to testify with Dr. Kittridge before the bureau regarding equal pilot licensing standards for both men and women. Uneasy with her friend's cavalier use of off-color language, Phoebe provided Pancho with a list of words she was not to use before the committee. Instead, Pancho impishly passed the list to the officials.[50]

In order to pay the doctors and support the research, Phoebe needed funds. She turned first to her friend, the first lady. At a meeting at the White House, Phoebe presented her plan and proposed budget. Her memo to Mrs. Roosevelt pointed out that heretofore all research done on pilots had been done entirely with men. But "the physiological difference of the sexes has made the problem more complex for women." The program she was proposing was "in no way intended to limit, by regulation, women's entry into any professional field," yet research had indicated a need for more study and more information. "Some study has been carried on by the medical profession in regard to the glandular connection with insanity at the time of the menopause," she wrote, but little was known "regarding the emotional reactions of women during the menstrual period." Phoebe suggested using women medical examiners to compile data from research and to engage in a series of examinations similar to those used for medical research by the U.S. Army Air Service. Her budget included $4,600 for each of two women medical directors, $23,000 for additional medical personnel (a female doctor and several nurses), $26,000 for equipment, and $52,000 operating funds, for a total of $108,700.[51]

Mrs. Roosevelt called Josephine Roche, assistant secretary of the Treasury Department in charge of Public Health. Roche explained that all her funds were earmarked by Congress. She suggested Phoebe talk with the only female senator, Senator Hattie Caraway of Arkansas. Phoebe met with the senator in her office and asked her to propose a bill to fund the project. The modest Senator Caraway responded, "You surely don't expect me to get up on the floor of the Senate and ask for such a fund." Phoebe similarly came up dry in her pleas to General Westover, chief of the Army Air Corps, who offered to hunt up any extant research on women, but no funds.[52]

In order to get the project going, Phoebe volunteered to be a guinea pig for a preliminary study by bureau medical examiner Dr. Roy E. Whitehead. She submitted to daily physicals for ninety days (three menstrual cycles). Her "chart showed almost straight lines during all of that time." When the pilot and doctor showed the chart to Cone, he dismissed it. "This doesn't prove very much, you're just a healthy horse." Despite the lack of funds, the Department of Commerce officially endorsed Phoebe's research plan.[53] Examinations of women pilots commenced; some data from related studies was gathered. The research went on for over a year, but ultimately, no regulation was ever proposed and the whole matter was allowed to "die a natural death."[54]

As Phoebe continued to travel for the bureau, she managed to get home to Memphis now and then and Vernon occasionally traveled to Washington to see his wife, but their times together were scattered and infrequent.[55] Despite the distance between them, Phoebe characterized her marriage to the press as a loving partnership. "We have shared everything together, and it has made for complete understanding."[56]

Nonetheless, Vernon and Phoebe's lives seemed to unspool in ways totally separate from each other. Her detailed flying itinerary coupled with her duties in Washington kept her very busy and away from home, while Vernon's business demanded his presence. Despite economic hard times, aviation in Memphis remained a popular avocation and his flying school was continuously booked. Vernon's most famous student was the author William Faulkner. He started taking lessons at Mid-South Airways in February 1933.[57] Faulkner had long been enamored with flying, at least since the age of twenty-one, when he joined the Royal Air Force with visions of becoming a flying ace in the Great War. The war was over before he could make his first solo flight, but that didn't prevent him from spinning tales about being shot down in France.[58] As barnstormers made their way across the South in the 1920s, Faulkner loved to don a white scarf and goggles for a "loop-the-loop in an open cockpit over the Mississippi River."[59] Vernon and Phoebe were the living embodiment of a way of life he found enchanting.

After several weeks and seventeen hours of dual instruction, Bill Faulkner soloed in Vernon's Waco biplane on 20 April 1933. Nearly every weekend, he would drive up to Memphis, stay at the Peabody Hotel, and spend all his spare time in the air with Vernon. Faulkner bought his own plane in the fall, and put up the money for his younger brother Dean's flight instruction as well. The three men, Dean and Bill Faulkner and Vernon Omlie became fast friends. Dean moved into Vernon's apartment, and after both brothers got their licenses, the three of them put together their own flying circus: "William Faulkner's (Famous Author) Air Circus." The group, with the addition of a black wing-walker named George "The Black Eagle" McEwen, followed the formula Vernon developed with Phoebe a decade before: a thrill show followed by passenger hops. The Faulkners flew the open-cockpit Wacos while Vernon and George did the stunts. The Faulkner Air Circus continued on weekends through two summers, 1934 and 1935, sometimes including William and sometimes not, doing shows in Tennessee, Mississippi, and Missouri. In 1935, they called themselves the Flying Faulkners, and McEwen was replaced by another black wing-walker and parachute jumper named Willie "Suicide" Jones.[60] Dean continued to live with Vernon in his apartment on Lamar, and after Vernon was a witness at Dean's wedding to Louise Hale, she moved in with the two men.[61]

All the flying and all the additional hangar flying (sharing tales of daring-do among pilots) provided valuable material for Faulkner's fiction. He wrote a series of short stories, including "Honor," "All the Dead Pilots," and "This Kind of Courage," based on his fascination with the skill and daring of barnstormers, and his eighth novel, *Pylon*, published in 1935, was loosely based on the adventures of the Omlies.[62]

In February 1933, Vernon and the Faulkner brothers flew to New Orleans for the dedication of Shushan Airport, which was celebrated with races and aerial events that featured numerous crashes and mishaps. Faulkner fictionalized that event as the setting for *Pylon*. In the novel, Faulkner rejects the romantic aspects of flying to focus on the tawdry lives of a clan of itinerant stunt fliers whose need for money ties them to a vocation that threatens their lives and whose mode of living has removed them from the moral strictures that bind everyone else. These barnstormers, Faulkner writes, "they ain't human like us; they couldn't turn those pylons like they do if they had human blood and senses and they wouldn't want to or dare to if they just had human brains . . . crash one and it ain't even blood when you haul him out: it's cylinder oil the same as in the crankcase."[63]

Pylon's main characters are Roger Shumann, a skillful but luckless racing pilot; a dull-witted alcoholic mechanic named Jiggs; Shumann's promiscuous wife, Laverne; her six-year-old son, Jack, a child of uncertain paternity; and parachute jumper, Jack Holmes, Laverne's lover. Laverne is strong and fearless, a mechanic, former wing-walker and parachute jumper, who dressed "in dungarees like the rest of them, with her hands full of wrenches and machinery and a gob of cotter keys in her mouth . . . and a smear of grease where she had swiped it back with her wrist."[64] Laverne is sexually aggressive, claiming at least two men as lovers, and unapologetic about her desires. Faulkner's description of her first parachute jump with Shumann as her pilot has them agreeing that she should wear a skirt because "her exposed legs would not only be a drawing card but that in the skirt no one would doubt that she was a woman." She removed her underwear as well. Standing on the wing, preparing to jump, Laverne suddenly crawls back into the cockpit to straddle Shumann in a sexual embrace as he struggles to control the plane. Then she climbs out, turns, and plunges into the open air, her body on full display as she descends to a "yelling mob of men and youths."[65]

As told through the observances of an unnamed newspaper reporter, who also lusts after Laverne, Faulkner's characters lead exaggeratedly unconventional lives of illicit sex and reckless flying that lead toward inevitable tragedy. In the end, Shumann dies in a fiery crash and Laverne is left bereft and alone.

There was little doubt that Roger and Laverne were based on the exploits of Vernon and Phoebe. She had loaned the author her early scrapbooks and clippings to use while writing the manuscript. When the novel was published, Phoebe was shocked and embarrassed by what he had done with them. Faulkner had taken the raw material of her achievements and twisted them into a grotesque tale of a sexually voracious usurper in the masculine world of aviation. Publicly, she said nothing except when she was directly asked about the veracity of the characterizations. Then she simply noted that she and her husband "disapproved of Bill's *Pylon*."[66] When Vernon privately admonished Faulkner with the comment that "aviation people are not like the way you portray them, and I doubt that it will be accepted by the majority of the people," the author allegedly replied that he was more interested in selling books than portraying historical accuracy.[67]

The Flying Faulkners continued throughout the summer of 1935, doing airshows around the mid-South. Dean earned his transport license and bought his brother's Waco. In one of the last events of the season, the troupe was scheduled for a show on Sunday afternoon, 10 November, at Pontotoc, Mississippi. Dean had been hauling passengers all day Saturday and continued to do so Sunday morning. He had three passengers with him who were viewing their farm from the air when the Waco suddenly plummeted to earth, killing all aboard. Witnesses said the plane was about 4,000 feet when the wing fell off and the plane dived into an open field, the wing landing in a cemetery about a mile away. Vernon, who had thoroughly inspected and certified the plane when Dean bought it just a few weeks before, rushed to the scene. Vernon's examination of the wreckage revealed that the control wheel, which was moveable, had been moved to the right, indicating that Dean's passenger had been flying the plane at the time of the crash. Devastated by the loss of his friend, Vernon told a friend that the accident "will always be a mystery. No one will ever know for sure exactly what happened." William Faulkner blamed himself for encouraging his brother to fly, for buying the plane, and ultimately for his death. Though they shared grief over the loss of Dean, how Vernon and Bill responded to each other after the accident is unknown.[68]

Phoebe's work in Washington took on new impetus after she conceived and developed a million-dollar program that she staffed with an all-women crew.[69] Aviation, she frequently told the press, was "a field where women have the same opportunities as men, where men will cooperate with women and help them get ahead."[70] She aimed to prove it while simultaneously solving a very serious problem for civil aviation.

Navigation, the seemingly simple matter of avoiding getting lost, had long vexed pilots. While the needs of commercial aviation were increasingly being addressed with aids like radio beacons and lighting systems, the private pilot still flew the way she always had, balancing a road map on her knees, tracing her route with a thumb. Whether flying over the trackless desert or the farm-country grid of the Midwest, there was little information to help her figure out where precisely she was. This became particularly acute during flights over strange and unmarked territory as storms closed in. Perhaps there was enough gas to reach the nearest airport, but only if the pilot knew where that airport was. During Phoebe's thousands of hours in the air she had often been lost and had witnessed countless other pilots who had to set down in unfamiliar and often dangerous terrain to ascertain where they were.

Local attempts to put "road signs in the air" had been started by some municipalities and aero clubs in the 1920s. In 1928, the Bureau of Air Commerce held an airway-marking conference to work on formulating a set of standard guidelines. Their report called for the name of the location in chrome yellow letters ten to thirty feet high, a north arrow, and the distance and direction of the nearest airport. Efforts were sporadic and funding depended upon the will and determination of local activists.[71] As she flew across the country in 1932, Amelia Earhart complained that she saw few towns properly named. "In some, the airway sign boards had been so neglected that the lettering was dirty and almost illegible; in others the only words visible from above spelled the names of certain kinds of pills or liniment."[72]

The program finally came together when a pilot with sensitivity to the situation was in a position of power to obtain federal funding. Shortly after Col. Walter Sumpter Smith, army pilot and former commander of the Alabama Air National Guard, was appointed head of the Airport Division of the Works Progress Administration, he dropped by Phoebe's office. As pilot's often do, they engaged in a bit of hangar flying, including tales of "railroad-track navigation" and "div[ing] down over depots" to figure out their location. Together they mapped out an air-marking plan to use the WPA to solve this problem and lobbied the WPA's new auditor, Corrington Gill, to approve the funds.[73] Unemployed men would be put to work, and pilots would have a road map in the sky to help them find their way. The plan was for twelve-foot black-and-orange letters to be painted on the roofs of barns, factories, warehouses, and water tanks. Visible from 4,000 feet, they identified the locale, gave the north bearing, and indicated by circle, arrow, and numeral the distance and direction to the nearest airport.

Phoebe was in charge of the program, working under Jack Wynne, director of airports for the bureau; her new title was assistant to the chief of the airport section.[74] Phoebe announced that the project would use women in multiple capacities to ensure its success. She requested approval to use women in local areas for liaison work. She wrote to Mr. Robert Lees of the Works Progress Administration that while "the actual painting would come under the labor of men . . . there is nothing in these approved projects that limits the liaison work necessary to obtain roof-top site releases to the male sex. This work could be done by women." She suggested that special efforts be made to involve women's organizations as well as the traditional male civic clubs in the project.[75] Phoebe was authorized to hire three fliers as field coordinators to work with state and local officials and WPA coordinators to set up the project. She immediately hired Louise Thaden to help her plan the project. Considerable research was required to determine the cost of materials, hours of labor involved, and general policy considerations.

Phoebe and Louise charted each state in fifteen-mile squares and designated the nearest towns to the intersecting lines as possible sites for markers. Phoebe then added "famed female flyers" Helen McCloskey and Nancy Harkness to aid Thaden as field representatives.[76] Ironically, the women pilots had no airplanes. The comptroller general would not allow WPA funds to be used for additional equipment for the project and the bureau did not have enough planes available for their own personnel. So the women traveled by bus, train, and airline when possible.[77] The women worked with state and area WPA coordinators, local leaders and civic clubs like the American Legion, the Shriners, numerous women's clubs, Lions' Clubs, chambers of commerce, Rotary and Zonta Clubs, to obtain permission and workers to paint rooftops on municipal buildings, businesses, barns, and factories. Sometimes multiple rooftops on groups of small buildings were used; in rural areas where buildings were not available, they built "shelters" to support the markings. Markers were painted on open highways and painted rocks were arranged to mark the tops of mountains.[78] *Newsweek* observed that the women "must be expert salesmen as well as pilots. A stubborn official can usually be convinced by flying him 15 miles from the airport and letting him try to find the way back."[79]

Fieldwork for the program began in October 1935 and less than a year later *Time* magazine announced that fully 58 percent of some 16,000 proposed markers were completed. All states had approved the program with an average of 300 markers being painted per state.[80]

In a nationwide radio address in the spring of 1935, First Lady Eleanor Roosevelt recognized Phoebe's achievement, naming her among "eleven women whose achievements make it safe to say that the world is progressing." Also included in the list were Amelia Earhart, novelist Dorothy Canfield, social worker Jane Addams, suffragist Mrs. Carrie Chapman Catt, Secretary of Labor Frances Perkins, Assistant Secretary of the Treasury Josephine Roche, New York settlement workers Lillian Wald and Mrs. M. M. Simkhovitch, industrialist Mary Dillon, and the late suffragist Dr. Anna Howard Shaw. These women, Mrs. Roosevelt said, "have been and are a constant inspiration to me."[81] Columnist Mary Margaret McBride also included Phoebe in her own list of eleven women who "have improved the 8,760 shining hours of 1934 by making new highs in human endeavor."[82]

With her air-marking program essentially complete, Phoebe was pleased to be able to release her women pilots to compete in the 1936 Bendix Trophy Race, a transcontinental race culminating at the National Air Races in Los Angeles.[83] Established in 1931 by industrialist Vincent Bendix, the prestigious race attracted the top pilots. Jimmy Doolittle won it the first year. Amelia Earhart became the first woman to enter the Bendix in 1935; she finished in fifth place.[84] As an added incentive to attract women, Bendix posted a special award of $2,500 for the female pilot who finished first regardless of her position in the race itself.[85] While Phoebe was not an entrant, she was the official representative for the National Aeronautical Association's Contest Board for the Bendix, and she enthusiastically encouraged her compatriots to take up the challenge.

The race was not until September. In early August, Phoebe was expecting Vernon to pick her up for a long-planned fishing vacation in Maine.[86] After her return, she would campaign again for FDR. She knew that, given the restrictions of the Hatch Act that prohibited federal employees from engaging in partisan political activity, she would have to resign her position. Nonetheless, as she wrote her congressman E. H. Crump, she would "consider it a privilege to do anything possible to help to bring about a victory for the Democratic Party."[87] Further, she hoped to return to the newly re-elected administration in a better position. She had her sights on becoming the new assistant secretary of commerce for aeronautics.[88] Her plans were in place; her future looked bright. But then "all the heavens caved in."[89]

1. Phoebe Fairgrave, circa 1920, shortly after graduating from high school. Phoebe Omlie Collection.

2. Phoebe Fairgrave in front of her new Curtiss Jenny, 1921, with her pilot, Vernon C. Omlie. Phoebe Omlie Collection.

3. Vernon Omlie pilots the Curtiss Jenny as Phoebe Fairgrave, having just exited the cockpit, makes her way along the wing to a vertical strut. Photo series by P. W. Hamilton, photographer for the *Minneapolis Tribune*. Phoebe Omlie Collection.

4. Phoebe stretches up to grab hold of the upper wing.

5. Phoebe secures a handhold and pulls herself up.

6. With her toes hooked under a wire, Phoebe rides on top as Vernon puts the Jenny through a series of stunts.

7. After landing in a lake during an early parachute jump, Phoebe began wearing a partially inflated inner-tube in order to make herself more buoyant. Phoebe Omlie Collection.

8. The Phoebe Fairgrave Fliers featured her famous Double Parachute Jump. Phoebe Omlie Collection.

9. Phoebe Fairgrave and her Monocoupe *Chiggers.* Phoebe Omlie Collection.

10. Phoebe Fairgrave at a stop in her hometown of St. Paul during the 1928 Ford Reliability Air Tour. She was the only woman competitor in the tour. Minneapolis Public Library.

11. At the end of the tour, Phoebe is hoisted on the shoulders of Edsel Ford and Michigan governor Fred W. Green. The Benson Ford Research Center, Dearborn, Michigan.

12. Pilots gather at the start of the 1929 National Women's Air Derby. *Left to right:* Ruth Nichols, Bobbi Trout, Blanche Noyes, Amelia Earhart, Dr. A. C. Rohrbach (German plane designer), Thea Rasche, Gladys O'Donnell, Phoebe Omlie. Cleveland Press Collection, Cleveland State University Library.

13. After winning in the CW class of the Women's Air Derby, Phoebe poses with her plane *Miss Moline* and her trophies. Left to right: trophy for winning closed-course race, the Aerol Efficiency Trophy, trophy for CW class win. Courtesy of Heather Taylor.

14. Phoebe preparing to meet President Herbert Hoover at the White House in 1930 to invite him to the National Air Races in Chicago. The Library of Congress, LC-USZ62-97332.

15. After winning the 1931 Transcontinental Handicap Air Sweepstakes, Phoebe is awarded with a horseshoe of roses. Minneapolis Public Library.

16. Phoebe Omlie, Free-for-All race winner at the National Air Races, 1931. Cleveland Press Collection, Cleveland State University Library.

17. Vernon and Phoebe Omlie circa mid-1930s. Phoebe Omlie Collection.

18. Phoebe Omlie meets with Amelia Earhart in Miami, 31 May 1937, the day before Earhart left on her fatal flight. Ninety-Nines Museum of Women Pilots, Oklahoma City.

19. Phoebe with Assistant Attorney General Stella Akin at Floyd Bennett Field as they leave for their Roosevelt campaign tour on 16 September 1936. Minneapolis Public Library.

20. Phoebe Omlie on the job. Minneapolis Public Library.

21. Phoebe Omlie stands with her plane *Miss Memphis* and her sweepstakes prize, a Cord Cabriolet automobile, after winning the 1931 Transcontinental Sweepstakes Derby. She and her dog pose in front of the family business at the Memphis Municipal Airport. Saint Louis University Special Collections.

Chapter Six

On 6 August 1936, "one of the famous romances of the air came to an end." Phoebe received the devastating phone call in the early hours of the morning telling her that Vernon was dead; he had been killed in a plane crash. As she caught her breath, she asked: was he at the controls? They told her no, that Vernon had been a passenger on a commercial flight.[1]

He had bought a one-way ticket. Vernon was on his way to Detroit to pick up a new plane. The flight originated in New Orleans; he climbed aboard at Memphis, the only passenger traveling with the two pilots until they reached St. Louis. There, five more men boarded the late-night flight to Chicago. They took off from Lambert Field at 9:56 PM. Weather conditions were good: partly cloudy, a 2000-foot ceiling, overcast skies, moderate fog, visibility 1½ miles, and a 4 mph wind. Six minutes after takeoff, the plane did not respond to a radio call. Controllers tried querying airports along the way. No word. They later learned that less than ten minutes after take-off, the plane crashed in an open pasture, engines wide open, wing digging into the dirt at top speed until it broke apart, killing all eight aboard. The sleek modern three-month-old Lockheed Electra *City of Memphis* had been routinely inspected during its stopover at St. Louis; investigators found no apparent mechanical failure.[2]

It was four hours before a search party located the shattered Electra. All the bodies were thrown clear of the wreckage; the pilot's watch had stopped at 10:02 PM. Given the condition of the wreckage, the best guess was that the pilot had become disoriented in the gathering ground fog over the Missouri River, made an attempt to turn back to Lambert Field, and had banked sharply to the left at full throttle while too near the ground. A wing-tip caught and tripped the plane into a cartwheel. The gear was retracted, indicating the pilot had not been trying to land. A full investigation led by Air Commerce director Eugene Vidal himself was unable to produce a better explanation than the one provided by Chicago and Southern Air Lines president Carleton Putnam: "It was one of those things that can't happen but still did."[3]

Captain Omlie had spent a lifetime in the air and was known as one of the most cautious fliers in the business. He had never crashed a ship in his entire career as a pilot. Articles about the tragedy noted the irony of Vernon meeting death as an air passenger on what was to have been a routine flight.[4] "How the evil Fates must have chortled that Vernon Omlie, who had worked so long and hard to lay a foundation for transport aviation, should thus be taken," his widow later wrote.[5] Phoebe, a reporter noted, demonstrated her own "undaunted faith in aviation" by booking the first available flight home after learning of her husband's fatal crash.[6] Her mother and father flew in from Iowa City and his mother, sister, and brother joined his widow in Memphis. Vernon Omlie was buried in his Reserve Officers Flying Corps uniform with full military honors in a donated grave at Forest Hills Cemetery. His grave was banked with flowers, many in the shape of wings; a firing squad fired a military salute and an American Legion bugler sounded "Taps."[7] Thirteen private planes, draped in black and flown by Vernon's friends, associates, and students, flew an aerial salute over the funeral party. One dropped roses. "Each gave the aviator's wing salute, dipped low over the cemetery, and 'went upstairs' with struts singing a final farewell."[8]

A stunned Phoebe struggled to go on. She later described her husband as "My Beloved Husband and Life's Greatest Inspiration." Vernon, she wrote, was "one of the most thoughtful pilots in the world—a trait he managed to hammer home to me—therefore, we had no inkling that we wouldn't in due time cross the threshold of old age together." Now she would have to carry on alone, and she was determined to be brave about it: "I have tried to be faithful to the code of smothering all personal grief."[9] She put Vernon's affairs in order as best she could. She was most concerned with stabilizing his business. The Faulkners offered assistance. Bill recommended his younger brother John for the post of manager of Mid-South Airways, Inc. Bill's mother, Maud Falkner, provided financial support for the transition.[10]

Phoebe then took off for New York to fulfill her duty to represent the NAA's Contest Board at the start of the Bendix Trophy Race from New York's Floyd Bennett Field.[11] The Bendix transcontinental dash was all about speed. There were no limitations on the design or power of the airplanes, and no limitations on the pilots' choice of route. The shortest time from point A to point B took the prize. The three women entries were all Phoebe's friends and close associates: Louise Thaden and her copilot Blanche Noyes flew a Beechcraft Staggerwing; Amelia Earhart took Helen Richey along in her new Lockheed Electra; and Laura Ingalls flew solo in her Lockheed Orion. Hampered by ground fog at the start and fighting thunderstorms and rain showers all the way across the continent, Thaden approached Los Angeles "believing I had lost all chance of landing in the money." Yet, in a joyous upset, Louise and Blanche finished first, defeating some of the world's best male pilots. Laura Ingalls finished second; Earhart and Richey finished fifth.[12]

At the finish line, Vincent Bendix and National Air Races director Cliff Henderson, noted Thaden, "looked so crestfallen" at the outcome: a woman had won the Bendix! Thaden captured the $7,000 grand prize as well as the original "consolation prize" of $2,500 for the first female pilot to complete the race. The prize money was "far less gratifying than the pleasure of beating the men," said Thaden, but pleasant nonetheless. The name of the consolation prize was changed to "Special Award" now that a female pilot had won. Helen Richey remarked that it took them fourteen hours and fifty-five minutes to make up their minds what to call the prize—the time it took for Louise and Blanche to fly from New York to Los Angeles.[13]

Phoebe returned to Washington after the races and resigned her position with the federal government in order to campaign for Franklin Roosevelt's reelection.[14] In her resignation letter to the National Advisory Committee for Aeronautics, she explained that "aviation, both military and civil, has been lifted from its former chaotic condition and prospered much under the able guidance of President Roosevelt . . . Therefore, I consider it my duty, as a pioneer of aviation and as an American citizen to lend my support to help make it possible to continue this upward trend in the aviation industry."[15] NACA secretary J. F. Victory accepted her resignation "without prejudice" while praising her "wealth of experience and judgment and keen zeal for the promotion of safety in flying."[16]

Many of Phoebe's cadre of women pilots were leaving the air-marking program as well. Louise Thaden had decided to spend more time with her small children, Helen McCloskey got married, and Amelia Earhart hired Helen Richey to work for her in planning some future flights. That left Blanche Noyes to carry on with the program.[17] As war heated up in Europe, the air-marking program stalled, and then suffered reversal as many of the completed markings were "obliterated to foil possible air invaders." Noyes found herself in charge of painting over the markings.[18]

For the 1936 campaign, Phoebe flew a Fairchild four-passenger plane called *Victory.* She took off from Floyd Bennett Field in New York on 16 September 1936 with Assistant Attorney General Stella Akin aboard.[19] Huge letters along the side of the plane read "Roosevelt Fliers," with "Win With Roosevelt" below that. The underside of the high wing was also painted with the name Roosevelt. Phoebe had wanted to equip the plane with neon lights that flashed "Roosevelt" when she flew at night, but this apparently did not work out.[20] From New York, the fliers headed upstate, then west through Pennsylvania, Ohio, Indiana, Michigan, Illinois, Wisconsin, North Dakota, South Dakota, Colorado, Nebraska, Iowa, flying back through the central states to New York, and ending their tour a few days before the election. Their "flying stump for the New Deal" covered 10,000 miles, twenty states, landed in 150 towns, and made one emergency landing in a farmyard in Pennsylvania. At each of their stops, including the farmyard where their unexpected arrival attracted a crowd, the women spoke for Roosevelt's re-election, citing the successes and unfinished business of the early New Deal. For towns where they did not land, Phoebe made it a point to fly low and slow overhead so that folks on the ground could clearly see their message to "Win With Roosevelt."[21]

About halfway through their journey, Akin was replaced by Izetta Jewell Miller, a former actress from West Virginia and the first southern woman to run for the U.S. Senate (in 1922 and 1924, both unsuccessfully). The Roosevelt Fliers were the featured guests of endless luncheons, receptions, rallies, and banquets. Miller did most of the speaking, said Phoebe. "I just fly her around. Pretty good team, too, don't you think?"[22] Miller returned the compliment: "Phoebe is a true bird-woman, a safe and sane pilot, and makes a dandy little talk on what the administration has done for aviation in the bargain."[23] Though she was reluctant to speak formally, when given the chance Phoebe spoke passionately about why she was campaigning again for the president:

In the first place, Mr. Roosevelt has done something for the forgotten men of aviation—the little fellow who have been sticking to flying all these years, hoping to make something of it. A great deal has been done for aviation concerns before Roosevelt was elected, but the little guy was being forgotten. Well, since 1932 the New Deal program has included the construction of some 2,000 small airports throughout the country. This has given the little man a new lease on life.[24]

After the election, she returned to Memphis and reconnected with her old friend, W. Percy McDonald. McDonald had been an original member of the Memphis Aero Club and maintained his close association with the Omlies. Indeed, when Vernon was killed, it was McDonald who offered a grave from his family plot at Forest Hills Cemetery. McDonald and Phoebe began to talk again about how to accomplish Vernon's dream of aviation training in the public schools. Since first establishing Mid-South Airways, Vernon had advocated making aviation ground school a part of vocational education in Memphis. At one point in the 1920s, he even convinced his congressional representative, Senator Kenneth McKellar, to request that the War Department establish such a program similar to ROTC. In spite of apparent enthusiasm for the idea, funding was never forthcoming. By 1937, even with the Depression, the prospect looked more promising. McDonald was then both the superintendent of Shelby County Schools and chair of the Tennessee Aeronautics Commission. He and Phoebe hatched an idea to dedicate the seven-cents-per-gallon tax on aviation fuel to furthering the aviation industry in Tennessee. This would entail applying 50 percent of the tax revenues to airport improvements and the other 50 percent to funding aviation ground schools in public high schools. Together, McDonald and Phoebe drafted legislation that would become the Tennessee Aviation Act of 1937.[25]

In January, following his inauguration, President and Mrs. Roosevelt invited Phoebe to the White House for a private informal Sunday night supper. When he asked about her future plans, she said she would very much like to continue working on the issue of aviation safety. She told the president about her work in Tennessee on legislation to fund pilot training with a transfer of fuel tax. They discussed the federal Aviation Act then making its way through Congress, and Phoebe suggested that she was particularly interested in two items: that the air-marking program be established as a permanent part of the airport division (it then existed only at the discretion of the WPA) and that a pilot training program be included. The president agreed.[26]

What he did not do was offer her employment. Since December, she had been trying to secure a new position, calling on the intercession of Molly

Dewson, First Lady Eleanor Roosevelt, and others, for an appointment to the Bureau of Air Commerce. In view of the coming reorganization of aviation agencies, she wrote, she would like to head up the aeronautics division with the title of assistant secretary of commerce. Dewson passed the suggestion on to J. M. Johnson at Commerce, who replied that he did not anticipate such a position being created, adding "Mrs. Omlie is a gifted woman and undoubtedly could be very useful. It would give me pleasure to give consideration to any plan to that end."[27] After Dewson shared this news along with her concern that the agency might not want a woman at the head, Phoebe responded:

> Really, Molly, any job connected with the development of aviation is a "he-man" job. It takes someone who has had varied experience and one who is not afraid to let the "chips fall where they may." . . . I am really interested in the Interstate Commerce Commission as I fully believe great study and work can be accomplished here, especially if Congress enacts legislation to turn airlines over to them. I have always, and now, more than ever will always devote my life's work to the development of safety in aviation. The Interstate Commerce Commission does not have one single member who has knowledge of aviation and its problems. Again, I quote you about "he-man." I agree with them one hundred per cent. But does that really mean sex?[28]

Dewson responded that she was doing the best that she could to lobby on Phoebe's behalf, but she was not hopeful.[29] Dewson turned to the first lady, reminding Mrs. Roosevelt that Phoebe "still thinks she would be better than the men in putting more safety into aviation if she were head of aviation for the Government." Given that Phoebe had resigned from her paying job to campaign for the president, furnished her plane free of charge, and honored her pledge to campaign even after learning of her husband's death, Molly suggested that the first lady at least invite Mrs. Omlie for tea to discuss the matter.[30]

Then came the break Phoebe had been waiting for. On 18 April 1937, she hastily posted a telegram to Molly Dewson:

MAJOR SHROEDER ASSISTANT DIRECTOR OF THE BUREAU OF AIR COMMERCE RESIGNED YESTERDAY STOP I AM NOT A HE MAN BUT I KNOW I HAVE MORE EXPERIENCE THAT ANY

OTHER IN THE BUREAU STOP I WOULD LIKE TO HAVE THIS
VACANCY STOP
REGARDS PHOEBE

Dewson promised to show her telegram to the first lady while cautioning Phoebe not to be overly optimistic. She observed that "in spite of our progress, every time we get a woman located in a prominent place, it's an achievement."[31] On her periodic list of concerns and messages that Dewson forwarded to Mrs. Roosevelt to share with the president, Dewson included her friend as Item No. 4: "Phoebe Omlie: Greatly discouraged because a College Professor with no commercial experience whatever in aviation has been appointed on the Safety Program in her place."[32] Mrs. Roosevelt privately responded to Dewson that she had been told that "Phoebe Omlie had come in with an attitude of knowing it all and had never been persona grata with anyone. Mr. Vidal came to see me Monday and said he thought it was going to be impossible for her to do any work there. The feeling was strongly against her before this had come up. I made the suggestion . . . that they try to get her something with an aviation company . . . There is no use of her trying to work with Commerce people."[33] Phoebe was a self-confident woman in a time when women were supposed to be quiet and self-deprecating. She was sure of her commitment and her skill, and proceeded accordingly. Apparently, her approach did not endear her to some important colleagues.

In the midst of all this, Phoebe flew to Miami to see her good friend, Amelia Earhart, off on her flight around the world. As a member of the NAA National Contest Board tasked to check and approve flight plans for record flights, Phoebe was concerned about the difficulties of the passage over the vast distances of the Pacific, where vital wind and weather information was inconsistent or unavailable. Still, Amelia was confident that all contingencies had been accounted for. Phoebe later recounted that she "agonized and studied that plan over and over again after [Amelia's] disappearance to find an answer." She feared that Amelia had encountered a tailwind that caused her to over-fly Howland Island (where she planned to refuel) during the night instead of at dawn. Amelia and her navigator, Fred Noonan, had planned to take advantage of the rising sun to make the tiny speck of an island (two miles long, half a mile wide, four feet elevation at high tide) easier to spot. After missing the island, Phoebe believed, Amelia had little fuel and no hope of reaching a safe landing.[34]

The Tennessee Aviation Act, proposed by Omlie and McDonald, passed 21 May 1937. The legislation replaced the Aeronautics Commission with a more centralized and powerful Tennessee Bureau of Aeronautics within the Department of Highways and Public Works.[35] McDonald was named director of aeronautics by the governor. By the time the Education section of the bill became operational the following March, Tennessee's Civilian Pilot Training Program (TCPTP) had established ground schools in Memphis, Nashville, Chattanooga, Knoxville, and the Tri-Cities, each of them designed to accommodate one hundred students per session. Open to any Tennessee citizen over the age of sixteen, the schools taught navigation, meteorology, aerodynamics, aircraft engines, and civil air regulations. Because there were no textbooks available for these subjects, Phoebe took on the task of developing the curriculum. She taught her own section of the ground school at Bellevue Junior High School in Memphis in October 1938.[36] Based on a merit system, the top fifteen students in each school (twelve boys and three girls) were granted scholarships for private pilot training.[37] By the end of the first year, the state had graduated 2,780 ground school students and 75 fliers.[38]

The first program of its kind, the TCPTP got a great deal of national attention. Phoebe's school was visited by representatives from the army and navy and members of the Bureau of Air Commerce. That December, President Roosevelt unveiled his own program to provide a boost to civil aviation by funding pilot training for college students. Though it was ostensibly aimed at stimulating the flagging private aviation industry, many recognized the program's potential for national defense. Critics charged that the president's real purpose was to build up aviation for war. Indeed, he did little to dampen that criticism, telling the National Aviation Forum that "hardly another civil activity of our people bears such a direct and intimate relation to the national security as does civil aviation. It supplies a reservoir of inestimable value to our military and naval forces in the form of men and machines, while at the same time it keeps an industry so geared that it can be instantly diverted to the production of fighting planes in the event of national emergency."[39]

The federal Civil Aeronautics Act of 1938 transferred responsibility for nonmilitary aviation from the Department of Commerce to a new independent agency, the Civil Aeronautics Authority. Under that agency's purview was the new Civilian Pilot Training Program, codified in the Civilian Pilot Training Act of 1939. Training began with the government paying for a 72-hour ground school course followed by 35–50 hours of flight instruction at facilities located near thirteen participating colleges and universities; 330 students between the ages of eighteen and twenty-five were selected for the first class.[40]

Modeled after the TCPTP, the program had three major differences from the one in Tennessee: ground school courses were offered in colleges rather than public schools, the minimum age of participants was increased from sixteen to eighteen, and the ratio of women to men fell from 20 percent to 10 percent.[41] By the end of the first year, 9,350 men and women were being trained at 435 colleges and universities. Overall, approximately 2,500 women were CPTP trained before America entered the war.[42]

After Pearl Harbor, the CPTP became the War Training Service (WTS).[43] From 1942 until the program ended in the summer of 1944, students continued to take college courses and private flight training, but all students were now required to sign agreements to enlist in the armed forces upon graduation. Once this took effect, women were automatically excluded. A number of women protested this development and Eleanor Roosevelt asked Robert H. Hinckley, assistant secretary of commerce and director of the Civilian Pilot Training Program, for an explanation. He noted the necessity to concentrate resources on training men for combat, adding "If, or when, the time comes when trained girls are needed in non-combat work to release men for active duty, that will be a different situation."[44]

In 1938, as she taught her ground school in Memphis, Phoebe was still struggling to try to secure a job in Washington. She tried again with a letter to Eleanor Roosevelt asking to be appointed as the third member of the Air Safety Board.[45] The first lady passed the request on to her husband, who responded: "She should have some job in the bureau tho [*sic*] I fear not this one." The president followed up with Edward J. Noble, chairman of the Civil Aeronautics Authority. Noble suggested he had found a possible position for her as assistant chief of the Flight Information Section. The description of the job made it clear that this would be strictly paper shuffling: preparing periodical bulletins, collecting and disseminating data on airport and navigational facilities, compiling weekly notices, and the like. Further, the position paid only about $3,000, a considerable cut from the $5,600 salary she earned in 1935. After the president forwarded this suggestion to Dewson, she dropped a note to the first lady saying that she had decided not to share this letter with Phoebe.

It might make her feel worse than the fact that others were preferred ahead of her for the Board. I really am enthusiastic about her for the

Board. She is keenly interested because of her husband's death in an air plane crash (when he was not piloting), because she has grown up in the industry, and because by nature she is sensible, practical and undramatic. From my experience a good woman does any group of men executives good. But I am not pressing you.

The first lady attached a note to her husband to Dewson's message reading simply "What about this? ER." The president passed it to Secretary Early with the message, "Will you take this up with the Chairman of the Air Safety Board and see if they can use Phoebe Omlie anywhere? FDR." A reply from the Civil Aeronautics Administration (CAA) administrator Clinton Hester asked James Rowe to look into the situation, asserting, "We have held up filling this position for several weeks in order that Mrs. Omlie might be considered should she be interested and should the President see fit to issue an executive order [in order to bypass a civil service exam] which would permit the appointment." When Rowe responded, he addressed his remarks to Secretary Early. The Air Safety Board cannot use her, he wrote, because "1. she has no civil service status and 2. their work is mostly field work at accident crashes and is too tough for a woman." He reiterated that the lower-paying position at Flight Information was still available. Otherwise there was no position for her "unless the president directs the authority to create a position." FDR forwarded this reply to his wife along with a memo responding to that final point. "Sorry but I cannot possibly make an exception. I have had many similar cases in the past."[46]

Attempting to eliminate at least one of the detriments to a Safety Board appointment, Phoebe took the civil service exam for senior air safety investigator and scored an 89 (including the widow's preference).[47] She appealed to her senator to help. In September 1940, Senator Kenneth McKellar wrote to the first lady about his concern that Phoebe's talents and experience had been overlooked. "[B]ecause aviation is more or less a profession for men, many people charged with policy making in our government do not know the vast experience and accomplishments of Mrs. Omlie." Given that the Civil Service Commission had informed him that "she heads one of their examination lists for aeronautics," he felt certain that if Mrs. Roosevelt would speak with the chairman of the Civil Aeronautics Board or the assistant secretary of commerce, that a position could be found. The first lady wrote to both Harlee Branch at the Civil Aeronautics Board and Robert Hinckley at Commerce to urge them to find a position for Phoebe Omlie.[48]

Phoebe, frustrated with trying to search for a federal job from Memphis, returned to Washington in mid-January 1941. Thanking the first lady for her kindnesses, Phoebe reported that Harlee Branch had been "very nice in try- ing to work me in with their safety division," but she had been told that their appropriation was so limited that such a place would have to be financed by Commerce.

> After many weeks I had a talk with Mr. Hinckley. He had me talk with Mr. Brimhall, who referred me to a Mr. Wright who informed me that he had just come over from the Census Bureau and would have to take the matter up with Mr. Hinckley . . . . I talked with one of the assistants in the office of Secretary of Commerce Jesse Jones. He asked me to submit a short resume of my career. After this I was informed that Mr. Jones was impressed and would take the matter up with Mr. Hinckley.

After spelling out the run-around she had received, Phoebe concluded with a plea. "As I have devoted the last four years in writing and working out the original public aviation instruction legislation for Tennessee (which did not carry a salary) I must make connections where I can be on a payrole [*sic*] . . . Will you advise me?" Mrs. Roosevelt immediately posted a short note to Secretary of Commerce Jesse Jones: "Phoebe Omlie tells me that her case has been brought to your attention. I do not know what you can do, but I do think she should have consideration because of the work which she has done."[49]

Apparently this time the pressure worked. In February 1941, Phoebe was appointed as senior private flying specialist assigned to the Research Division of the Civil Aeronautics Administration to coordinate all aviation work done by various agencies of the federal government.[50] Shortly after- ward, the president met with Phoebe and told her that he was particularly concerned about the paucity of trained ground personnel to service planes being readied for war.[51] She was immediately put in charge of the Aviation Ground Servicemen's Training Program, a position for which she was high- ly qualified, given her mechanical knowledge, her familiarity with airport management, and her experience setting up aviation schools and writing curricula. Her job was to systematize the efforts of the CAA, the WPA, and the Office of Education in establishing a 1.5-million-dollar defense train- ing program to provide specialized training for airport ground personnel in skills required by expanding civil and military aviation. She was charged with inspecting 250 key airports around the country as potential training sites, as well as outlining the appropriate courses of instruction. Working with the Office of Education, Phoebe designed and established a ninety-day course of study that included airport safety practices, reading blueprints, airport management, care of equipment, fuel facilities, cleaning planes, clerical work, and the numerous other jobs around an airport that did not require highly skilled aviation mechanics. Although the leader of the program was a woman, the trainees were limited to men.[52]

"It's a program that's urgently needed," she said. "As the number of airplanes increases, the demand for ground personnel becomes greater. In civil aviation it is estimated that at least nine ground men are needed to keep one pilot in the air. Military aviation requires a much larger ground crew per pilot."[53] Phoebe spent eight weeks setting up 120 schools in thirty-eight states. After the initial program to train 5,000 men in the first year and a half was organized, Phoebe served as the CAA's technical advisor and liaison with the schools. Ultimately the program was expanded to 620 schools that graduated 9,000 mechanics and ground personnel for the war effort.[54] In May, she was again in the air, traveling over 20,000 miles to establish flying schools to teach primary aviation around the country for the CPTP program. Among the schools she got up and running was one at Tuskegee, Alabama, "the first of its kind for negroes."[55]

As all able-bodied men were being drafted for war and the need for trained pilots significantly increased, the Civil Aeronautics Authority predicted a critical shortage of flight instructors. The CAA press spokesman Charles E. Planck expressed grave concern that the CPTP programs and civilian schools that were training pilots for the army might have to cease operations. "Draft boards continue to draft civilian instructors into the foot army or else, with threat of draft, the instructors volunteer for the Air Transport Command, get into airline cargo carrying, or into some branch of service aviation. If draft boards cannot be dissuaded, women are going to have to fill the breach."[56] W. McLean Stewart, director of the War Training Service, concurred: "The Army is going to take every qualified man between the ages of 18 and 37. Every possible man must be released for the service, and from the standpoint of the manpower problem alone it makes sense to use women instructors when we can."[57]

This discussion of women flight instructors occurred at the time when women in many capacities were stepping up to aid the war effort, volunteering for war industry jobs, or joining the Women's Army Auxiliary Corps (WAAC). The Women's Auxiliary Ferrying Squadron (WAFS), the predecessor of the Women's Airforce Service Pilots (WASPs), had begun training female pilots for noncombat missions in support of the Army Air Forces.[58]

Percy McDonald also saw "no reason women could not be trained so that they could be used in the training of pilots, both as ground and flight instructors."[59] Without waiting for the federal government to do something about it, he and the Tennessee Bureau of Aeronautics decided to act. Before making their proposal, though, the bureau cautiously investigated the possible "psychological reactions of young student fliers towards women instructors." They interviewed students at aviation schools that used them and found that "especially new students react very favorably under the patient guidance of women. The fear of altitudes and speed in the air is more quickly overcome [with a woman instructor]." The TBA was satisfied that their survey supported their own conclusions that "there is a definite place that women can take in the all-out war effort in the training of needed personnel in divisions of our aviation training schools when specialized aeronautical knowledge is required."[60] In 1942, McDonald persuaded the CAA to loan Phoebe Omlie to the state in order to establish an experimental program to fully train ten women flight instructors with the anticipation that the program would serve as a pilot project for later adoption by the Civil Aeronautics Administration and the U.S. military.[61]

The Tennessee Women's Research Flight Instructors' School was launched in September 1942 with a spartan budget of approximately $15,000, out of which the residence, subsistence, uniforms, and equipment, including three training planes, were bought or rented. Though the CAA provided no funds, besides loaning Phoebe's services, the agency lent rhetorical support. Robert Hinckley wrote to McDonald that "women have always been the fundamental background for teaching, and I feel that when they are properly trained to teach aviation subjects then they can contribute much toward relieving man-power for actual combat flying."[62]

Applicants for the school were required to be single or married to husbands in active military service, hold a private pilot's license or better, and have at least 120 flying hours.[63] They would be chosen on the basis of their "attitude toward women's part in the war, physical fitness, previous flying experience, and willingness to serve where needed."[64] In return, they were promised "62 hours of flying, 216 hours of ground school instruction, 162 hours of flight instructors ground school, a hard eight hours of work a day for six days a week for 12 weeks, uniforms, food, and an enormous old southern colonial house for a dormitory."[65]

Calling it a southern colonial was a bit grand. Phoebe acquired an old farmhouse near Nashville's Gillespie Field which she cleaned, painted and renovated into an army-style barracks. She begged blankets from the factory at the state penitentiary, commandeered some war-surplus cots, and set about hiring instructors. She immediately ran into the very shortage her school was seeking to overcome. Finding it impossible to get an instructor who could teach all the ground school classes she wanted to include (meteorology, aerial navigation, aircraft structure, aircraft engines, and civil air regulations), she had to hire five different instructors to teach in their particular areas of expertise.[66]

Ten students were selected from over 250 applicants. Six were chosen from Tennessee: Margaret Josephine Wakefield, a Vanderbilt graduate and teacher in Nashville Schools who had flying experience in six different types of aircraft; Martha E. Childress of Columbia, a recent Vanderbilt graduate who took her civilian pilot training there; Mary Elizabeth Pigg, another Vanderbilt University graduate and secretary with extensive experience in the Civil Air Patrol; Jennie Lou Gower of Murfreesboro, a former assembly line inspector for Vultee Aircraft; Lucille Biggs, a former schoolteacher and employee of Gill Dove Airways in Martin, Tennessee; and Cora McDonald of Bristol, an aeronautical engineer who worked for Bristol Aircraft Company and had flown twelve types of planes. The others were Elizabeth Moody Hall of Lexington, Kentucky, daughter of missionaries to India and the wife of a military man, with 150 hours in her logbook; Helen Jean Johnston of Birmingham, Alabama, married to a major with the 127th Observation Squadron stationed in Tullahoma, Tennessee, had 300 logged flight hours; Dorothy Moselle Swain of Asheville, North Carolina, a ferrying pilot for Piper Aircraft; and Emma Jean Whittington of Hot Springs, who already held a ground instructor's rating.[67]

Speaking to the press on women's proper role in wartime aviation, Phoebe said,

> The greatest contribution they can make to the all-out war effort is to prepare themselves for and accept jobs as teachers in the primary training of aviation pilots. It's hard work and it isn't a glamorous job, but women in America have never failed when they had to adapt themselves to meet emergencies. They will not fail today. Indeed, because of the high standards set up and their knowledge that they must be perfect to convince the skeptics, I feel that they will become the best instructors in aviation.[68]

Phoebe was particularly concerned that her trainees not be perceived by the press and the general public as frivolous or glamorous.

We need a new appraisal of women in war, particularly in aviation. The whole program of women in war work always gets distorted by excess publicity, until you can't see the jobs for the women, uniforms and window dressing. I'm eager to add here that it is not the fault of the women, either. The first women in the factories had to smear grease on their faces and pull their hair down to satisfy the art editors of the newspapers. Later, as each new and different job for women opened up, the photographers dressed it up and the writers elaborated upon it, until we hardly know today what the important jobs are.[69]

Trips to the beauty shop were discouraged and the women wore drab uniforms of khaki-gray trousers, a dark-brown coat, and a dark-brown overseas cap.[70] The young women studied "under similar conditions of discipline and curricula" as that afforded in a regular army cadet training school.[71] Their six-day-a-week schedule began when they were awakened by the clang of an old plantation bell at 6:45 AM. They engaged in calisthenics on the lawn and a quick breakfast before their two-mile march in formation to the airport where they stayed until suppertime. Their days were filled with flight instruction, classroom instruction in aerodynamics, meteorology, navigation, and civil air regulations. Phoebe incorporated her ground servicemen's "mechanics helper" course into the curriculum, including engine overhaul and repair, and recovering wings and flight surfaces in the shop, to ensure her instructors could service and fix their own aircraft. After supper the women had study time for two hours before collapsing into bed.[72] The drill continued, good weather and bad. When the Cumberland River flooded and marooned the school, Phoebe borrowed a boat and rowed her students to the airport.[73]

Phoebe was tough, demanding, and "definitely not one of the girls."[74] She held to very rigid rules and pushed her students hard because, she said, these women would be training men to fight and lives would depend upon their skills. "I want that instruction to be as perfect and tough as possible because the men's lives may depend on it. If we aren't tough with them, these women, they won't be tough on the men."[75] Moreover, Phoebe knew that, as women, her students would be held to higher standards than comparable men and that, as McDonald told them at their welcoming dinner, "Yours is a great responsibility. Whether or not you succeed or fail in this course may prove the turning point for women in aviation in the United States."[76]

While Phoebe always referred to her trainees as women, the press inevitably called them girls and remarked on their attractiveness. For example, one reporter reassured readers that the students' "good looks are above the average with blue eyes and brown hair prominent."[77] A *Washington Daily News* feature captioned a photograph of the women marching in formation in their dress uniforms as "Ten little girls from the Tennessee school."[78] An article featuring graduate Emma Hall in the *Atlanta Journal* called her "pert and pretty" under a headline reading "90-Pound Career Girl Teaches Navy Boys How to Fly Planes."[79]

Each woman had logged a minimum of 120 hours before entering the school and each logged 165 additional hours or more before she graduated. Each qualified for a commercial pilot's license as well as qualifying as a pilot instructor. In addition, each had at least five ratings in the ground school subjects of meteorology, aerial navigation, aircraft structure, aircraft engines, and civil air regulations. In case of an emergency, Phoebe told the newspapers, any one of her students would be able to manage an airport.[80]

The ten women graduated with great ceremony 3 February 1943, as Phoebe Omlie stood proudly by. Gov. Prentice Cooper commended the graduates and the Tennessee Bureau of Aeronautics, saying that he could "imagine no more important work than that of training fighter pilots."[81] Then C. I. Stanton from the Civil Aeronautics Authority took the podium:

> It is my opinion that, since women have always excelled in instructing and have done most of the teaching of our nation, this should be their natural function in aviation. Our problem is to give the 1,000,000 boys who will graduate into the draft each year flight training. I believe we should train at least 200,000 of them each year. To do that, we shall need at least 5,000 women instructors.[82]

The graduates were immediately in very high demand since few instructors were highly and broadly qualified. The Embry-Riddle School in Miami, Florida, wanted to hire the whole class, as did a school in Kansas City; other requests came in from Missouri, El Paso, New Orleans, Atlanta, and several others. Jackie Cochran tried to recruit the whole class for the WASPs.[83] In the end, the women were assigned to various aviation training schools across the country where the CAA held contracts with the armed forces.

Tennessee Bureau of Aeronautics executive director Col. Herbert Fox celebrated the successful completion of the school as a model for a national initiative. "Our job was to prove that women can do flight instructing. It is now the job of the federal government to train them. I believe they intend to do that."[84] The Tennessee Bureau of Aeronautics and the Civil Aeronautics Authority asked Congress for a supplemental appropriation of $2.5 million to train 500 more women instructor pilots within six months with 400 more in training. About a month after the first class graduated, the House Appropriations Committee was hearing testimony on the bill in closed session.[85] A year later, McDonald declared that, despite the apparent success of the Tennessee school whose graduates had by then trained an estimated 500 men and the eagerness of over 1,000 women pilots who had contacted his agency seeking training, there had been no action on the bill.[86]

Given discussions about the acute need for flight instructors, it is difficult to discern why the initiative was not funded, but it appears that a number of factors were involved. Among them was the bubbling controversy over the heavily funded women's ferry service, a discomfort by the military in having civilians train military pilots that was exacerbated by their reluctance to use women to train male pilots, and a rapidly dwindling evidence of need, due largely to stepped-up efforts by the military to provide and train flight instructors of their own.

As the closed hearings continued, some of the debate between the CAA and the military played out in the newspapers. While "private schools in [the] CAA program say they could put 1,000 women pilots to work," the army was demonstrating great reluctance to use civilian training schools. The army announced that they would not use women flight instructors in the CAA schools for training their Army Air Force cadets. Further, in a point disputed by the CAA, the army contended that they had "several thousand enlisted men in reserve waiting to be trained as instructors in the Army's 'continuing' training program."[87] Funding concerns had also arisen in the hearings. The TBA director Herbert Fox complained that the ferry service had been given funding priority even though the cost of training women as service pilots cost about $25,000 apiece while the bureau had trained women flight instructors for about $1,000 each.[88]

At bottom was the military's longtime skepticism of the value of civilian programs for flight training, a concern that affected congressional commitment and appropriations. Once the war began, the military, especially the army, more actively opposed civilian training and moved to undercut its effectiveness by building their own training facilities and staffing them with military personnel.[89] Apparently prompted by criticism that they had allowed thousands of qualified male flight instructors to be swept up in draft calls, the army aggressively moved to "reclaim" for the air forces those instructors who had been reassigned, inducted, or called to active duty in nonflying capacities. In short, before Congress could act in funding more women flight instructors to alleviate a shortage, the shortage, according to the army, no longer existed.[90]

Phoebe's job as senior operations supervisor with the War Training Service was abolished when the war ended. She was transferred to the lower-rated job of research liaison officer in the Administrative Office for Research.[91] In that capacity, she worked on a variety of research projects for the CAA. One major study involved a survey of fatal air accidents resulting from stall conditions of aircraft. A stall occurs when the angle of the wing relative to the air traveling over it becomes too great to sustain lift and the wing stops flying, causing the aircraft to fall. The study concluded that about half of all fatal private flying accidents before 1945 resulted from stalls. The CAA's technical division subsequently devised several devices to serve as stall warnings, activating a horn or flashing light in the cockpit to warn pilots of an approaching stall. Though designed primarily for private aviation, these devices were critical additions to the safety equipment of all aircraft.[92]

In the years following the end of the war, the Civil Aeronautics Administration struggled to redefine its priorities among competing aviation interests, primarily those of the airlines, military aviation, and private pilots. This resulted in a good deal of chaos at the agency. Many personnel changes, some accompanied by charges of malfeasance and corruption, roiled the agency; budgets were held to wartime levels despite the increasing pressure to expand its responses to a burgeoning commercial sector.[93] Still, at least for a time, the CAA saw its mission to support civil aviation as an important one. Given the large numbers of pilots trained during the war, the CAA anticipated a postwar boom in civil aviation. When the postwar market for private planes appeared to be stalled, Director Theodore P. Wright tried to determine the cause. Part of this investigation involved Phoebe's survey of the financial status of persons investing in aircraft at various age levels. Her data revealed that for the average individual the advantages of flying were only cost effective for trips over 100 miles, so it was impractical for a pilot to own a plane unless he used it frequently for long trips. Given this contingency, flying was rapidly becoming luxury recreation for the wealthy.[94]

It was Wright's contention that government support was needed to expand the private flying sector, in the form of airport development, improved airways and navigational systems, and subsidies for aircraft manufacturers.[95] Congress was not receptive to these advances, however. Despite Wright's personal interest in private aviation, the CAA's primary obligation would increasingly be to commercial and military users. As the World War evolved into the Cold War, federal funding focused on those aspects of aviation that had potential value for national defense. The CAA began research, for example, on how transport planes could be adopted to military needs in an emergency, finding ways to standardize commercial and military communications and navigation infrastructure and protocols, and designing airways for maximum efficiency in the event of war.[96]

In May 1947, Phoebe took a six-month leave without pay. She later extended the leave by three months and then another three months.[97] She wrote a memo (with no indicated recipient) concerning questionable activities at the CAA and her concerns about investigations of communist influence in Congress and the agency. The stress of working there, she maintained, affected her health to the extent that her doctor suggested she take a leave.[98] In August, she underwent what the press called "a major operation."[99] Since she had been suffering with ovarian cysts for many years, it is likely to have been some sort of female surgery. Ladies in the 1940s did not talk about such things, even euphemistically as "female troubles," except to their closest friends.[100] Phoebe spent some time recuperating at the home of her old flying friend Janette Rex in Cleveland and told the press that she had taken a leave to write her memoirs.[101] She enlisted an old friend, Swanee Taylor, to help her get started writing. Taylor had been a wing-walker with the Gates Flying Circus in the 1920s and a participant in a number of cross-country air races. He had most recently worked as a script-writer for CAA training films in Washington. Together they produced about 135 pages of manuscript, covering the first five years of her aviation career, before her leave expired.[102]

When she returned to work in mid-1948, Phoebe resumed her former position as research liaison officer in the Administrative Office for Research. After being gone so long, the changes in the agency had become even more apparent. In the interim, many of its functions, like pilot certifications, ground schools, and repair stations, were being decentralized and some divisions cut. What remained was increasingly unsympathetic to civil aviation, those "little guys" Phoebe had championed her whole career. In the interests of safety, the CAA was tightening restrictions on the private flier, requiring expensive electronic equipment for navigation and communication in private planes. To Phoebe, these were efforts to stifle and regulate private flying right out of business. Even more disturbing to her was the direction the country appeared to be heading. The Truman administration seemed to be riddled with corruption and communism. Like others who worked in the government, she was now required to sign an oath of loyalty and list all organizations with which she was affiliated.[103] Her work assignments had shifted away from direct involvement in aviation projects to designing and formulating cooperative efforts between the federal government and the states for search and rescue operations in times of emergency. Her job entailed investigating all the standard practices and legislative responsibilities of the agencies and the governments of the various states to ensure a more uniform effort could be made to save life and property in time of disaster. While this was undoubtedly worthy work, it was not the kind of work she found satisfying and was only peripherally about aviation.[104]

Once that study was completed, she was transferred to the Office of Aviation Development, a catch-all division devoted to the needs of private aviation, created after a major reorganization by the new director, Delos W. Rentzel, a former communications officer with American Airlines. Rentzel was decidedly airline oriented, and several administrators sympathetic to private aviation resigned in protest.[105] Phoebe remained, but there seemed to be little for her to do here. She was briefly loaned to the Civil Defense Administration to assist in formulating plans for using civil aircraft in civil defense. These were later codified in a uniform state plan for Civil Aviation Mobilization and Civil Defense.[106]

In the increasingly tense atmosphere following the beginning of the Korean War in 1950, the CAA was engaged in planning mobilization of all aviation in the event of a major conflict. One component of this effort was a press for a single military-civilian standard measurement for speed and distance used in air navigation. In August 1950, the CAA announced that after 1 July 1952, knots and nautical miles would be the standard for all aircraft, thus imposing a single standard for civil and military aviation and one that would conform to the practice of other nations. The air force and navy had already adopted the system. The CAA anticipated that the nearly two years' advance notice would be sufficient for pilot education and instrument modification.[107] But they met with considerable resistance among private pilots, represented by the Airplane Owners and Pilots Association (AOPA), who vowed to resist the expensive change that was being "jammed down our throats."[108]

For Phoebe, it was the last straw. She was now convinced that her agency was no longer supporting private aviation, but was in fact actively working against it. On 21 January 1952 she sent a letter of resignation to commerce secretary Charles Sawyer, effective 1 April.[109] She told the press:

I'm resigning from CAA because—after devoting 31 years of my life to aviation—I can no longer willingly sit by and watch the Truman administration socialize civil aviation in the United States. The present trend in CAA policy committees can lead only to the liquidation of America's aviation industry, forcing it into Government ownership. For some time now I have sat in planning discussions controlled mostly by bureaucrats who have no actual experience in civil aviation, and watched them agree to regulations and taxing policy that must eventually force civil aviation to the wall.[110]

Phoebe was fifty years old; she was now retired. She left Washington, severing her connections with all those who remained.

Chapter Seven

Almost as soon as she touched down in Memphis, Phoebe joined the staff of Free Enterprises, Inc., an organization dedicated to saving "this country from socialism and communism." She was put in charge of a television "Freedom Series," a Sunday afternoon talk show. "It was a real thrill," she told the press, "to come back home and find that our people here have not been unaware of the dangers confronting them . . . I am instilled with the old spirit and am now joining the fight to help in any way I can to re-establish constitutional government in this country."[1]

At present I am not committing myself as to what I think should be done, but one thing I am certain of, and that is that there must be drastic changes made in our Government if we are to keep our way of life. I have always been a great believer in States Rights. To me that has always been the balance wheel that has protected this country from the entanglements that have caused the rest of the world to be in such constant turmoil. Personally, I am a Democrat. I have always been a Democrat but my country will always come first before party and before any kind of world government.[2]

In October, she undertook a three-day tour of twenty mid-South towns distributing 100,000 invitations to attend presidential candidate Dwight

Eisenhower's riverfront speech in Memphis.[3] She was soon disillusioned with Eisenhower as president, however, for not reversing the course of what she saw as socialism.[4] Over the next few years, she flirted with a variety of right-wing groups as she became increasingly concerned with the direction of the country.

During her first summer home, Phoebe fulfilled a dream she and Vernon had long shared of retirement to a farm. She bought 427 acres in Panola County, Mississippi, near the small town of Como, investing her $22,000 savings and assuming a $47,000 mortgage.[5] She christened her new home Rancho Fairom, combining the first few letters of her maiden and her husband's name.[6] The property of rolling grassy hills sprinkled with small ponds included a ranch-style home. She stocked her ranch with cattle and settled in. The place was lovely, but lonely. Since she was less than fifty miles from Memphis, Phoebe returned frequently, leaving the day-to-day operations of the cattle ranch in the hands of a foreman.[7]

Things did not go well for Phoebe in Mississippi. She had problems seeking honest and reliable help; her cattle business foundered as unpaid bills mounted. She decided to try something else. Five years after she bought her ranch in Como, she traded her property to Mrs. J. L. "Flossie" Koger for a hotel and cafe in Lambert, Mississippi, another small community about forty miles to the southwest.[8] The business, located on a trapezoidal lot beside the railroad tracks, included the twenty-one-bed Lambert Hotel and the City Café, located in the same building, with seating for thirty and a vintage jukebox. She borrowed $5,000 from the Bank of Lambert to help establish her business.[9] Just over a year later, a tornado scored a direct hit on Lambert. The twister, according to the local newspaper,

> picked up a Negro house believed vacant and smashed it against the home of J. L. Koger, a white man who lived in a brick house across the street. Koger was bruised by bricks sent flying by the impact . . . the winds ripped out the back part of the post office and pulled down the awnings in front of the building before skipping three blocks and knocking a tree into another house. It also threw a small shed into a field and demolished it . . . debris littered most of the town and many stores and many buildings suffered minor damage to windows and doors.[10]

While the extent of damage to the Lambert Hotel and City Café is unclear, Phoebe's business apparently never reopened. She wrote to friends that "a tornado wrecked everything."[11] In 1960, she disposed of what was left of the property and its contents for the sum of $2,339 and the assumption of her indebtedness to the Bank of Lambert and Union Planters National Bank in Memphis.[12]

After eight years in Mississippi, Phoebe's original investment of $22,000 had been reduced by 90 percent. She was fifty-eight years old. She was broke. She returned to Memphis and began living with friends. She made a few public appearances, some speeches to service clubs, and was the subject of a handful of retrospective articles in local newspapers. These sometimes mentioned her desperate circumstances but more often recounted her illustrious public life. Though most of the attention looked to her past, she was passionately interested in the future. In a speech to the Whitehaven Kiwanis Club in May 1962, which was reprinted by her congressman, Clifford Davis, in the *Congressional Record*, Phoebe described her recommendations for moving the country forward. The key, she said, would be increased trade with Latin America so that America could stimulate her economy and train the nation's young people to seize the opportunities of free enterprise. Such trade would require a commitment to developing those impoverished countries with whom we wished to trade, and training our own people to take advantage of those opportunities. She expressed her concern with America's declining educational system, saying that too much emphasis was focused on a college education. Those seeking most of the jobs that would be available in the manufacturing sector would be better served through vocational training. Train young people to work with both their hands and their minds, she argued, then free their entrepreneurial spirits to move into Latin America and help build the infrastructure and the trading opportunities, "directing their abilities toward pioneering the underdeveloped areas of the world."[13]

The American economy, she observed, always prospered in times of war. Now America should make a commitment to "develop and train for peace like we develop and train for war." Vocational education was a bargain and a very sound investment. "Industrial colleges could be established to cover subjects that deal with manufacturing, sales and services, construction and languages, especially Spanish and Portuguese to enhance the value of the Alliance for Progress program." This kind of government-funded training had precedents in the civilian pilot training program and the aviation ground servicemen's training program, she said, both of which put well-trained people to work in meaningful and productive jobs. "If we concentrate on planning for our goal, full employment, and use training methods for peace like we do for war, peace will come."[14]

Phoebe's last press interview in Memphis was with Eldon Roark in February 1962. After the requisite recap of her aviation career, he said that she was "living quietly" in Memphis, flying only occasionally with friends in their private planes. As she looked back upon her career, Phoebe took the most pride, Roark wrote, in the vocational training program she established in 1938. "Her great dream now is to see Memphis develop an international airport and become a great air export-import center. She would like to have a part of it, for aviation will always be her life."[15]

Phoebe was clearly still interested in having a public forum for her ideas, but it is difficult to tell if anyone was listening. She was no longer a celebrity with a platform. When her old friend Louise Thaden visited in mid-1963, Phoebe was pessimistic and frustrated. Louise and her daughter Pat flew into Memphis on their first leg of the Amelia Earhart Stamp Lift. Phoebe met them at the airport; they attended a luncheon with the mayor of Memphis where the Thadens presented him with a First Day cover of the memorial stamp. The date, 24 July 1963, would have been Amelia's sixty-sixth birthday, and was twenty-six years since the famed flier vanished in the Pacific. After the banquet, Louise told her daughter that it broke her heart to see her friend in such despair. Phoebe was in dire financial circumstances, and she was very discouraged by her inability to get support for her important ideas and projects. Still, Phoebe remained fiercely independent and refused all offered assistance.[16]

Sometime in 1964, Phoebe left Memphis on what would become a seven-year journey during which she resided in at least a dozen different locations.[17] The record is blank until the spring of 1967. On 10 July of that year, the women's-page columnist for the *St. Paul Pioneer Press*, Mary E., declared the day "Phoebe Fairgrave Omlie day." She recorded the story of forty-six years earlier when "a skinny little 18-year-old climbed out on the wing of a big red Curtiss and dropped 15,200 feet to make a new world's record for women." The article recapped Phoebe's colorful career through World War II.[18] In a follow-up column two weeks later, Mary E. wrote that Phoebe had long since dropped out of sight, and somebody suggested she may have died. But a reporter in the newspaper's Washington bureau had located her living in the Capitol, where she had apparently gone to lobby for her paramount cause: state control of education. "Mrs. Omlie has jumped, minus her parachute, into the states-versus-federal government wild blue yonder," Mary wrote. Calling herself a crusader, Phoebe indicated that she had been working with "small groups in the Middle West and Southern states. These are solid citizens who . . . dislike federal controls. Now our greatest fears have become reality. So last fall we concluded it was time for a Constitutional amendment, one that will simply clarify the Constitution."[19]

The amendment she proposed would codify state and local control of schools. Each state, it read, shall have "complete, absolute, direct and indirect control of all schools and training" within its borders. Secondly, "All federal educational and training appropriations funded by the Congress shall be allocated, as the states' agreed-upon formula—per student, direct to the states and local school districts without any kind of federal control, except for reports on the expenditures." Section three mandated that "No more than one-half of one percent of all funds for education and training appropriated by the US Congress shall be used for administration and State-Federal Relations in any department of the federal government."[20] "I think this is going to save our country," Phoebe declared. "The states are closer to the people; they understand their problems."[21]

It should be noted that this whole debate was taking place within the context of the country's turmoil over civil rights, desegregation, and efforts to ensure racial balance within the schools. "States rights" and "local control" functioned as euphemisms for states' desires to maintain segregation. A constitutional amendment, in this context, was an attempted end run around legislative and judicial enforcement of civil rights.

While in Washington, Phoebe sought the assistance of Senator Everett Dirksen to press for "the enactment of a Constitutional Amendment that would clearly define the powers of the States and local School Districts. It is my opinion that drastic actions must be taken *now* to quell the unrest that exists in our country today. We are committed to shed the blood of our youth around the world to provide self-determination to everyone, yet, here at home our present leaders are gradually whittling away at all pretense of self-determination in our educational system." Dirksen's reply reminded her that the passage of an amendment required a two-thirds vote by the Senate, which, he said, would be unlikely given the "rather close vote" on the education bill.[22] The vote to which Dirksen referred was the reauthorization of the Elementary and Secondary Education Act (ESEA), passed in 1965, which funded primary and secondary education. Opposition to federal aid to the schools was based primarily on the contention that federal aid meant federal control. To mollify these critics, the act as passed explicitly stated that there was to be no federal control over the curriculum, selection of books, or personnel of any school aided by the ESEA. After another bitter partisan battle in 1966, Congress added language prohibiting the federal government from requiring the transfer of students or teachers to overcome racial imbalance, but left intact the government's authority to withhold federal funds from schools that did not comply with the non-discrimination requirements of Title VI of the Civil Rights Act of 1964. Again, during another contentious reauthorization process in 1967, though Congress did not directly address the racial issue, it did rewrite some provisions to expressly give most of the control for the dispersal of funds to state education agencies.[23]

Phoebe had been following these developments closely, even campaigning for the approval of the ESEA and the similar Vocational Education Act of 1963, which authorized a major expansion and redirection of vocational education.[24] But, as she complained in numerous letters over the years, "The Acts were passed, but the ink on the Presidents' [*sic*] signature was hardly dry before 'guidelines' were issued by HEW. First, to apply only in the South, using the double-school system as an excuse, but with the full intention of eventually covering the entire country."[25] Again, the primary issue here was school desegregation. The guidelines referenced included the mandate for "categorical aid" geared primarily to upgrade the education of low-income pupils and the provision, based upon Title VI of the 1964 Civil Rights Act, that no federal funds would be expended in support of segregated schools. These limitations imposed upon the separate states' total control of the schools within their borders amounted to, in Phoebe's way of thinking, Soviet-style "thought-control."[26]

Phoebe left Washington sometime after writing Dirksen in mid-1967. Aviation journalist H. Glenn Buffington gathered a stream of forwarded and returned letters to various friends and acquaintances of Phoebe's that help to account for her wanderings over the next few years. After he wrote to her in Washington seeking her permission to publish an article about her, Phoebe responded from Montgomery, Alabama, several months later, but when he tried again to reach her there, his letter was returned with a note by the occupant, Lillian Fields, saying that Phoebe had left Montgomery, and was heading for Florida. She supplied the Florida address but noted that she felt sure Phoebe was no longer there.[27] Phoebe apparently caught a bus to Florida where she worked as a companion for an elderly woman for a time in Jacksonville before relocating to the home of an old friend, Marie Ryan in Silver Springs. "She arrived in Silver Springs all bedraggled and worn out from bus travel," reported one friend to another. "Her stay there was brief. Miss Ryan was, herself, old and ill. While there, Phoebe received money and clothes from her friend in Miami. She would not accept the money, but did take the clothes."[28]

Phoebe spent some time during the summer in Atlanta, then headed north to visit an old acquaintance, Richard Cornell, in Chagrin Falls, Ohio. Meanwhile, Buffington exchanged letters with Percy McDonald in early 1969, asking if he had any information about her whereabouts. McDonald replied that he didn't know where Phoebe was, adding:

> Phoebe had accumulated some money and left a very satisfactory job in Washington to come down here and against advice of her friends bought a plantation and lost every cent. She has been practically destitute every [*sic*] since that time. The last time I heard anything about her was from a lawyer in Jacksonville, Florida who wanted to hire her for a companson [*sic*] for his mother. When I knew Phoebe she was OK, and I told him I had not heard from her in quite a number of years. I do not know whether she secured the job or not.[29]

In fact, by that time Phoebe had already moved on. She placed an ad in the *Chicago Tribune:* "Situations Wanted-Women. Companion to elderly lady. I will live in, drive, light housework, travel. $50 a week." She worked for three months as a companion in Chicago, then moved to Cleveland, living presumably in the home of a friend for a time and then for several months at the Quad Hall Hotel in the city.[30] Buffington finally caught up with her there. She replied to him:

> I am pretty much on-the-go, still fighting for a more practical approach in starting the youth of America toward a goal that can bring them contentment and happiness. It has been a long, hard, rough and rugged road, but I think the people are beginning to see the futility of listening to the professors and young "diploma-holders" and their philosophies. Their thinking that money will solve everything just is NOT true. If we used the funds already appropriated to train people, instead of for high-salaried personnel in the federal government, we would have an entirely different outlook from our youth. I have spent the 1960's talking with hundreds of people representing all sections of the country, and feel that I really know how they think. They are fed-up!!! . . . The great mistake that many of the so-called leaders make is that, people are "dumb." They are years ahead of the leaders. Well, anyway, there is a beginning of a little light on the horizon. Thank you again for remembering me.[31]

After he heard from her, Buffington contacted Glenn Messer in Birmingham, telling him he had found Phoebe and urging her old friend to contact her. "We believe Phoebe has been having a rather rough time of it lately, so I imagine she would be happy to hear from some of her old-time friends."[32]

At about the same time, Louise Thaden flew into Memphis asking about Phoebe. The *Press-Scimitar's* aviation writer, Orville Hancock, wrote that the latest word received from Phoebe was from Florida, but she had reportedly moved to California. "If anyone knows Phoebe Omlie's whereabouts, the aviation community would like to know how to reach her."[33] Phoebe later contacted Louise from Cleveland, saying she'd been busy working on political issues for free, and would stop now and then to take odd jobs until she had saved enough to start again. She was meeting lots of folks, she said, who were urging her to write about these issues. She had come to Ohio "because there has been so many 'school bond' failures. The people are just fed up with the squandering and waste in education funds that have already been appropriated."[34]

While she had been traveling about, Phoebe told Buffington, she had been working on a book, but had been unable to find a publisher who would contract to market it "the way I think it should be handled, a direct-mail distribution."[35] She initially called her book *S.O.S.: Save Our Schools from Federal Control*, but changed the title to *The Silent Majority Speaks Out*, after Nixon's characterization of patriotic Americans who did not join in public demonstrations. Based upon her "personal contacts with thousands of people throughout the entire country during the past ten years and from actual experiences of the author," the book represented the culmination of her quest.

"When I resigned from a federal government job in Washington," she wrote in her foreword, "I willingly gave up my future security to help alert the American people to the threat of the federal government to brain-wash the youth of the country through the public schools. Hundreds of letters poured in from every State in the country thanking me for trying to alert the people to what was taking place."[36] Her "introductory" set the tone for the work. "This book will concentrate on why it is necessary that the people take a good look at the bureaucrats in Washington, how they want to control the schools in our country, to 'brain-wash' the youth to accept federally-controlled ideologies and philosophies in every phase of government."[37] In addition to taking on the "ultra-liberals" and "intellectual morons" who misled people about the need for a college education at the cost of vocational training, she also raised alarms about "foreign ideologies" infiltrating education at all levels and posited that "much of the trouble in the schools today is caused by the gradual breakdown of the homes, which has been engineered psychologically by those who are out to capture the country from within."[38] In the ten chapters of her manifesto, she also critiqued Social Security, the Alliance for Progress, government funding of the transportation system, as well as the "one-worlders" and the United Nations. All of these were part of a conspiracy to crush independence and individualism, leading to "the conquering of the minds of the masses."[39]

Throughout the manuscript, she defined the development of aviation as the epitome of rugged individualism and entrepreneurship, and its takeover by the federal bureaucracy as the forerunner of the decline and fall of America. Her concern about excessive regulation of civil aviation, combined with her distaste for forced racial integration in the schools, had evolved, in the overheated anticommunism climate of the period, into an obsession with looming federal control over every aspect of American life.

Her manuscript concluded with a proposal for a Constitutional Convention to create a new Bill of Rights that included provisions to ensure unfettered state control of schools, welfare programs, and voter requirements; a balanced federal budget; limits on all taxes to 25 percent of the Gross National Product and the return of 10 percent of all income taxes to the states. Congress members would be forbidden to hold outside employment or take expense-paid junkets; all Supreme Court decisions would be limited to "Constitutional issues (no legislative actions)." Federal civil service retirement was to be placed under the rules and regulations of Social Security and "the United States shall remain on the existing system of measurements" (a reference to her continued hostility to the adoption of the nautical mile).[40]

Phoebe designed the cover and guidelines for publication. She estimated the printing costs for her 150-page paperback, including mail solicitations and a royalty of six cents per volume, at forty-nine cents each. The cover price of $1.00 would result in a net profit for a million copies of $510,000.[41] She repeatedly sent out the manuscript with her guidelines for publication to conservative publishing houses, beginning in 1968 and continuing through the mid-1970s, and was just as repeatedly rejected.[42] Many rejected it without comment, but one who did offer a critique was managing editor Donald Graff of the Newspaper Enterprise Association in Cleveland.

The major problem, briefly, is that it comes through more as an expression of highly personal opinion, a lengthy letter to the editor, than as a coherently organized and thoroughly documented expose, which is apparently what you are attempting . . . You have stated a case—or a number of cases, but not made one . . . A guarantee of a million sales would require quite a bit in the way of advance orders to make it convincing. Bibles and cookbooks sell in that range, but there are few, if any, other such sure things.[43]

When her efforts to lure a publisher were unavailing, she drew up a plan to form her own company, to be called Grass-Roots America Press, to publish and distribute her book. The press would be incorporated for $20,000, ten shares at $2,000 per share. Her plan called for mass mailings to school boards, PTA organizations, "dedicated teachers throughout the country," the American Legion, the Daughters of the American Revolution, and "many, many small groups of concerned citizens who have joined together to save the public schools from federal control." She predicted "a conservative estimate for the first year's publication would be over a million copies if the above mentioned memberships were properly alerted." There is no evidence she ever followed through on this plan.[44]

Despite the difficulties in doing so in the midst of her peripatetic life, Phoebe kept up a lively correspondence with a broad array of political figures, editors, aviation writers, and journalists, as well as with contemporaries like Louise Thaden, Pancho Barnes, Bobbi Trout, Jimmy Doolittle, Cliff Henderson, and Karl Voelter, who ran an air service in Miami.[45] Many of them could not understand why she was spending all her energies on political issues at the expense of writing her memoirs. She responded that it was far more important to find a way to deter the infiltration of foreign ideology into the schools that could ultimately destroy the American system. She told Louise, in a typical retort, "This is, probably, the most crucial time in our history—whether we will sink into socialistic—bureaucratic—dictatorship or stay in the pattern laid down by our forefathers in the Constitution."[46]

Louise Thaden was her most constant correspondent. They exchanged numerous letters about the "old days," and Louise repeatedly urged Phoebe to write down all she knew before it was too late. To aid in this effort, she suggested Phoebe contact aviation writer Philip Wendell about assisting her with her writing. Phoebe relocated to Wendell's home in Burr Oak, Michigan, in mid-1970. When she insisted that she wanted to publish the *Silent Majority* book first, Wendell told her she had it backward. "We're going to need exposure to the Omlie tome to really sell the education tome," he told her, emphasizing that the autobiography must come first because it is "the springboard . . . For Crysakes, finish it!"[47] Wendell also expressed his frustration to Buffington:

> To the best of my knowledge, Phoebe has not attacked the manuscript one bit since she finished page 134 [with Swanee Taylor]. She simply won't let anything interfere with her pursuit of her first interest, the publication of a 10-year work on solving the nation's Education mess . . . Her autobiography is a solid, tender, commercial seller—so far. BUT she's covered only the first four flying years from 1920 to 1925. As she says, "That leaves 10,000 pages to go." Her funds are low but her spirits aren't. I'd like to figure a way of getting her back up here in a warm cubicle for the winter, typing. It would call for a grant of some kind; I can't afford the pleasure and she won't listen to charity.[48]

Wendell was in poor health and exasperated with trying to work with Phoebe, who accused him of not listening to her.[49] He suggested that Robert McComb, another early aviation pilot, then living in Fort Wayne, Indiana, might be a better writing companion. So Phoebe relocated once again. McComb later revealed what happened between them in a letter to another mutual friend and pilot, Bobbi Trout. He wrote that he thought that Phoebe had come to Fort Wayne to seek his help in shaping the final draft of her autobiography, but soon learned that she wanted his help in "promoting, underwriting, funding, finding a sponsor" for her *Silent Majority* manuscript. He found her to be "very guarded in her manner of revealing the subject-matter. She carefully weighed every word before and as she spoke." After three weeks, she finally allowed him to read a few excerpts. From those, "I had gathered just enough information to realize the entire text was perhaps too controversial" for him to find anyone willing to underwrite the publication. He told her he knew "no one willing to stand beside her and share the brunt of any repercussion which might result." McComb told Trout that "the best thing I could think to do to help Phoebe was to get her acquainted with my nephew who was in the state legislature at that time and possibly make some worthwhile connections—going that route—to further her quest toward getting published."[50]

Phoebe moved to Indianapolis in April 1971 to be nearer the seat of power, hoping she could accomplish through the political system that which she cared so passionately about. She wrote to friends that she had come to the capitol and intended to "headquarter here for some time, as it is in the middle of an area that is very important in helping solve the school situa-tion."⁵¹ She moved into the York Hotel, a fading downtown transient hotel, renting a room for $21 a week.⁵² Louise wrote plaintively to Phoebe, saying she hoped that her friend "won't get lost again," adding that it was too bad she didn't settle in Burr Oak where people "are pulling for you with sincere interest . . . . Do you stay with itching feet or wouldn't putting down (even shallow) roots have merit?"⁵³

Indianapolis had long been an incubator for conservative and libertar-ian politics. There Phoebe encountered a host of like-minded individu-als and groups, including the American Conservative Union, whose then chairman was the editor of the *Indianapolis News*; the American Party of Indiana, an incipient ultraconservative third party; the Indiana chapter of Pro America, an anticommunist and antifeminist women's organiza-tion; the John Birch Society, an ultraconservative advocacy group founded in Indianapolis in the 1950s that equated communism with socialism and liberalism; the Taxpayer's Lobby of Indiana, whose agenda was clear in its name; and others. These groups were strongly anticommunist but also animated, as she was, by the issue of states' rights. They believed that the federal government had usurped the powers delegated to the states by the Tenth Amendment to the Constitution. Phoebe was actively supportive of the Liberty Amendment, which was designed to limit the powers of the fed-eral government, restore power to the states and to the people, and to abol-ish all taxes.⁵⁴ Pro America's literature, in their STOP ERA (Equal Rights Amendment) campaign, claimed a conspiracy between the feminists and the communists, with destruction of the family being one of the prerequi-sites of a communist takeover. Phoebe drew parallels with her earlier con-cerns, as she wrote Louise that "Both in the ERA and the school situation the main drive is geared to nationalizing and centralizing all power to the US Congress and the bureaucrats in Washington."⁵⁵ She wrote a number of letters to local and national representatives in opposition to the ERA. To her, it was yet another federal imposition on states' rights.⁵⁶ She supported George Wallace as "the only national leader who would lay the cards on the table," praised Spiro Agnew for "telling it like it is," and deplored what she called the "Watergate Frame-Up."⁵⁷

Phoebe engaged with conservative groups in various capacities during her years in Indianapolis, collecting their literature, drafting supportive let-ters to friends, newspaper editors, state and national political figures, at-tending meetings and conventions, and sometimes serving on their boards. She was, for example, listed as a "Director at Large" on the letterhead of the National Council Against Forced Busing.[58] She proudly wrote to Louise that the Congress of Freedom had presented her with their annual "Liberty Award" for her work in "helping to save our schools from federal control."[59]

Phoebe carried on these lively political activities in spite of her poverty and worsening health. Her rent consumed nearly half of her meager income, and she was beginning to feel the consequences of her lifelong smoking habit.[60] While continuing to try to publish her manuscript, she also tried to seriously pursue writing her autobiography. She wrote numerous inquiries seeking assistance with the writing, contacting friends and old aviation acquaintances seeking confirmation for some of her own memories, and trying to recover lost documents and photographs that she had left here and there over the years as she moved.[61] One major motivation for getting started was to correct what she saw as persistent misrepresentations about the history of early aviation and particularly that of the origins and development of the Ninety-Nines and the activities of their charter members. Her memoirs would be a way to correct these falsehoods and tell the true history of early aviation, particularly women's part in it.[62]

In her exchange of letters with Louise Thaden and with Glenn Buffington, Phoebe frequently complained about those who persisted in distorting the early history. She was, she said, on an "Aviation True History Crusade." When either of them, however gently, disagreed with Phoebe, she would lash out. Indeed, her mostly cordial five-year correspondence with Buffington came to an abrupt halt in an angry exchange over his characterization of the genesis of the Ninety-Nines. She found his comments "asinine" and wrote, "It seems that you believe what you want to, and discredit that which you do not want to believe." She closed with "As you know so little about all of this, let's call it 'quits.'"[63] By the same token, Louise endured Phoebe's complaints about false history, but admitted that sometimes Phoebe tried her patience. After Buffington told her of his altercation with their mutual friend, Louise responded: "Phoebe has always been an odd character and those of us who have known her for a long time let her opinions etc. slide off and forget it. However, her obsession with 'the truth' over the past several years (blindly) and her rudeness to folks (I've not escaped either) is considerably accelerated, to the point it seems where all are out of step except herself. Regrettable."[64]

Phoebe was hospitalized in 1973 for what was likely the beginning of her battle with lung cancer. Her doctor began radiation treatments in July, to which she seemed to be responding "quite well."[65] But a subsequent hospitalization a year later convinced her to prepare for her own demise. She wrote a letter to Mr. and Mrs. John Bieschke, founder and president of the Pioneers of American Heritage in Indianapolis: "As you know, the trip to the hospital was rather sudden. If this is the final landing, please take over." She instructed the manager of the York Hotel to release her things to them and suggested that they act "as manager of my auto-biography, try to find a writer that has some 'feel' of the days that will be depicted in this story." She enclosed a memo for a sample agreement with an author for her autobiography, adding that "Two volumes will be necessary to cover over fifty (50) years of the auto-biography." Phoebe closed with: "Best of luck, and don't worry about me. I have lived a very full life and, more or less, done what I wanted to do."[66]

After that scare, she apparently rebounded to write a more upbeat Christmas message to friends. She apologized for its late posting, which was caused by her two weeks "sojourn" in the hospital. "I have had a sore throat for six months and they can't find out the cause of it. The doctor even asked me if I ever had a broken neck." The x-rays and the radiation treatments had made her weak but, she reported, she was feeling better now.[67] She was, in fact, continuing to receive cobalt treatments on her throat. A few days later, she wrote Pancho that she had spent the last ten years trying to save the schools from federal control, "but since a recent physical check-up I realize that time is running out." She asked her friend if she knew anyone who could help in editing her autobiography. "Do you know any writer who would be willing to work on a percentage, and who would not question the truth of the background of aviation's development?"[68]

A few months later, Phoebe made contact with author Jeanira Ratcliffe, an Indianapolis native who had recently published two books, *Will There Really Be a Morning?*, the ghostwritten autobiography of troubled actress Frances Farmer, and *The Kennedy Case (The Intimate Memoirs of the Head Nurse to Joseph P. Kennedy During the Last 8 Years of His Life)* written with Rita Dallas, R.N. Intrigued with the possibility of working on the aviator's story, Ratcliffe asked a friend's cousin, Della May Frazier, to pick Phoebe up at the York Hotel and bring her to Jean's home. Della May was dismayed by conditions she found at the York, a dilapidated structure next door to a burlesque theater. Phoebe lived in one small room with a hot-plate and kept her milk on the windowsill in winter. "I don't know what she did in the summertime," Della May said.[69]

Ratcliffe was initially unwilling to commit to producing Phoebe's story in its current state. She made it clear that she "did not work with the subject I am writing about except to hone up the story and draw out the stronger points." She suggested Phoebe and Della May draw up an agreement to work together to get her memoirs in that condition before she would take it on.[70] While the discussion continued, Phoebe issued a power of attorney putting Della May in charge of her personal and financial affairs and signed a new will leaving all of her estate to Della May Frazier. Article II reflected her intentional distance from her family (an estrangement that had apparently begun when she split with her brother Paul in the 1920s and maintained over the many years since their parents' death): "I am aware that I have blood relatives and it is my demand and my firm will that no blood relative nor any of their heirs receive or any way participate or enjoy benefits or inheritance from my estate, be it personal or real, tangible or intangible."[71] The three women eventually signed a collaborative proposal Phoebe drew up at the end of the month, in which Della May promised that she would "in all ways act as I [Phoebe] would act in regard to the preparation and eventual sale of the manuscript." They all recognized that the clock was running out for Phoebe.[72]

The course of her cancer had been swift, but her doctor remained optimistic. The previous month, Dr. Woerner indicated that following Phoebe's first course of "irradiation" for lung cancer in 1974, a new nodule in the left lung was found in February 1975, and she was again "treated with irradiation." Both times she responded well. "The stress on her heart has increased . . . [but] Her appetite has improved, and she has started to gain a little weight. It is impossible to say at this time how long we will be able to control her problem."[73]

After visiting the York Hotel, Della May tried to get Phoebe into a better living environment; she offered to help her apply for assistance to live in a low-income apartment complex. Given Phoebe's storied distrust of others and her proud rejection of any kind of assistance from friends, much less from the government, her transformation here is remarkable. For reasons we'll never know she responded positively to Della May's compassion. Phoebe had so little income (just over $2,000 a year) that her application was easily approved. Her rent in her new place in Pine Needle Court was $134.50 ($50 less than at the York) of which $99 would be covered by the Federal Housing Authority. With so few belongings, Phoebe was easily and quickly moved. Jean and Della May furnished her apartment and got her a telephone (the one in the York was in the lobby). Phoebe took possession of her new apartment on 7 June. Less than three weeks later, Phoebe called Della May to tell her that she had lung cancer and that she was going to the hospital.[74]

Jean called Louise, then Louise wrote Glenn describing Phoebe's desperate circumstances: "Phoebe Omlie is in an Indianapolis hospital, dying . . . . Phoebe is destitute; the hotel where she lived was on Skid Row and in a very small room at that; malnutrition; deaf; no possessions. Of course, no family. Phoebe has been as controversial as she is proud—and this period of last years' finish of her life is heart-breaking."[75]

Phoebe checked into St. Vincent's Hospital for the last time on 27 June. She died there three weeks later, at 2 AM on 17 July, of "lung cancer with metastasis."[76] Della May had visited her the day before, but regretted that Phoebe died alone. She took her favorite red nail polish to the funeral home. Phoebe had $837 in her bank account when she died. Della May made up the difference in paying for the doctor, hospital, the local undertaker to prepare the body, the airfare, and the bill for her funeral in Memphis.[77] Phoebe had told Della May that she wished to be buried next to her husband in Memphis. Since Della May did not know any of Phoebe's friends in Memphis, she contacted the Ninety-Nines in Oklahoma City, who referred her to the Ninety-Nines chapter in Memphis to meet the body and make arrangements there. She sent along a floral arrangement in the shape of a propeller.[78] A brief graveside service put Phoebe to rest beside her husband in Forest Hills Cemetery.

Obituaries that followed celebrated her amazing career while only mentioning, if at all, the circumstances of her final years. One exception was published in the local paper by a writer who apparently had intimate knowledge of Phoebe's life in Indianapolis. Phoebe, she wrote,

> walked briskly . . . her head held high with an air of dignity . . . she wore silver wings on her lapel. She met acquaintances for good conversation at the YWCA or in a busy hotel lobby. Seldom did she invite guests to her $21 a week shabby room. She ate one full meal a day, and kept eggs, butter and milk in her window. Her small Social Security check and much smaller amount from her husband's pension sustained her. She would have no part of welfare or food stamps . . . . She treasured scrapbooks and pictures of the golden days of her life in space, and carried them with her in a courier case. Without a plane, she was like a bird with a broken wing.[79]

Epilogue

Soon after Phoebe returned to Memphis for the last time, local colum-nist Eldon Roark suggested naming the Memphis International Airport for the Omlies. The Memphis chapter of the Ninety-Nines enthusiastically endorsed the idea, saying that Memphis-Omlie International "has a nice ring, don't you think?"[1]

Aviation enthusiast James T. Kacarides, editor of the *Memphis Flyer*, the publication of the Memphis Experimental Aircraft Association, had already been working for several years on a fitting memorial for Memphis' most famous woman aviator.[2] Kacarides had widespread support from the avia-tion community. Groups like the Experimental Aircraft Association, the Civil Air Patrol, the Ninety-Nines, the Antique Airplanes Association, the Aircraft Owners and Pilots Association, and the Confederate Air Force re-sponded enthusiastically to these efforts. First, they attempted to get the Shelby County Airport named for her in 1970, but the County Quarterly Court named it for their chairman, Charles W. Baker.[3] Next, when the Mud Island Downtown Airport was relocated and hence would be renamed in 1971, Kacarides submitted a long brief outlining her career to justify the name change. It was because of the Omlies' "unbounded energies and hard work [that] aviation was rooted to Memphis," he wrote. Instead, the downtown airport was named to honor local war hero Brigadier General DeWitt Spain, who died in 1969.[4] This most recent call, in 1975, to include Phoebe Omlie in the title of the Memphis International Airport was rejected by the Airport Authority. Instead, they created an Aviation Historical Room in the Terminal Building "to perpetuate the memory of the Omlies."[5]

The issue was raised again in the centennial edition of the *Memphis Press-Scimitar* in 1980 that featured a detailed article about Phoebe Omlie's career from her high school graduation until her husband died in 1936, closing briefly with her sad end and her "battle with the bottle."[6] Kacarides responded to the *Press-Scimitar* with a letter to the editor that extended the highlights of her career post-1936 and suggested that the time was right to establish a lasting memorial to Phoebe Omlie.[7] He proposed "the new air traffic control tower at Memphis International Airport be named in memory of Phoebe Fairgrave Omlie in recognition of her outstanding accomplishments and contributions to the field of American aviation. Towering into the sky she loved so dearly, it would be a magnificent tribute to a magnificent woman."[8] Carolyn Sullivan, representing the Memphis chapter of the Ninety-Nines, enthusiastically endorsed the idea, adding, "I can see a beautiful bronze likeness of her, gazing skyward, on an appropriate natural stone or granite base. This object would be facing, and near, the road which passes the tower, where thousands and thousands of people would see, read, and be inspired by it."[9]

While Kacarides campaigned for naming the tower for Phoebe Omlie alone, particularly emphasizing her work in government on behalf of general aviation long after her husband had died, the Airport Authority clearly preferred naming the tower for both the Omlies. In their December meeting, they officially "agreed to name the airport tower after Vernon C. Omlie and his wife, Phoebe Fairgrave Omlie, if the move is approved by Federal Aviation Administration officials."[10] In response to their inquiry, the FAA pointed out that "Federal Aviation Administration facilities are not usually named in honor of people, living or dead, in or out of aviation. As a matter of fact, it takes an act by the Congress of the United States to name a government facility after a person."[11] The Airport Authority promptly informed Kacarides that the FAA had rejected the proposal, but Kacarides saw not rejection but a suggestion that they pursue congressional action.[12] He pressed that the issue be included in the next meeting's agenda, and after a favorable vote by the Airport Authority, chairman Ned Cook contacted the members of Tennessee's congressional delegation to request that they initiate a bill to name the new FAA control tower "Omlie Tower."[13]

Senators Howard Baker and Jim Sasser filed the bill S.896 in the Senate. Representatives Harold Ford, Robin Beard, and Ed Jones sponsored the matching bill, H.R. 3072, in the House. "A bill to designate the control tower at Memphis International Airport the Omlie Tower" easily passed the Senate in May 1981. It was held up in the House over Department of Transportation concerns that "Confusion could arise because the airport approach control, VOR, air route traffic control center, and flight service station at that location are all identified as 'Memphis.' Additionally, considerable cost would be involved in reprinting documents such as approach plates, enroute and sectional charts, the Airman's Information Manual, and the airport facility directory." In order to minimize this confusion the bill contained language that any references to said tower would be "held and considered to refer to 'Omlie Tower.' Therefore, "Pilots would still 'call in' to 'Memphis Tower' and maps would still read 'Memphis Tower'—but this would be deemed to refer to Omlie Tower. We were further advised that report language to accompany the bill would make clear that no impact on air traffic control operations was intended."[14] With these clarifications, the Department of Transportation satisfied their objections and the Committee on Public Works and Transportation moved to take up the bill. "During debate on the bill on the House side, the sponsors agreed that the renaming of the tower would not mean that federal officials would have to reprint any maps or air charts to show the new name of the tower."[15] In short, despite the name change, no one would be required to use the designation.

H.R. 3072 passed the House in early June, and President Reagan signed the measure 21 June 1982.[16] In making the announcement of the president's signing, Senator Howard Baker said,

> This legislation recognizes the enormous contribution to our state and region and to the development of commercial aviation across the country by two famous aviation pioneers, Phoebe and Vernon Omlie . . . We have all marveled at the technological and human magnificence manifested in our space shuttle program. We would do well to remember that such would not be possible were it not for the aviation pioneers of a previous generation, such as Phoebe and Vernon Omlie.[17]

In August, two months after the president signed the legislation, Kacarides, who had been appointed by the Airport Authority to be chairman of the dedication ceremony, began writing letters trying to find out what the FAA Regional Office planned for the ceremony.[18] The Regional Office, he was told, "were non-committal on any plans for a dedication ceremony."[19] At the end of August, the *Press-Scimitar* reported that the lack of a plaque was holding up a planned dedication ceremony for the newly named Omlie Tower. Until it arrived, no dedication ceremony would be scheduled.[20] Continued letters from Kacarides throughout the fall yielded a notice that the FAA estimated the dedication would be set up within two to three months.[21] Still, the plaque never arrived, and the ceremony was never held.

When I approached the Memphis–Shelby County Airport Authority about the issue, they averred that the control tower was indeed officially named the Omlie Tower. Still, if there was no plaque, no dedication, and the airport did not use that designation, what did that mean? What it meant was that they considered the matter closed.

Further investigation revealed the general consensus among representatives of the Federal Aviation Administration that the name change had been pushed aside in the turmoil surrounding the PATCO (Professional Air Traffic Controllers Organization) strike in 1981. PATCO went on strike on 3 August 1981, in violation of a law that banned strikes by government unions. Although other government unions had declared strikes without penalty, this time President Reagan declared the strike a "peril to national safety" and ordered the air traffic controllers back to work within forty-eight hours. When they failed to comply, the president fired over 11,300 striking controllers and banned them from federal service for life. The FAA was then faced with the massive task of replacing all these controllers in order to keep the nation's commercial aviation system moving and safe. In short, the FAA was distracted by significant other priorities in 1982.

After numerous attempts over several years to reach the appropriate authorities in the FAA to address the problem, the question of the name is about to become moot. A new control tower is under construction at Memphis International Airport, scheduled to be dedicated in 2011. The Omlie Tower will be destroyed. According to the FAA, since the Omlie name had been affixed by law to the old tower, it could not legally be transferred to the new tower. At the same time, the FAA's Southern Regional administrator Doug Murphy emphasized his agency's desire to officially recognize Phoebe's "extraordinary career and contributions to aviation in Memphis and the nation." When the new tower opened, Murphy proposed to unveil a "prominent, permanent display" in the main lobby of the airport.[22] This matter is still pending.

In the interim, in November 2008, Phoebe was officially inducted into the Tennessee Aviation Hall of Fame.[23] Her commemorative plaque immortalizes the words of James Kacarides in deftly summarizing her career: "Her place in the pages of aviation history is unchallenged. A woman of daring, courage, intelligence and devotion to the 'air age,' she ranks as one of the greatest participants in American progress."[24]

Afterword

FINDING PHOEBE

*P*hoebe *Omlie came into my life in 1994.* I had no sooner begun my new job as assistant professor of history at the University of Memphis when a colleague, who had noted from my resume that I had a private pilot's license as well as an abiding interest in the history of women, told me that the control tower at Memphis International Airport had been named for a woman.

I was just finishing up a very large project, a biography of Senator Margaret Chase Smith, to which I had devoted nearly ten years of graduate and postgraduate work. Looking for a smaller project with which to take a breather from the heavy lifting of academic study, I found this one intriguing: a nice local story to produce a small, engaging book.

As I began to look for information on Phoebe, I found newspaper clippings in the Memphis Public Library covering, for the most part, her early barnstorming days, a bit of information about some work in government during the New Deal, and her death in Indianapolis in 1975. The Memphis Airport had a few items in a tiny museum under the stairs in the main terminal: some yellowed newspaper clippings, a couple of trophies, the leather bit she held in her teeth as she twirled in the slipstream of a plane. There was no indication that the control tower was named for her, and no one seemed to know anything about it. The Pink Palace Museum had a small display as well: more yellowed clippings, a couple of trophies, a small model airplane, her pilot's license and that of her husband, Vernon. Intriguing tidbits to be sure, but hardly the stuff of biography.

I posted a query on an internet listserv for historians interested in women in the military and other nontraditional occupations. I received a few responses from scholars suggesting I check archives in several areas of the country. A few listed publications that might be helpful. Several months after the posting, I got a telephone call from a screenwriter, Patrick Pidgeon, who hoped to make a movie about her life. After being assured that my project would not compete with his, he generously offered to share his research with me. His gift of a large spiral-bound folder filled with photocopies provided me with a very useful chronology and overview of Phoebe's accomplishments. The documents were a revelation. This was not a small, local story. This was the story of a woman of spirit, courage, and national importance.

I traveled to Minnesota where Phoebe began her aviation career. The Minneapolis Public Library had some clippings and a handful of photographs. The Minnesota Historical Society supplied some pages from her high school yearbook. Phoebe had been inducted into the Minnesota Aviation Hall of Fame in 1988. I visited the facility and photographed the plaque, but my research was not much enhanced. From there I headed for the Quad Cities (Davenport and Bettendorf, Iowa; Moline and Rock Island, Illinois) in search of records from the Mono Aircraft Company. From what I had learned, Phoebe was a sales representative for the company when she took up air racing in their signature Monocoupe in the late 1920s. I figured if I could find the company records, I would learn a bit more about Phoebe and her connection with them. At the Quad Cities airport, decorated with a restored Monocoupe suspended from the ceiling, I was granted access to some "old papers" in the basement, where I found some company files, specifications, advertising copy, and the like. Between those records and a trip to the library to peruse the microfilm of the *Moline Dispatch* for the years Phoebe was active locally, I got a pretty good handle on Phoebe's activities with the Mono-Aircraft Corporation. Things were looking up.

With the information I'd gathered, I was able to piece together a brief overview of her life. While it lacked scholarly authority, it was liberally embellished with descriptions of airborne stunts, serious crack-ups, and pithy quotes. In an effort to find people who had once known her or known of her, I offered free talks to any local group that would have me. At one such talk, a woman came forward with a battered pewter loving cup. On the side was etched: "Presented to PHOEBE FAIRGRAVE for Women's Record Parachute Jump by Grafton Aero Club." She also had a small tattered photograph album containing snapshots, some of which included Phoebe. She told me the story of acquiring these items: her husband had once owned a small airstrip in Mississippi, and one day a man stopped by, asking $75 for the items. Her husband, she said, wasn't interested but she was, because it had to do with a woman. She paid the money and put the items on her mantle where they had been ever since. She had not known who the woman was, she said, until she saw the notice about my talk on Phoebe Fairgrave Omlie. Now she wanted me to have them.

Of course I loved having these items, and I had found some very interesting materials during my travels, but I was getting pretty discouraged with the project. Doing the research was like trying to put together a giant jigsaw puzzle. A piece of sky here, a bit of personal information there, a few notices of her accomplishments. This puzzle had such a large number of pieces missing that I didn't think I'd ever fill in enough blanks to uncover enough of her life's story to tell. The pieces were tantalizing indeed, but far too few. And much of what I did have was not the stuff of "legitimate" history. Newspaper clippings, often undated and unattributed, were at best unreliable and often in conflict with each other over the specifics. Most important, because of the circumstances of her death, her personal effects had apparently vanished. Periodically over the years I put the project aside, convinced that I would never be able to complete it.

I worked on other projects. One of them was for a series on public intellectuals published by the University Press of Mississippi. When the director Seetha Srinivasan asked me to consider doing a second book for the series I demurred, saying that I was immersed in another project. When she asked about it, I shared a handful of Phoebe stories. She said that her press would be very interested in publishing the biography and offered to send me a contract. I emphasized everything that I didn't know, but she urged me to tell what I could, reminding me that if I didn't tell the story, however incomplete, it would be lost to history. So I agreed to sign a contract, as long as they were willing to wait what could be a long while.

I had learned that Phoebe was a founding member of the Ninety-Nines, an international organization of women pilots. In 1999, a museum dedicated to the Ninety-Nines opened at the Oklahoma City airport. I immediately contacted them about their archives. They stressed that their primary focus was on the museum, but I was welcome to come check out what they had. My five-day stay in Oklahoma City yielded disappointingly little—a few clippings, a couple of photographs, some articles from aviation publications. I also found a few letters referring to a manuscript about Phoebe composed by Gene Slack Scharlau. The exchange made it clear that she had tried to get it published but had died before that happened. One of her letters was to John McWhorter, an attorney in Memphis, requesting his help in seeking a publisher. I looked him up when I got home. McWhorter had a couple of cardboard boxes of things he said he recovered when he acquired a house in Memphis at auction. These materials had been in the attic. He couldn't remember precisely where the house was. He mentioned vaguely having had more materials at one time but had given them away to people who inquired. And he promptly gave these two boxes to me. One contained a hand-made rug with a wing design in the center and the words *Rancho Fairom*. The other contained many old clippings, undated, unattributed, yellow and crumbling. There was also a yearbook from Vernon's military aviation training at Ellington Field in Texas, a small disintegrating photograph album, a couple of logbooks, some letters of condolence addressed to Phoebe on the occasion of Vernon's death, and his 1930 pilot's license signed by Orville Wright. Great stuff, all of it adding a few more pieces to the puzzle.

When I asked him about Scharlau's manuscript, McWhorter sent me back to one of my colleagues, Dr. Charles Crawford. McWhorter had asked him for an opinion as to its potential for publication. After locating it in his files, Dr. Crawford passed the manuscript to me. He had not recommended its publication, citing concerns about its lack of documentation. The piece was apparently written by someone who knew Phoebe many years before. I later learned that Gene Slack had been an aviation writer for the *Nashville Tennessean* in the 1930s and 1940s. The style of the biography was chatty and anecdotal and supplied Phoebe's internal thoughts and invented dialogue. I use some of this material in the story, mostly for information that seemed credible and was unavailable to me elsewhere.

A trip to the Franklin Delano Roosevelt presidential library in Hyde Park, New York, yielded a handful of letters between Phoebe, Eleanor Roosevelt, and Molly Dewson, head of the Democratic National Committee's Women's Division, concerning Phoebe's appointments to a series of aviation-related positions in the federal government. Phoebe had worked in Washington, with a few breaks, from 1933 to 1952. I needed to find out what she did.

I obtained Phoebe's death certificate from Indiana, which provided her social security number, from which I was able to obtain a copy of her federal personnel file. These records helped me navigate through her employment history, including her titles, pay grades, and years of service. But they didn't reveal what she did in those positions. A trip to the National Archives yielded a bit more information. Unfortunately, the entities for which she worked had been repeatedly reorganized and folded into other agencies. None of the finding aids nor the archivists I met had any information about these organizations' files. When I met with the fifth archivist, one who specialized in transportation records at College Park, he surprised me by saying he had heard of Phoebe Omlie. He said he might be able to locate something for me, surmising that they could be in records someone had recently used and hence would be sitting in a holding area waiting to be refiled. After a couple hours, he brought me a folder. It had come from the Amelia Earhart files. But tucked inside were carbons of letters detailing Phoebe's tours of aircraft manufacturers and her survey of the federal airways system in 1934—a few more pieces of the puzzle aimed toward understanding her work in government.

I took a trip to Dearborn and the Ford Museum to look at the records of the Ford Reliability Air Tours, and to Cleveland, the scene of her air-race triumphs. The Ford Museum had documentation about the Air Tours and a terrific photograph of Phoebe at the end of her tour in 1928. More records at the Case Western Reserve Historical Society in Cleveland helped me clear up some confusion and inconsistencies in the press coverage regarding Phoebe's other races.

A chance meeting at a reception put me in contact with a young woman from Como, Mississippi, where Phoebe had retired. Meg Bartlett told me her husband's family had deep roots in the area. Moreover, her husband's father had worked with Phoebe in Washington and may have influenced her decision to settle there. We visited the site of Phoebe's ranch, and I traced her property in the county records. A series of misfortunes left Phoebe, at the end of 1960, essentially broke. And there the trail ended. Fifteen years of Phoebe's later years remained unaccounted for, and she was no longer a celebrity I could trace through newspaper coverage.

At an aviation writers' conference in Memphis, I was introduced to an experienced genealogist who offered to help me find Phoebe's family. With her help, I found one of Phoebe's nieces and two grandnieces. From them I learned lots of family gossip, but it was clear that I knew more about Phoebe than her relatives did. I was happy to share with them some pieces I'd written and some photographs, but for all practical purposes, they could add little to my research.

Over the years, every six months or so, my editor at the University Press of Mississippi would send me a gentle inquiry. I always answered the same: I was very busy with other responsibilities, but I had not abandoned the project; I had found some more information, but not nearly enough, and I still didn't know if I would be able to complete the biography.

I took a sabbatical in the fall of 2007. I would dedicate this time to one last push to find out about her last years. If I failed, I'd either abandon the project or write the biography with an explanation that this was all I knew and would likely ever know about the life of Phoebe Fairgrave Omlie. I started writing the manuscript in that manner even as I pressed on with my investigation.

Despite the strong possibility of disappointment, I decided to return to the Ninety-Nines Museum in Oklahoma City. Perhaps they had gotten better organized by now, and this time I would try to look at files of other fliers who might have stayed in touch with Phoebe over those later years. After about a week in the archives, I thought I had gotten about all I could. I had found more information in her file, and some tidbits in others'. Nearing the end of my stay, I learned that the records of aviation journalist H. Glenn Buffington had been donated to the museum. Buffington was the author of several of the articles about women fliers that I'd collected, including a few about Phoebe. Although they had not yet been organized, I was allowed to see the records, and they provided the final key I needed.

In those files I found several letters Buffington had written to Phoebe in the late 1960s. They had been forwarded, sometimes several times to addresses around the country, but eventually returned as undeliverable. Also in his files were copies of letters sent to Louise Thaden asking: where's Phoebe? While Louise frequently replied that she didn't know, I now knew who had kept in touch with Phoebe during those lost years. Thaden's papers were not housed there, but the museum provided me with the name and contact information for Louise's daughter, Pat Thaden Webb. She would ultimately lead me to the breakthrough I had long been seeking.

On my behalf, Pat contacted a former chairman of the Ninety-Nines Museum, Lisa Cotham, about my quest. Cotham sent me an email:

> While with the Museum, I received a letter with information as to the whereabouts of Phoebe's last worldly possessions, who had them, etc.

My interest was in acquiring Phoebe's memorabilia for the Museum. My initial conversation with the "owner" was that she would not release anything because she promised Phoebe on her deathbed that she would see to it that her biography was written. That has been several years. With your permission, I'd like to approach this woman again with information about your book. You may obtain more information from her, and maybe we can work together to achieve all our goals—Phoebe's story told and her memorabilia preserved.

Lisa supplied me with the name and contact information for the woman who was with Phoebe when she died: Della May Hartley-Frazier. It had been over thirty years since Phoebe's death, and nearly that long since Lisa had been contacted about the possessions. What were the chances that she'd still have them?

I called Della May to introduce myself. It took several conversations and sending her copies of my books and pieces I'd written about Phoebe to convince her that I was a serious scholar and writer. I assured her that I had no designs on the materials. All I wanted to do was see them and use their contents to write the very best biography I could. She said I sounded like a very nice person (a good sign), but that she wanted some legal advice (maybe not a good sign).

I impatiently waited the two weeks she requested before calling her back. She said that the papers were a mess, and that she would have to get her niece to help her sort them out before I could see them. (Sort them out!? Terrible words to a historian.) I gently suggested that I might be a better judge of what was valuable in the papers than her niece. I offered to come to Indianapolis, go through everything, sort and organize what had value. Della May told me about her deathbed promise to Phoebe and her concerns about the final disposition of the papers, saying she had been "praying to God every day to help" her resolve her dilemma. I said, "Della May, we are the answers to one another's prayers. Without you, I cannot finish this biography, and without me, you cannot fulfill your promise to Phoebe." Okay, she said, come on.

At Della May's home in Indianapolis, I found four large cardboard boxes and a small pile of personal items, including a battered suitcase, a traveling typewriter, and some clothes still in the dry cleaner's bags. Among the treasures were stacks of crumbling clippings about her career and the political concerns that consumed the last years of her life; photographs covering a span of seventy years, from a formal baby picture to snapshots of her taken two weeks before she died; her first scrapbook, begun in 1921, in which she called herself an "air nut"; pieces of her autobiography and extended essays describing her role in federal projects, and why she left government in 1952; dozens of letters to friends and contemporaries and their replies, many neatly clipped together. These materials helped me fill in many of the missing puzzle pieces.[1]

Although there remain many things about Phoebe that I do not and can never know, her story here is as complete as I can make it.

Notes

Chapter 1

1. Marriage between Madge Traister and H. J. Park listed in *Iowa Marriages, 1851–1900*, Appanoose County, 30 April 1898; divorce listed in *Des Moines Daily News*, 7 July 1908.
2. Federal Census, 1910 Polk County, Des Moines, Iowa, lists Madge Park as widowed with two children: Paul Park and Phebe Park (Madge's mother was named Phebe Jane Corder). A copy of Phoebe's birth certificate lists her as Phoebe G. [*sic*] Park, Omlie Collection, Memphis Public Library.
3. Paul's daughter, Deloris Navrkal, reports that until the knock on his door in 1943, Paul thought his father was dead. Author telephone interview with Navrkal, 5 November 2007. The story of Park and his daughter is in unpublished manuscript, Gene Slack Scharlau, *Phoebe: A Biography*, 1, in author's possession.
4. Andrew Fairgrave married Rose McIntyre in 1895 and divorced three years later. Fairgrave listed as living in Des Moines and operating a saloon in 1915 Iowa census; Fairgrave saloon listed in St. Paul City Directory for 1915 until 1919; "soft drinks" thereafter. Phoebe's request for a copy of her birth certificate noted that she was "born Phoebe Jane Park, my mother later married Andrew Fairgrave whose name I adopted," Omlie Collection. There is no evidence that Andrew formally adopted Madge's children. Andrew ran a "near-beer" saloon in St. Paul in 1921 according to Glenn Messer, interview by Gene Scharlau, 1982, International Women's Air and Space Museum, Cleveland (IWASM).

5. The 1920 Senior Class statistics listed nationalities of the graduates: eight Swedish, seven German, four ½ Norwegian, three ½ French, two ½ Irish, two ½ Scotch, two Danes, two English, fourteen Jewish, and twenty-eight American, in *The M* (newsletter of Mechanic Arts High School) 21 June 1920. Graduates of Mechanic Arts included civil rights leader Roy Wilkins (class of 1919) and Supreme Court justice Harry Blackmun (class of 1925). John W. Larson, "'He Was Mechanic Arts': Mechanic Arts High School: The Dietrich Lange Years, 1916–1939," *Ramsey County History* 41, no. 2 (Summer 2006): 4–17.

6. Thomas Minehan, *The M*, February 1919, in Larson, "'He Was Mechanic Arts,'" 7.

7. Class notes in *The M*, June 1919, 60.

8. *The M*, June 1920, 21.

9. Phoebe averred that dramatic lessons bolstered her self-confidence "maybe a bit too much," in an early attempt at autobiography she called *The Omlie Story*, 12. *The Omlie Story*, and a similar piece labeled "third draft," in Omlie Collection.

10. *The M*, June 1920, 52, and November 1920, 33; *The Omlie Story*, 19.

11. *St. Paul Pioneer Press*, 10 September 1919.

12. Ibid.

13. *St. Paul Pioneer Press*, 9 September 1919. The planes, owned by the Curtiss-Northwest Airplane Company, were flown by V. C. Omley (this is Vernon C. Omlie), C. F. Keyes, Ray S. Miller, and M. A. Northrup.

14. *The Omlie Story*, 9–10.

15. Katherine Stinson also did exhibition flying in the Midwest at this time. She had been flying since 1912, and on 18 July 1915, at Cicero Field in Chicago, Stinson became the first woman to perform a loop. Noel E. Allard and Gerald N. Sandvick, *Minnesota Aviation History 1857–1945* (Chaska, MN: MAHB Publishing, 1993), 41.

16. Allard and Sandvick, *Minnesota Aviation History*, 29–31, 41–42.

17. Information on Curtiss Headless Pusher from Albuquerque Museum, www.airminded.net.

18. *Oneonta (New York) Daily Star*, 20 November 1916. This flight also discussed by Amelia Earhart in *The Fun of It*, (Chicago: Chicago Academy Publishers, 1992 [reprint of 1932]), 186–188.

19. *Kokomo Daily Tribune*, 5 December 1916; incident also described by Amelia Earhart in *The Fun of It*, 188.

20. http://www.ctie.monash.edu.au/hargrave/law.html.

21. *Lancaster (Ohio) Daily Watch*, 5 August 1918.

22. *Fort Wayne Journal-Gazette*, 5 July 1917.

23. *Fort Wayne Daily News*, 8 June 1917.

24. *Fort Wayne Journal-Gazette*, 6 January 1917.

25. Playbill detailing stunts published in *Des Moines Sunday Capital*, 14 August 1921.

26. *St. Paul Pioneer Press*, 7 September 1919. Phoebe's name was not among those listed as attending or going for a ride that day; these girls were described as members of "local society" at White Bear. Lieutenant Miller would later provide Phoebe with her first airplane ride.

27. The JN4D, powered by a 90 horsepower Curtiss OX-5 engine, was the first mass-

produced American aircraft, purchased in quantity by the U.S. military during the war, and used as a primary trainer. The Jenny was notoriously unstable. The plane's huge wings made it very susceptible to wind gusts, its controls were very stiff, and the plane was easy to spin but difficult to recover. About 6,750 Jennys were produced by war's end. Joe Christy, *American Aviation*, 2nd ed. (Blue Ridge Summit, PA: TAB Books, 1994), 16. Curtiss-Northwest Field was on Snelling and Larpenteur Avenues near the state fairgrounds in St. Paul. *The Omlie Story*, 16–17.

28. *The Omlie Story*, 19–22.

29. *The Omlie Story*, 22–25; this story repeated by Flora G. Orr, "Phoebe Fairgrave Omlie: Special Assistant to Air Intelligence, N.A.C.A.," in *Holland's: The Magazine of the South*, September 1935, 32, clipping in Tennessee State Library and Archives.

30. This is an astonishing amount of money in 1920, when the average annual income for all workers was $1,489. Inflation Calculator, U.S. Bureau of Labor Statistics, http://data.bls.gov/cgi-bin/cpicalc.pl. Curtiss-Northwest had bought the planes from the government for a few hundred dollars each, then resold them for the princely sum of $3,500. The cost of Jennys quickly plunged as more flooded the market; by the mid-1920s one could be had for as little as $300. *Omlie Story*, 3rd draft, 66; Nick A. Komons, *Bonfires to Beacons: Federal Civil Aviation Policy Under the Air Commerce Act, 1926–1938* (Washington, D.C.: Smithsonian Institution Press, 1989), 10–12.

31. The $15 fee verified in a description by William Kidder of the airport's opening in 1918, when they had such a large crowd vying for rides at this fee that the management took in several thousand dollars that day. Allard and Sandvick, *Minnesota Aviation History*, 140; *The Omlie Story*, 26.

32. Locklear appeared at the Minnesota State Fair in 1919, where he did wing walking and a plane-to-plane transfer. Some 200,000 attended the fair that day and it is possible Phoebe was one of them. Allard and Sandvick, *Minnesota Aviation History*, 41. Phoebe had a picture postcard of Locklear "entertaining Mack Sennett's Bathing Beauties at Curtiss Field—St. Paul, Minn." in her Scrapbook, Omlie Collection. Locklear was killed in 1920 during the filming of a nighttime crash for William Fox's film *The Skywayman*. Apparently blinded by the studio's searchlights, he spun into the ground. Don Dwiggins, *The Air Devils: The Story of Balloonists, Barnstormers, and Stunt Pilots* (Philadelphia: J. B. Lippincott Company, 1966), 152; Robert Wohl, *The Spectacle of Flight: Aviation and the Western Imagination, 1920–1950* (New Haven, CT: Yale University Press, 2005), 113.

33. Hardin's new design featured a series of springs between the pack bottom and a fiber board that ejected the canopy from the pack. The military rejected Hardin's chute as "too weak, bulky and uncomfortable." Dan Poynter, *The Parachute Manual: A Technical Treatise on Aerodynamic Decelerators* (Santa Barbara, CA: Para Publishing, 1984), 163; *The Omlie Story*, 27–28.

34. The Hardin Parachute Company, Inc., was located at 515 Metropolitan Bank Building, Minneapolis.

35. *The Perils of Pauline* was an episodic cliffhanger serial that ran in weekly installments at movie theaters beginning in 1914 and running throughout the 1920s. Only a few episodes survive, none of them, alas, involving aerial stunts. Movie studios often gen-

erated "generic" footage of the drama and dangers of flying that were used in newsreels and in many, mostly undistinguished, films with titles like *Broken Wing*, *Speed Girl*, and *Wings Outstretched*. Fox produced a host of aviation films, including *The Air Hawk* (1925), *Aflame in the Sky* (1927), and *Air Circus* (1928), as did other motion picture companies. For a list of films featuring flying during the 1920s and 1930s, see H. Hugh Wynne, *The Motion Picture Stunt Pilots and Hollywood's Classic Aviation Movies* (Missoula, MT: Pictorial Histories Publishing Company, 1987), 171–176.

36. *The Omlie Story*, 28–29.

37. Fox Film Corporation, William Fox (New York) president, local manager M. J. Weisfelt, at 807 Produce Exchange Building, *Minneapolis City Directory*, 1920 and 1921. William Fox founded Fox Film Corporation in 1915 and produced hundreds of early silent films, serials, and feature films. Fox merged with Twentieth Century Pictures in 1935 to become Twentieth Century Fox Film Corporation.

38. *The Omlie Story*, 29–31.

39. Ibid., 31–32.

40. The first recorded parachute jump from an airplane was executed by Grant Morton, who jumped from a Wright Model B airplane flying over Venice Beach, California, in 1911. He carried his folded parachute in his arms; as he jumped, he threw his folded canopy into the air. The parachute opened and he landed safely. Australian Parachute Federation, "History of the Parachute," www.apf.asn.au/history.

41. *The Omlie Story*, 72.

42. Throughout her career, every story about Phoebe asserts that she launched her career with a $4,000 inheritance from her grandfather. In her memoirs, she confesses that she gave reporters that "white lie" to cover up the real terms of the deal made with her mother. She claims that her father never suspected the truth as she paid off the loan rather rapidly and always made the payments at Christmastime so as not to arouse his suspicions. *The Omlie Story*, 35–36, 39–48.

43. Ibid., 44–45.

44. Ibid., 54–61.

45. Ibid., 61–65.

46. Ibid., 67–68.

47. Omlie enlisted in the infantry in June 1916 and served with Pershing on the Mexican border chasing Pancho Villa. He transferred to the Air Service when war came in 1917, learned flying at Kelly Field in San Antonio; he later transferred to Ellington Field outside Houston where he became a bombing instructor, serving there until his discharge in April 1919. Biographical data form for *The International Cyclopedia of Aviation Biography*, completed by Omlie, 28 February 1930; summary in Phoebe's Personnel File, apparently submitted to secure civil service classification in 1939, Omlie Collection.

48. Allard and Sandvick, *Minnesota Aviation History*, 42, 61–63, 94.

49. From essay by Phoebe Fairgrave Omlie, "About the Author," in her unpublished manuscript *The Silent Majority Speaks Out*, Omlie Collection.

50. The Non-Partisan League (an organization with which Charles Lindbergh's father was connected) was formed in 1915 to lobby political parties on behalf of farmers; it

was especially active in Minnesota and North Dakota. Its influence faded following the indictment and conviction of Townley and his manager Joseph Gilbert for opposing the war effort and discouraging the sale of Liberty Bonds. Motions for a new trial were denied by the Supreme Court. See unattributed clipping, 24 October 1919, Omlie Collection.

51. *The Omlie Story,* 70.
52. Phoebe was barely five feet tall and not quite 100 pounds. *Minneapolis Morning Tribune,* 10 July 1921. Glenn Messer, who flew stunts with Phoebe, pegged her weight at 86 pounds. Messer interview, IWASM.
53. *The Omlie Story,* 71–75.
54. Charles E. Planck, *Women with Wings* (New York: Harper & Brothers, 1942), 55.
55. *The Omlie Story,* 79–80.
56. Ibid., 83–84.
57. Ibid., 80–82.
58. Vernon began work for Curtiss-Northwest on 1 April 1920 for $25 a week and $35 expenses; Vernon Omlie Datebook, Omlie Collection.
59. While some jumpers tied the chute to a wing strut, this made the plane extra unstable due to the interruption of airflow over the wings.
60. *The Omlie Story,* 87–91.
61. Ibid., 86.
62. Ibid., 90–92. Phoebe Fairgrave, "Jumps I Have Made," *The M,* February 1922, 23–24.
63. One of them was Lena Hickok, then working for the *Minneapolis Morning Tribune.* This is the same Lorena Hickok who served as first lady Eleanor Roosevelt's traveling companion during the New Deal. Phoebe reconnected with Hickok when she campaigned for FDR in 1936; Hickok was then working for the National Democratic Committee. See *The Omlie Story,* 99, 101.
64. *Minneapolis Morning Tribune,* 18 April 1921; *St. Paul Pioneer Press,* 19 April 1921.
65. There apparently was a good deal of jealousy and animus between Paul and Vernon. Paul allegedly once told Phoebe that if she married Vernon, he would never speak to her again. Whether for this reason, or others, Phoebe and Paul were estranged for the rest of their lives. Telephone interview by author with Phoebe's niece, Deloris Navrkal, 5 November 2007; Messer interview, IWASM.
66. Vernon Omlie Datebook, Omlie Collection. *The Omlie Story,* 102.
67. *The Omlie Story,* 29–31. By 1921, David Wark Griffith, Associated First National Pictures, Goldwyn Film Company, Selznick Pictures Corporation, Universal Film Company, and William Fox Studios were producing films in which flying and airplanes were an essential part of the action. See Jim and Maxine Greenwood, *Stunt Flying in the Movies* (Blue Ridge Summit, PA: Tab Books, 1982), 38–41.
68. *Minneapolis Morning Tribune,* 10 July 1921.
69. Charley Hardin probably taught her this trick. Charles Lindbergh, during his barnstorming days in 1925, did a double parachute drop with a Hardin parachute. Fairgrave, *The M,* February 1922, 23.
70. Fairgrave, *The M,* February 1922, 23–24. See also yellow typed notes dated 15 December 1934, Omlie Collection.

71. *St. Paul Pioneer Press*, 11 May 1921.

72. *Minneapolis Morning Tribune*, 10 July 1921.

73. She wrote, "I was supposed to be fortunate in having basketball shoes on—the rubber attracting the current and the hole in the shoe permitting it to go out. How true this is I do not know." Phoebe's account of the accident in handwritten notes, Omlie Collection.

74. He did put it in the papers, *Des Moines Register*, 30 July 1921.

75. Phoebe's handwritten notes, Omlie Collection.

76. Ibid. See also Charles Land Callen, "There's No Stopping a Woman with Courage Like This," *American Magazine*, August 1929, 144. In response to requests for biographical information about his wife, Vernon Omlie referred inquirers to this article.

77. *St. Paul Pioneer Press*, 11 July 1921; Fairgrave, "Jumps I Have Made," 23–24.

78. *Des Moines Evening Tribune*, 11 July 1921.

79. Mabel Cody was Buffalo Bill's niece. Ron Dick and Dan Patterson, *Aviation Century: The Golden Age* (Erin, Ontario: Boston Mills Press, 2004), 204.

80. Letter, Phoebe Omlie to Louise Thaden, 5 June 1973, Omlie Collection.

81. List of "towns made during the 1921 season," Omlie Collection.

82. The term "barnstorming" came from traveling theatrical groups who often performed in barns. Dominick A. Pisano, "The Greatest Show Not on Earth: The Confrontations between Utility and Entertainment in Aviation," in *The Airplane in American Culture*, ed. Pisano (Ann Arbor: University of Michigan Press, 2003), 51.

83. Their net profit for the summer of 1921 was $159.32. Vernon Omlie's Datebook lists expenses and income, Omlie Collection.

84. Undated clipping from Quincy, Illinois, Scrapbook, Omlie Collection.

85. Messer interview, IWASM.

86. Yellow typed notes, 15 December 1934, Omlie Collection; story also recounted by Planck, *Women with Wings*, 53–55, and referenced in Messer interview, IWASM.

87. *Memphis Evening Appeal*, 28 March 1929.

88. *Fairfield (Iowa) Daily Ledger-Journal*, 5 August 1921. Yellow typed notes, 15 December 1934, Omlie Collection; Planck, *Women with Wings*, 53–55.

89. Undated story by John White, photocopy in Personnel File, Omlie Collection.

90. Unattributed newspaper clipping, Scrapbook, Omlie Collection.

91. Glenn Messer indicated that Phoebe worked with him on at least one film entitled "Price of Honor." Messer interview, IWASM.

92. *Mexico (Missouri) Intelligencer*, 20 October 1921, Scrapbook, Omlie Collection.

93. *Fairfield (Iowa) Daily Ledger-Journal*, 5 August 1921; other unattribued and undated clippings, Scrapbook, Omlie Collection.

94. Undated clipping from Cedar Rapids, Scrapbook, Omlie Collection.

95. *Des Moines Register*, 30 July 1921, Scrapbook, Omlie Collection.

96. In 1923 alone, 85 barnstormers died in 179 recorded accidents. In the five-year period, 1921–1925, 354 people lost their lives in aircraft accidents. Dick and Patterson, *The Golden Age*, 204; Komons, *Bonfires to Beacons*, 23; Pisano, *The Airplane in American Culture*, 57.

97. Clippings in Scrapbook, Omlie Collection.

98. "Harrison—Obit on Phoebe Fairgrave, written March 21, 1922" in *St. Paul Dispatch* files, St. Paul, Minnesota.

99. Paul Fairgrave left the group in late summer; the last entry about him was on 29 August in Vernon's Datebook; "About the Author," *The Silent Majority Speaks Out*, Omlie Collection. Messer established the first flying field at Birmingham. He soloed Lindbergh when he sold the young flier his first Jenny. The Birmingham Museum of Flight has an extensive collection and exhibit space dedicated to his career. Messer died 13 June 1995 at the age of one hundred.

100. Unattributed clipping, 4 November 1921, Scrapbook, Omlie Collection.

101. *Cairo (Illinois) Bulletin*, 5 December 1921, Scrapbook, Omlie Collection.

102. *Memphis News-Scimitar*, 30 December 1921; poster in Omlie Collection.

103. Park Field had been decommissioned by the government in 1919, buildings were torn down and the site turned to agriculture. So it stayed until 1942 when another war prompted the U.S. Navy to establish an aviation base there. John Norris, "Park Field—World War I Pilot Training School," *West Tennessee Historical Society Papers* (1977): 75–76; "About the Author," Omlie Collection.

104. *St. Paul Pioneer Press*, 19 February 1922.

105. Western Union Telegrams, 14 February 1922 and 17 February 1922, Scrapbook. Interestingly, only a month later, Ruth Law abruptly retired. When the press asked why she quit, Law responded, "Because I'm a normal woman and want a home, a baby and everything else that goes with married life." She'd been married for ten years to Charlie Oliver, her business manager, who apparently asked her to stop. "It was a matter of choosing between love and profession. Of course, I'm crazy about flying. But one's husband is more important . . . It's my husband's turn now," she said. "I've been in the limelight long enough. I'm going to let him run things hereafter and me, too." *Waterloo (Iowa) Times-Tribune*, 22 March 1922. Ruth Law died in 1970 at age eighty-three.

106. *St. Paul Daily News*, 26 March 1922.

107. Newspaper clippings, Scrapbook, Omlie Collection.

Chapter 2

1. "If it hadn't been for the Isele brothers, who managed the old Arlington Hotel, now the Claridge, we would have been completely out." Phoebe interview with Betty Jeanne Claffey, *Commercial Appeal*, 11 October 1945.

2. Vernon Omlie's presence at Park Field during the war was revealed in an advertisement for his operation at the new Memphis Municipal Airport; ad in *Commercial Appeal*, 14 June 1929, 14. In his history of Park Field, John Norris notes that when Park Field opened in November 1917, 300 men were transferred from Kelly Field in San Antonio; Omlie was stationed at Kelly Field during this period. Norris, "Park Field," *West Tennessee Historical Society Papers*, 65, 71.

3. Joseph J. Corn, *The Winged Gospel: America's Romance with Aviation, 1900–1950* (Oxford: Oxford University Press, 1983), 34.

4. In addition to Corn, see Robert Wohl, *A Passion for Wings: Aviation and the Western Imagination 1908–1918* (New Haven, CT: Yale University Press, 1994), 2.

5. Corn, *The Winged Gospel*, 5–8; Wohl, *A Passion for Wings*, 19.

6. Glenn Curtiss and the Wright Brothers both formed exhibition companies to pro-mote sales of their airplanes in 1909. Tom D. Crouch, *Wings: A History of Aviation from Kites to the Space Age* (New York: W. W. Norton & Co., 2003), 142; Corn, *The Winged Gospel*, 9.

7. The French led aviation development during this period, organized the first avia-tion competition, hosted the first aviation exhibition, opened the first flight training schools, and led the world in the manufacture of airplanes prior to 1914. Almost every innovation to flying machines between 1908 and 1914 originated in France. Wilbur Wright tested and demonstrated his invention in France in 1908. Wohl, *A Passion for Wings*, 2, 20; Dick and Patterson, *The Golden Age*, 36.

8. At Rheims, twenty-two aviators flew ten different types of airplanes; 500,000 paid attendance while thousands more watched from the surrounding hills. A detailed description of the meet at Rheims in Wohl, *A Passion for Wings*, 100–110.

9. Bleriot crossed the English Channel on 25 July 1909; Rheims Air Meet began 22 August; the two men competed against each other on 28 August. This was the first time airplanes raced around a circuit that was marked with prominent towers called pylons. Bill Gunston, *Aviation: The First 100 Years* (Hauppauge NY: Barron's, 2002), 32. Note that $5,000 in 1909 had the same purchasing power as $122,000 in 2010. See measuringworth.com for conversion tables.

10. Wohl, *A Passion for Wings*, 113.

11. *Memphis News-Scimitar*, 11 April 1910; Emily Yellin, *A History of the Mid-South Fair* (Memphis: Guild Bindery Press, 1995), 132–135; *Memphis Press-Scimitar*, 28 October 1980. (Note the *Memphis Press* merged with the *News-Scimitar* to become the *Press-Scimitar* in 1926.)

12. *Commercial Appeal*, 8 April 1910; Jim Fulbright, *Aviation in Tennessee* (Goodlettsville, TN: Mid-South Publications, 1998), 11.

13. The *New York Times* devoted six pages to this remarkable feat. Curtiss made the jour-ney of 150 miles in 2 hours 46 minutes at an average speed of 54.18 mph. *New York Times*, 30 May 1910.

14. Despite the title, the Moisant brothers were Americans, sons of French-speaking immigrants from Canada. Their sister, Matilde E. Moisant, would later become the second woman pilot certified by the Aero Club of America. (Her friend, Harriet Quimby, was the first.) But this was in 1911, after the Moisant circus flew in Memphis. Doris L. Rich, *The Magnificent Moisants: Champions of Early Flight* (Washington, D.C.: Smithsonian Institution Press, 1998), 135–137.

15. Chattanooga planned to host a Moisant three-day aviation meet featuring speed, altitude, and distance contests with daily plane versus automobile races between the 35 hp Demoiselle and a 110 hp Fiat racer. *Knoxville Daily Journal and Tribune*, 28 November 1910. Finding Chattanooga's Olympia Park too small, the stands dilapi-dated and the strong winds off the mountains too dangerous, the company left after one disappointing day. Rich, *Magnificent Moisants*, 80–81.

16. In 1913, Garros flew an astonishing 450 miles across the Mediterranean. He went on to become one of the first French "aces" during the war, downing three German

planes in aerial combat before he was shot down and killed in October 1918. Wohl, *A Passion for Wings*, 208–210; Ron Dick and Dan Patterson, *Aviation Century: The Early Years* (Erin, Ontario: Boston Mills Press, 2003), 54–55.

17. Rich, *Magnificent Moisants*, 68–76; *Memphis Press-Scimitar*, 28 October 1980.

18. Poster in Wohl, *A Passion for Wings*, 206; Rich, *Magnificent Moisants*, 82.

19. *Commercial Appeal*, 2 December 1910.

20. Ibid., 8 December 1910.

21. Ibid., 2 December 1910.

22. Exhibition companies typically charged sponsoring organizations $5,000 for each aircraft used. Memphis got a bargain at this rate. Flying exhibitions were a profitable business during these early years; the Curtiss Company reportedly grossed nearly a million dollars in 1911. Pisano, *The Airplane in American Culture*, 48; *Commercial Appeal*, 8 December 1910.

23. John Moisant crashed and died on December 31 while preparing for a competition in New Orleans. His first flight to his final crash was only five months. The international airport in New Orleans was originally named Moisant Field in his honor; it has since been renamed Louis Armstrong New Orleans International Airport. Rich, *Magnificent Moisants*, 85, 94.

24. Racetracks served as the first hosts for air meets. For example, Moisant's Statue of Liberty Race flew out of the famous Belmont Park near Queens.

25. Senate Bill No. 72, "An Act to Prohibit Gambling on Races," 1905. Carroll Van West, ed., *Tennessee Encyclopedia of History and Culture* (Nashville: Rutledge Hill Press, 1998), 437.

26. Although no longer part of the Grand Circuit, the Driving Park was used for training and racing trotters until the property was sold off in 1928. Charles Bobbitt, "The North Memphis Driving Park, 1901–1905: The Passing of an Era," *West Tennessee Historical Society Papers* (1972): 40–55.

27. Paul R. Coppock, 23 January 1977, in Helen R. Coppock and Charles W. Crawford, eds., *Paul R. Coppock's Mid South*, Vol. 3, 1976–1978 (Memphis: The Paul R. Coppock Publication Trust, 1993), 143.

28. Fulbright, *Aviation in Tennessee*, 21.

29. The capacity of the Driving Park was estimated at "20 machines and 50 cadets, with the necessary instructors." *Commercial Appeal*, 7 January 1918; Norris, "Park Field," *West Tennessee Historical Society Papers*, 68.

30. The Memphis Aerial Company mentioned by Paul R. Coppock, 10 June 1973, in Coppock and Crawford, *Coppock's Mid South*, Vol. 2, 1971–1975, 159.

31. Memphis Business Men's Club was an ancestor of the Chamber of Commerce. Paul R. Coppock, "The Flying Machines," in Paul R. Coppock, *Memphis Sketches* (Friends of Memphis and Shelby County Libraries, 1976), 123. The Omlies also did exhibitions away from Memphis, mostly in southern Missouri. One example, in Dresden, Missouri, on 16 March 1923, clipping in Scrapbook, Omlie Collection.

32. Norris, "Park Field," *West Tennessee Historical Society Papers*, 75.

33. W. Percy McDonald, "Growth of Aviation in Tennessee with Emphasis on Memphis and Shelby County," Memphis and Shelby County Airport Authority.

34. About the Author, Omlie Collection.

35. *Commercial Appeal*, 27 June 1926.

36. *Commercial Appeal*, 12 November 1926; Poster for "Armistice Day Aerial Derby," 11 November 1926, Omlie Collection. This was to be Phoebe's three hundredth parachute jump and the last one, she promised her mother. However, she did jump one more time, on 4 July 1927, after the boy who was to make that jump broke his hand. *Commercial Appeal*, 27 August 1929.

37. The plane was named for Byrd's backer, Edsel Ford's daughter. *Commercial Appeal*, 17 November 1926.

38. Daniel Guggenheim, head of a wealthy family that made its money in the mining industry, created the $2.5 million Daniel Guggenheim Fund for the Promotion of Aeronautics in 1926 to speed the development of civil aviation in the United States. The fund supported expeditions by Byrd and Lindbergh, established schools of aeronautics and research centers at numerous universities around the country, and supported the development of commercial aircraft and aircraft equipment. Claire Gaudiani, *The Greater Good* (New York: Times Books, 2003), 112–115.

39. Commander Byrd did not make the tour. *Commercial Appeal*, 17 November 1926.

40. After the tour, the *Josephine Ford* went on display in the window at Wanamaker's department store in Philadelphia. Corn, *Winged Gospel*, 15.

41. In October 1927, for example, the Omlies were engaged in mapping routes for proposed power lines in the northern portion of west Tennessee. *Commercial Appeal*, 1 November 1927; Max Stern, "Aviation's Nursemaid," *Today*, 23 February 1935, 19.

42. Career chronology, Personnel File, Omlie Collection.

43. Scharlau, *Phoebe*, 54.

44. WACOs (from the acronym of the Weaver Aircraft Company) were easy-to-fly small airplanes prized for their rugged design and safety record. *Memphis Press-Scimitar*, 12 June 1929.

45. Official Report of the Relief Operations, *The Mississippi Valley Flood Disaster of 1927* (Washington, D.C.: American National Red Cross, 1928), 3–5. See also Bette B. Tilly, "Memphis and the Mississippi Valley Flood of 1927," *West Tennessee Historical Society Papers* 24 (1970): 41–47; John M. Barry, *Rising Tide: The Great Mississippi Flood of 1927 and How It Changed America* (New York: Simon & Schuster, 1997), 173–182.

46. Relief Headquarters remained in Memphis from April 25 until May 26, when it was transferred to New Orleans. Red Cross Official Report, 24–25.

47. *Commercial Appeal*, 20 April 1927 and 24 April 1927.

48. Stern, "Aviation's Nursemaid," 19; Earhart, *The Fun of It*, 177.

49. Both local newspapers carried dozens of photographs for months during the flood, most of them unattributed. The *Press-Scimitar* on occasion credited staff photographer William Day, noting that the photos were taken from a Waco plane piloted by V. C. Omlie; see, for example, *Memphis Press-Scimitar*, 16 April 1927 and 20 April 1927. See also "About the Author," Omlie Collection; reference to Phoebe's photography of the flood in *Commercial Appeal*, 27 August 1929.

50. Phoebe's remark to Edwin Williams, "The Thrilling Experiences of a Pioneer Woman

Flyer," *Southern Aviation*, July 1932, 15. The Red Cross's official report on the disaster was dedicated to Officer Kilpatrick.

51. Unattributed newspaper clipping, Scrapbook, Omlie Collection.

52. William Alexander Percy wrote about the flood around his home in Greenville, noting that the waters did not recede for four months. W. A. Percy, *Lanterns on the Levee* (New York: Alfred A. Knopf, 1941), 248.

53. Red Cross Official Report, 3–5; Barry, *Rising Tide*, 285–286.

54. Stern, "Aviation's Nursemaid," 19.

55. The Aero Club of America and the Fédération Aéronautique Internationale (FAI), a sanctioning body for aviation records and attempts, began issuing licenses to pilots participating in sporting events and demonstrations sanctioned by the ACA and FAI in 1911. The ACA was succeeded by the National Aeronautic Association in 1922. Komons, *Bonfires to Beacons*, 7–26.

56. Press release, 26 February 1927, Donald E. Keyhoe, Editor, Air Information Division, Aeronautics Branch Department of Commerce; *St. Paul Pioneer Press*, 28 February 1927. See also letter, Phoebe Omlie to Joe Field of Bradford, Pennsylvania, 14 October 1971, reminiscing about how Parker "Shorty" Cramer put her "through-the-grill" for her licenses in 1927. She notes that during the flood they were flying from dusk to dawn, but he was very cooperative in giving her and Vernon their written exams at night, Omlie Collection.

57. From press release, 28 October 1929, Ninety-Nines scrapbook Vol. I, Ninety-Nines Museum, Oklahoma City.

58. Ruth Nichols received the second, #326, on 22 July. Ruth Nichols also received the second mechanic's license; even though hers was #401, it was issued after Phoebe's. They were both issued their licenses on the same day. Because Phoebe had obtained a Letter of Authority authorizing her to operate as a mechanic pending official examination, dated nearly three weeks earlier, hers was officially the first woman's mechanic's license. Copy of letter to Ruth Nichols from Bruce Jones, Aeronautics Branch of the Department of Commerce, in response to her inquiry as to which woman had the first mechanic's license issued; letter in Phoebe Omlie file, Ninety-Nines Museum.

59. The race was variously referred to as the National Air Tour, the Air Olympics, the Caravan of the Sky, the Ford Reliability Air Tour, and other titles. The official title was The National Air Tour for the Edsel B. Ford Reliability Trophy. The most comprehensive source on the tours is Lesley Forden, *The Ford Air Tours, 1925–1931* (New Brighton, MN: Aviation Foundation of America, 2003).

60. Des Moines, for example, built a new field after being passed over by the 1925 air tour, and Tulsa chose the arrival of the tour in 1928 to dedicate its new airport. Forden, *Ford Air Tours*, 24, 27; *Tulsa Tribune*, 4 July 1928.

61. Competition for the Edsel Ford trophy, a three-foot-tall structure of gold and silver that was said to have cost $7,000, depended upon the pilot's ability to keep to a planned 80 miles-an-hour schedule. The air tours later adopted a more complicated scoring system based upon landing and takeoff times ("stick and unstick") and the greatest payload per horsepower in the shortest time. Forden, *Ford Air Tours*, 2–5, 157–158; Official rules booklet, Commercial Airplane Reliability Tour Collection, Benson Ford Research Center, Dearborn, Michigan.

62. Forden, *Ford Air Tours*, 25–47.

63. Ibid., 42–61; *Commercial Appeal*, 8 July 1927.

64. The official report indicated that the plane went into a power spin at 800 feet, insufficient altitude to recover. Cause was blamed on "material and personnel." Senate Doc. 319, Department of Commerce, 17 February 1931, 18.

65. Phoebe detailed her injuries in a letter to Louise Thaden, 6 December 1973, Omlie Collection. She later told the *Washington Times Herald* that the accident had "completely scalped her." 24 February 1948. See also Earhart, *The Fun of It*, 175–176.

66. Annotated outline for *The Omlie Story*.

67. Lindbergh's tour was sponsored by the Daniel Guggenheim Fund for the Promotion of Aeronautics, who paid Lindbergh $50,000 for the trip plus $18,721 in expenses. In order to demonstrate that planes could perform on schedule, Lindbergh arranged to arrive at each stop at precisely 2 PM. The tour covered 22,350 miles, visited each of the 48 states, with 82 stops and 68 overnight stops. Lindbergh rode in 1,285 miles of parades, attended 69 official dinners, delivered 147 speeches, and dropped 192 messages of regret to cities in which he did not stop. Robert Wohl estimates that 30 million people turned out to see Lindbergh on the tour, one out of every four Americans. The entire tour is described, accompanied by great photographs by Lt. Donald E. Keyhoe, "Seeing America with Lindbergh," *National Geographic*, January 1928, 1–46. Wohl, *The Spectacle of Flight*, 37–41.

68. *Commercial Appeal*, 3 October 1927.

69. Ibid., 4 October 1927.

70. Ibid.

71. Ibid.

72. The sum of 100,000 might have been a bit of an exaggeration, as that would have been about half of Memphis's total population. *Commercial Appeal*, 4 October 1927.

73. Ibid.

74. Crump had become convinced, at least in part by Vernon's lobbying, that Memphis needed a municipal airport. Watkins Overton, a descendant of one of Memphis' founders, Judge John Overton, was a member of the inner circle of the Crump political machine and entirely comfortable with his role as Crump's proxy. G. Wayne Dowdy, *Mr. Crump Don't Like It: Machine Politics in Memphis* (Jackson: University Press of Mississippi, 2006), 53–54.

75. McDonald, "Growth of Aviation," 3.

76. Fulbright, *Aviation in Tennessee*, 22; Paul R. Coppock, "Mid-South Memoirs: Those Daring Young Aviators," *Commercial Appeal*, 19 September 1982.

77. After a friend of his was killed in a Ford flying flivver in 1928, Henry Ford stopped manufacturing the small planes. *New York Evening Sun*, 7 August 1926, as cited in Corn, *Winged Gospel*, 95.

78. Billy Sunday abandoned the tabernacle to "take up the hallelujah trail" so Don Luscombe and Clayton Folkerts "liberated" it for their purposes. John W. Underwood, *Of Monocoupes and Men: The Don Luscombe, Clayton Folkerts Story* (Glendale, CA: Heritage Press, 1973), 4–8; annotated outline for *The Omlie Story*.

79. By contrast, restored Monocoupes now sell for about $150,000 up to $225,000; see

for example, Pietsch Aircraft Sales on the web: pietschaircraft.com. Underwood, *Monocoupes and Men*, 7. Advertisement in *Moline—The Quad City Airport*, circa 1927, Quad Cities Airport archives.

80. Velie's mother was John Deere's daughter.
81. Underwood, *Monocoupes and Men*, 8–11.
82. Altogether 350 Velie Monocoupes were built between 1927 and 1931. Underwood, *Monocoupes and Men*, 11, 14.

Chapter 3

1. In the 1930s, airplane manufacturers often hired female salespeople to demonstrate that flying was easy and safe. Phoebe was one of the earliest women to take on this role. See Corn, *The Winged Gospel*, 76–77. "Ambassadoress" used in promotional ad copy for Velie Monocoupe, Quad Cities Airport archives.
2. Promotional ad copy, Quad Cities.
3. Hours listed in *Memphis Press-Scimitar*, 2 July 1928; *Velie Long Life* pamphlet, Quad Cities.
4. Official rules booklet, Commercial Airplane Reliability Tour Collection, Ford Research Center.
5. Forden, *Ford Air Tours*, 63–65.
6. Scharlau, *Phoebe*, 61; *Aero Digest*, September 1928, 82.
7. Map in Forden, *Ford Air Tours*, 66.
8. The first air navigational charts were published in June 1927, but they were "Strip Airway Maps," covering only the main air routes. Sectional charts did not arrive until the 1930s. www.avn.faa.gov.
9. Quoted in Gene Nora Jessen, *The Powder Puff Derby of 1929* (Naperville, IL: Sourcebooks, 2002), 146.
10. *Moline Dispatch*, 30 June 1928.
11. Rules indicated that the first entry registered would be first ship to take off, but this rule was apparently ignored in this instance. Official rules booklet, Commercial Airplane Reliability Tour Collection, Ford Research Center.
12. Standard instruments listed on Velie application for airworthiness certificate, Department of Commerce. Copy in Quad Cities; enameled ring described in Scharlau, *Phoebe*, 64; the ring is in the collection of the International Women's Air and Space Museum, Cleveland.
13. In all there were twenty-seven planes on the tour including the pathfinder ship and the army's twelve-passenger plane, which brought up the rear. Several other planes joined the caravan for short legs. Forden, *Ford Air Tours*, 84–85.
14. Telegram, 6 July 1928, Phoebe Omlie file, Ninety-Nines Museum.
15. *Minneapolis Morning Tribune*, 25 July 1928.
16. Crash description and analysis in Senate Doc. 319, Department of Commerce, 17 February 1931, 80.
17. *New York Times*, 10 July 1928.
18. Telegram quoted in *Memphis Press-Scimitar*, 10 July 1928.

19. *St. Paul Pioneer Press*, 10 July 1928; *Moline Dispatch*, 6 August 1928.
20. *Moline Dispatch*, 6 August 1928.
21. Underwood, *Monocoupes and Men*, 12.
22. *Ford News*, 15 August 1928.
23. *Ford News*, 16 July 1928; *Washington Post*, 1 July 1928.
24. Tour events described by Forden, *Ford Air Tours*, 63–68; photograph showing Phoebe and Estelle in the front row at MGM Studios in Forden, *Ford Air Tours*, 83.
25. *St. Paul Daily News*, 24 July 1928.
26. Scharlau, *Phoebe*, 65.
27. Forden, *Ford Air Tours*, 68.
28. *Minneapolis Morning Tribune*, 25 July 1928.
29. *Ford News*, 15 August 1928; Forden, *Ford Air Tours*, 68.
30. Forden, *Ford Air Tours*, 201; *Detroit News*, 29 July 1928.
31. She was the first woman to fly a light plane over the Great American Desert and the Rocky Mountains. Reprint from *Detroit News* in *Moline Dispatch*, 6 August 1928.
32. *Memphis Press-Scimitar*, 6 August 1928.
33. Ibid.
34. "Given up for gone, but recovered," annotated outline, *The Omlie Story*.
35. *Atlanta Constitution*, 15 October 1928; telephone interview with pilot Donis B. Hamilton, Paragould, 6 January 2009.
36. Many Monocoupes did not survive. In 2009, two Monocoupes, including a 1928 Velie Monocoupe 70 similar to *Chiggers*, were owned by Golden Age Air Museum in Bethel, Pennsylvania. One of them had been restored by a Berks County, Pennsylvania, aviation pioneer, R. Harding Breithaupt, and hung from the ceiling of his Antique Airplane Restaurant at his Dutch Colony Inn in Exeter Township. There it remained for forty years until the inn and restaurant closed in 2007 when Breithaupt donated the Monocoupe to the Golden Age Air Museum. In the spring of 2009, stunt pilot Andrew King of Virginia "portray[ed] famed female aviatrix Phoebe Omlie behind the stick of the 1928 Monocoupe 70 at the annual Flying Circus Air Show." http://readingeagle.com.
37. *Memphis Evening Appeal*, 28 February 1929. Official cause of the crash listed as a jammed aileron control wire in Senate Doc. 319, Department of Commerce, 17 February 1931, 25.
38. NR8917, *Miss Moline*, exists today as a stripped fuselage awaiting restoration in a facility outside Wichita, Kansas. It was salvaged from a farmer's field in 1987.
39. *Commercial Appeal*, 6 April 1928; announcement also in *Moline Dispatch*, 24 April 1929.
40. *Memphis Press-Scimitar*, 1 July 1929. Louise Thaden set her record in a Travel Air with "souped up" Hisso engine. Louise McPhetridge Thaden, *High, Wide and Frightened* (Fayetteville: University of Arkansas Press, 2004 [reprint of 1938]), 15–24.
41. *Memphis Press-Scimitar*, 27 May 1929.
42. Annotated outline, *The Omlie Story*; *Commercial Appeal*, 30 June 1929.
43. Coppock, *Memphis Sketches*, 126; *Commercial Appeal*, 19 June 1934.
44. Ad for Curtiss Flying Service, *Commercial Appeal*, 14 June 1929.

45. *Memphis Press-Scimitar*, 15 June 1929.

46. Michael Finger, "Flying a Steady Course," *Taking Flight* (a supplement to *Memphis* magazine), 2005, 10–11.

47. *Moline Dispatch*, 1 July 1929.

48. *New York Times*, 30 June 1929; *Commercial Appeal*, 30 June 1929.

49. *Moline Dispatch*, 1 July 1929.

50. *Commercial Appeal*, 30 June 1929.

51. *Memphis Press-Scimitar*, 1 July 1929.

52. *Moline Dispatch*, 24 July 1929.

53. Ibid., 23 July 1929. Such a discrepancy was apparently not that unusual. When Louise Thaden set her record, she carried two altimeters. One indicated 27,000 feet and the other nearly 29,000 feet, yet the official barograph recorded a maximum of 20,200 feet. Thaden, *High, Wide and Frightened*, 22–24.

54. *Moline Dispatch*, 24 July 1929.

55. Ibid., 19 July 1929.

56. Ibid. Des Moines to Hastings is roughly 300 miles, to Manhattan 300 miles, to Dodge City 550 miles, to Albany about 1,200 miles. She flew the distance in less than twelve hours. *Moline Dispatch*, 22 July 1929.

57. The other Monocoupe pilots took first, second, and third against "the Middlewest's foremost fliers" in the light plane races. *Moline Dispatch*, 22 July 1929.

58. A meet in Los Angeles in 1928, attended by an estimated 300,000 people, launched the era of the National Air Races and established their format: a ten-day program of races, exhibits, and stunts. In 1929, the races moved to the newly completed Municipal Airport at Cleveland. Over the next ten years, most of the National Air Races were hosted by Cleveland, except for 1930 in Chicago and 1933 and 1936 in Los Angeles. "The National Air Races and Aeronautical Exposition," *Aero Digest*, September 1929, 55–56, 120; Henderson Collection, Western Reserve Historical Society, Cleveland.

59. Quoted in Susan Butler, *East to the Dawn: The Life of Amelia Earhart* (Reading, MA: Addison-Wesley, 1997), 228.

60. Louise Thaden quoted in Corn, *Winged Gospel*, 75.

61. Ruth Elder quoted in *Cleveland Plain Dealer*, 18 August 1929.

62. Rasche quoted in Valerie Moolman, *Women Aloft* (Alexandria, VA: Time-Life Books, 1981), 13.

63. *New York Times*, 12 July 1929, quoted in Butler, *East to the Dawn*, 229; Earhart quote in "Flying Clubs," *Time*, 24 June 1929.

64. Lap prizes were usually between $200 and $250 each. "The complete purse involved in this race is one of the richest in the history of aviation," noted "The National Air Races and Aeronautical Exposition," *Aero Digest*, September 1929, 56; Planck, *Women with Wings*, 81.

65. There were also five other shorter races set to converge on Cleveland: the All-Ohio Derby, Rim-of-Ohio Derby, races from Philadelphia, Oakland, California, and the Canadian Derby from Toronto. "The National Air Races and Aeronautical Exposition," *Aero Digest*, September 1929, 56.

66. In 1929, the 776-foot-long Zeppelin traveled around the world at an average speed of 70 miles per hour. R. G. Grant, *Flight: The Complete History* (Washington, D.C.: Smithsonian National Air and Space Museum, 2007), 121.

67. Total pilots' licenses issued and renewed by the Department of Commerce in 1929 was 9,824. United States Department of Commerce, Aeronautics Branch, *Annual Report of the Director of Aeronautics to the Secretary of Commerce for the Fiscal Year Ended June 30, 1929* (Washington D.C.: U.S. Government Printing Office, 1929), 8; Kathleen Brooks-Pazmany, *United States Women in Aviation 1919–1929* (Washington, D.C.: Smithsonian Institution Press, 1991), 34; Komons, *Bonfires to Beacons*, 26.

68. Brooks-Pazmany, *Women in Aviation*, 38.

69. Jessen, *Powder Puff Derby*, 26.

70. Thaden, *High, Wide and Frightened*, 132.

71. Earhart, *The Fun of It*, 154.

72. Thaden held the altitude record for less than six months; Marvel Crossen topped 23,996 feet on 28 May 1929. Margaret Whitman Blair, *The Roaring 20: The First Cross-Country Air Race for Women* (Washington, D.C.: National Geographic, 2006), 29.

73. Brooks-Pazmany, *Women in Aviation*, 37–39.

74. Jessen, *Powder Puff Derby*, 44–47; Brooks-Pazmany, *Women in Aviation*, 39–44.

75. Brooks-Pazmany, *Women in Aviation*, 35.

76. Elinor Smith, *Aviatrix* (New York: Harcourt Brace Jovanovich, 1981), 100–101.

77. Phoebe's Monocoupe had a closed cockpit. So did Amelia Earhart's Vega and Edith Foltz's Eagle Rock Bullet.

78. CW class in order of takeoff: Phoebe Omlie in Warner Monocoupe; "Chubby" Keith-Miller, New Zealand, Fleet-Kinner 5; Claire Fahy, Los Angeles, Travel Air (with OX-5 engine); Thea Rasche, Germany, Gypsy Moth; Bobbie Trout, Los Angeles, Golden Eagle; Edith Folz, Portland, Oregon, Alexander Eagle Rock Bullet. *New York Times*, 19 August 1929.

79. DW class in order of takeoff: Marvel Crosson, San Diego, Travel Air; Florence "Pancho" Barnes, San Marino, Travel Air; Blanche Noyes, Cleveland, Travel Air; Louise Thaden, Pittsburgh, Travel Air; Mary Von Mach, Detroit, Travel Air; Amelia Earhart, New York, Lockheed Vega; Margaret Perry, Beverly Hills, Spartan; Ruth Nichols, Rye, New York, Rearwin Curtiss Challenger; Opal Kunz, New York, Travel Air; Neva Paris, Great Neck, New York, Curtiss Robin; Ruth Elder, Beverly Hills, Swallow; Gladys O'Donnell, Long Beach, Waco; Vera Dawn Walker, Los Angeles, Curtiss Robin. *New York Times*, 19 August 1929.

80. Rules for 1929 Women's Air Derby, Henderson Collection, Western Reserve Historical Society.

81. Thaden, *High, Wide and Frightened*, 132–133; Planck, *Women with Wings*, 81; Jessen, *Powder Puff Derby*, 25.

82. *Cleveland Plain Dealer*, 25 August 1929.

83. Jessen, *Powder Puff Derby*, 59, 66.

84. *Cleveland Plain Dealer*, 18 and 19 August 1929.

85. Rules for the 1929 Women's Air Derby, Henderson Collection.

86. Thaden, *High, Wide and Frightened*, 54.

87. Scharlau, *Phoebe*, 75.

88. Elapsed times for the various legs of the Women's Air Derby found in Herbert F. Powell, "The 1929 National Air Races Get Underway," *Aviation*, 31 August 1929, 466.

89. Jessen, *Powder Puff Derby*, 84.

90. Thaden, *High, Wide and Frightened*, 48; Jessen, *Powder Puff Derby*, 94.

91. *Cleveland Plain Dealer*, 20 August 1929.

92. Thaden, *High, Wide and Frightened*, 48.

93. Jessen, *Powder Puff Derby*, 101; Brooks-Pazmany, *Women in Aviation*, 46.

94. Jessen, *Powder Puff Derby*, 113.

95. Thaden, *High, Wide and Frightened*, 46; *Cleveland Plain Dealer*, 20 August 1929.

96. *Cleveland Plain Dealer*, 22 August 1929; Brooks-Pazmany, *Women in Aviation*, 46.

97. Thaden, "The Women's Air Derby," *Aero Digest*, October 1929, 62.

98. Jessen, *Powder Puff Derby*, 106.

99. Thaden, *High, Wide and Frightened*, 49–50.

100. Blair, *The Roaring 20*, 91.

101. Thaden, *High, Wide and Frightened*, 51.

102. *Ogden City (Utah) Standard Examiner*, 20 August 1929.

103. *Cleveland Plain Dealer*, 22 August 1929. Rasche would be plagued with dirty gas throughout the race.

104. *San Antonio Express*, 22 August 1929. Thaden thought Crosson might have succumbed to carbon monoxide poisoning, a problem with the Travel Air design with which Thaden had struggled. Before the race, Thaden had installed a four-inch pipe through which she could breathe fresh air. Thaden, *High, Wide and Frightened*, 43–45. Jessen wrote that Beech's factory crew agreed, noting that there was evidence that Crosson had vomited over the side of the plane. Jessen, *Powder Puff Derby*, 153.

105. Quoted in Blair, *The Roaring 20*, 12.

106. Thaden, *High, Wide and Frightened*, 51.

107. Earhart, *The Fun of It*, 138. In all, five people were killed in accidents associated with the 1929 National Air Races: Marvel Crosson, Thomas G. "Jack" Reid (making a solo endurance record), Edward "Red" Devereaux, Mrs. Devereaux and Edward Reiss (killed at Boston racing from Philadelphia); five others were seriously injured. "Cleveland Races and Show," *Time*, 9 September 1929.

108. Thaden, *High, Wide and Frightened*, 51; also quoted in Jessen, *Powder Puff Derby*, 129; Brooks-Pazmany, *Women in Aviation*, 46.

109. *Memphis Press-Scimitar*, 21 August 1929.

110. Ibid.

111. *Cleveland Plain Dealer*, 22 August 1929.

112. Ibid.; Louise Thaden, "The Women's Air Derby," *Aero Digest*, October 1929, 299.

113. *Cleveland Plain Dealer*, 23 August 1929.

114. Jessen, *Powder Puff Derby*, 151–152.

115. Blair, *The Roaring 20*, 85.

116. *Cleveland Plain Dealer*, 25 August 1929.

117. Blair, *The Roaring 20*, 96.

118. Ibid.
119. Jessen, *Powder Puff Derby*, 186.
120. Crowd estimate in *Cleveland Plain Dealer*, 29 August 1929. "The National Air Races and Aeronautical Exposition," *Aero Digest*, September 1929, 55–56, 120; Russell C. Johns, "Observations at the National Air Races and Exposition," *Aero Digest*, October 1929, 66–70.
121. "Cleveland Races and Show," *Time*, 9 September 1929.
122. *Cleveland Plain Dealer*, 26 August 1929.
123. Blair, *The Roaring 20*, 94–95.
124. *Cleveland Plain Dealer*, 26 August 1929.
125. Thaden, *High, Wide and Frightened*, 56.
126. Ibid., 57.
127. Photo in Brooks-Pazmany, *Women in Aviation*, 48.
128. Thaden, *High, Wide and Frightened*, 59.
129. Ibid.
130. Fourteen women finished the race 26 August; Bobbi Trout arrived the following day to also finish. Blair, *The Roaring 20*, 108.
131. Thaden won $3,600 for first place in the DW class. Official Standings of the Contestants in the 1929 National Air Races, Henderson Collection.
132. Final standings in DW class: Louise Thaden, Gladys O'Donnell, Amelia Earhart, Blanche Noyes, Ruth Elder, Neva Paris, Mary Haizlip, Opal Kunz, Mary Von Mach, and Vera Dawn Walker. Light plane finishers: Phoebe Omlie, Edith Foltz, Chubby Keith-Miller, and Thea Rasche. The remaining six in the field did not finish: Pancho Barnes (crashed), Claire Fahy (broken wires), Ruth Nichols (crashed), Margaret Perry (typhoid fever), Bobbi Trout (finished untimed), and Marvel Crosson (killed).
133. In 1929, the National Air Races adopted the "race-horse start" (all entrants starting at once) for closed course races over the previous method of starting entrants at intervals and having them race against the clock. "The National Air Races and Aeronautical Exposition," *Aero Digest*, 56.
134. John T. Nevill, "The National Air Races, Day by Day and in Summary," *Aviation*, 7 September 1929, 525.
135. *Cleveland Plain Dealer*, 28 August 1929.
136. Johns, "Observations," 68.
137. Brooks-Pazmany, *Women in Aviation*, 54.
138. Phoebe was still in braces from her crash in Paragould. Phoebe described breaking her ankle to the *Minneapolis Tribune*, 2 September 1931, and in *The Omlie Story*.
139. *Cleveland Plain Dealer*, 28 August 1929; *Moline Dispatch*, 14 September 1929; Smith, *Aviatrix*, 142.
140. Nevill, "The National Air Races," 525.
141. The trophy was delivered to the chapter of the National Aeronautic Association to which the entrant belonged, to be held for one year. The Aerol Trophy was awarded only twice for a cross-country women's derby: 1929 and 1930 when Gladys O'Donnell won it. Beginning in 1931, the trophy was awarded to the winner of the women's free-for-all closed-course race. News Release, National Air Races, August 1932, Henderson Collection.

142. Booklet, 1929 Women's Air Derby, Henderson Collection.
143. National Air Race Briefs, microfilm, Western Reserve Historical Society.
144. *Dallas Morning News*, 22 September 1929.
145. Several sources say Amelia wrote a letter to Ruth Nichols in 1927 discussing the need for a female pilots' association. Phoebe is credited in the official history of The Ninety-Nines; Lu Hollander, Gene Nora Jessen and Verna West, *The Ninety-Nines: Yesterday, Today, Tomorrow* (Paducah, KY: Turner Publishing Company, 1996), 11. Phoebe passed credit to Peggy Rex, who suggested the idea at a breakfast held at the "Hostess House" the day after the races. Letter, Phoebe to Pancho Barnes, 29 December 1968, William E. Barnes Collection (private).
146. Letter, Phoebe Omlie to Glenn Buffington, 28 December 1974, Omlie Collection.
147. Clara Trenchman, who worked for the Women's Division of the Curtiss Flying Service and edited a newsletter called *Women and Aviation*, contacted four female Curtiss demonstration pilots (Neva Paris, Frances Harrell, Fay Gillis, Margery Brown) who drafted the invitation. Brooks-Pazmany, *Women in Aviation*, 51.
148. Transcript of letter signed by Faye Gillis, Margorie [*sic*] Brown, Francess [*sic*] Harrell, and Neva Paris, posted on www.ninety-nines.org/letter.htm.
149. Hollander, Jessen, and West, *The Ninety-Nines*, 11; Kay Menges Brick, "The Ninety-Nines: A Glance Backward," 1959, posted on www.ninety-nines.org/thirty.htm. See also, Brooks-Pazmany, *Women in Aviation*, 51–52.
150. Phoebe was described as chairman of the middle-west division and member of the governing board of the Eighty Sixes, *Moline Dispatch*, 16 December 1929.
151. Hollander, Jessen, and West, *The Ninety Nines*, 11–12.

Chapter 4

1. *Minneapolis Morning Tribune*, 2 September 1931.
2. *Moline Dispatch*, 4 June 1930 and 7 July 1930; *The Omlie Story*.
3. The new plane, NR518W, powered by a 140 hp Warner engine, was considerably faster than the 110 hp NR8971, *Miss Moline*. *Moline Dispatch*, 12 August 1930; *Commercial Appeal*, 10 September 1930.
4. This iconic photograph was used for many years in various newspaper articles about Phoebe. *Moline Dispatch*, 2 August 1930.
5. *Milwaukee Sentinel*, 2 August 1930; *Moline Dispatch*, 2 August 1930.
6. A photograph of the women with an enormous arrangement of flowers in *Olean (New York) Evening Times*, 7 August 1930; *Moline Dispatch*, 31 July 1930.
7. The National Air Races returned to Cleveland in 1932 where they remained (except for 1933 and 1936 when they were held in Los Angeles, and suspended for the war between 1940 and 1946) until they were discontinued in 1949. Thomas G. Matowitz Jr., *Cleveland's National Air Races* (Charleston, SC: Arcadia Publishing, 2005), 7; *Moline Dispatch*, 12 August 1930.
8. Six women and planes entered each race. Hollander, Jessen, and West, *The Ninety-Nines*, 432–433; Planck, *Women with Wings*, 86. Course of the race reflected in 1930 Engine Log, Omlie Collection.

9. *Moline Dispatch*, 22 August 1930, 23 August 1930; Phoebe Fairgrave Omlie, "Women in the Air Races," *Aero Digest*, October 1930, 40–42.
10. *Chicago Daily Tribune*, 27 August 1930.
11. Ibid., 24 August 1930.
12. Ibid., 24 August 1930; Nancy Hopkins Tier, "All Woman's Dixie Derby—1930," Phoebe Omlie Collection, Ninety-Nines Museum.
13. *Chicago Daily Tribune*, 24 August 1930.
14. News accounts reflect Phoebe's insistence upon giving Bowman the lap money: *Moline Dispatch*, 26 August 1930; *Washington Post*, 26 August 1930; *Commercial Appeal*, 27 August 1930. Also see Letter, Phoebe Omlie to Clifford Henderson, 25 August 1973, Omlie Collection.
15. *Memphis Press-Scimitar*, 25 August 1930.
16. Gladys O'Donnell, flying a Taper Wing Waco, won the Pacific Derby and the Aerol Trophy in 1930. *Moline Dispatch*, 29 July 1930.
17. Ibid., 27 August 1930.
18. *Time*, 1 September 1930.
19. *Chicago Daily Tribune*, 27 August 1930.
20. *Memphis Evening Appeal*, 25 August 1930 and 27 August 1930.
21. *Memphis Evening Appeal*, 27 August 1930; *Moline Dispatch*, 28 August 1930; Underwood, *Of Monocoupes and Men*, 20. At a time when the national hourly wage was about 50 cents, this was big money. The purchasing power equivalent in today's money is approximately $57,200.
22. Fulbright, *Aviation in Tennessee*, 38.
23. Ibid.
24. "Air-Rail Line Spans America in 48 Hours," *Modern Mechanics*, November 1929, 167.
25. T.A.T. lost $2.75 million during its eighteen months of operation; it was rescued by a merger with Western Air Express to become TWA. Christy, *American Aviation*, 119. For details on this merger, see Gore Vidal, "Love of Flying," *New York Review of Books*, 17 January 1985.
26. Article and ad in *Commercial Appeal*, 19 October 1930; annotated outline, *The Omlie Story*.
27. A 1931 press release, folder 45, Henderson collection; *Cleveland Plain Dealer*, 30 August 1931.
28. A 1931 press release, Henderson collection.
29. Quoted by H. Glenn Buffington, "Phoebe Fairgrove [sic] Omlie: USA's First Woman Transport Pilot," *Journal of the American Aviation Historical Society* (Fall 1968): 187.
30. *Moline Dispatch*, 31 August 1931.
31. *New York Times*, 23 August 1931.
32. Phoebe's log book from 28 November 1930 through 16 July 1932, in Omlie Collection.
33. *New York Times*, 23 August 1931.
34. Phoebe quoted by Edwin M. Williams, "How Phoebe Omlie Won the 1931 Air Derby," *Southern Aviation*, April 1932, 15–16, 31.
35. *Dallas Morning News*, 25 August 1931.
36. Phoebe's race journal quoted by Scharlau in *Phoebe*, 79–80; Williams, *Southern Aviation*, 16.

37. *Dallas Morning News*, 26 August 1931.

38. Ibid.

39. Ibid., 27 August 1931.

40. Ibid., 28 August 1931.

41. Phoebe's race journal, Omlie Collection; *Cleveland Plain Dealer*, 31 August 1931.

42. R. H., "Just Between You and Me," 1 September 1931, clippings in Annetta Sands scrapbook, National Air Races collection, Western Reserve Historical Society.

43. Ibid.

44. *Dallas Morning News*, 28 August 1931.

45. Ibid., 29 August 1931.

46. Quoted in Williams, *Southern Aviation*, 31.

47. *Cleveland Plain Dealer*, 31 August 1931.

48. Ibid., 30 August 1931 and 31 August 1931.

49. Ibid., 31 August 1931.

50. Ibid.

51. Ibid.

52. Ibid., 30 August 1931.

53. *New York Times*, 1 September 1931.

54. The framed fabric is now on display at the Air Force Museum in Dayton, Ohio. Bill Meixner, "1931 National Air Races," posted at http://www.airrace.com/1931Nat.htm.

55. *Dallas Morning News*, 1 September 1931.

56. *New York Times*, 1 September 1931; *Chicago Daily Tribune*, 1 September 1931.

57. *Cleveland Plain Dealer*, 1 September 1931.

58. *New York Times*, 1 September 1931.

59. Ibid.

60. Official race results in Henderson Collection.

61. Phoebe protested the changes, but to no avail. Press release, 1931 Air Races, Henderson Collection; *Moline Dispatch*, 29 July 1930.

62. Claudia M. Oakes, *United States Women in Aviation 1930–1939* (Washington, D.C.: Smithsonian Institution, 1985), 42, 58.

63. The Cord L-29 Cabriolet convertible with rumble seat was the first production automobile with front-wheel drive. It had a mile-long hood capped with a V-shaped radiator grill. Weighing 4,500 pounds with a 137.5-inch wheelbase, the Cord was introduced in 1929, only two months before the stock market crashed. Built from 1929 to 1932, about 5,000 were produced. The Cabriolet convertible sold new in 1931 for $3,295. Only eight are known to still exist; a restored Cord was advertised at $105,000 on www.signigicantcars.com, where most of this information was found.

64. "Grandstand Observations," *Aero Digest*, October 1931, 36.

65. Official race results, National Air Races, Western Reserve Historical Society. This was an astonishing amount of money in 1931; $7,000 in 1931 had the equivalent purchasing power of $98,600 in 2010.

66. The Monocoupe company was reorganized several times during the 1930s and 1940s. The last Monocoupe rolled out of a Melbourne, Florida, plant in 1950. In all, 870 Monocoupes were built, about 155 remain, and fewer than 30 are active and flying. Underwood, *Of Monocoupes and Men*, 20–21.

67. *Commercial Appeal*, 18 September 1931.
68. Ibid., 14 June 1931.
69. Fulbright, *Aviation in Tennessee*, 38.
70. This sounds like an early version of Federal Express forty years before the company was established at Memphis in 1973. *Commercial Appeal* Sunday magazine, 11 June 1933.
71. *Commercial Appeal* Sunday magazine, 11 June 1933.
72. Phoebe listed her titles as Secretary, Director of Public Relations, Airline Traffic Representative, Test Pilot, Airplane Sales and Assistant to the President, Mid-South Airways, Inc. Personnel File, Omlie Collection.
73. *Memphis Press-Scimitar*, 3 December 1931.
74. Copy of the telegram, 12 September [1932], Omlie Collection.
75. W. B. Courtney, "Wings of the New Deal, *Collier's*, 17 February 1934, 12.
76. Komons, *Bonfires to Beacons*, 225. After she became first lady, Eleanor Roosevelt and three friends aboard a large transport plane circling over New York City played a rubber of bridge in the company of a host of reporters, who of course duly reported on the safety and novelty of air travel. Corn, *Winged Gospel*, 57.
77. *New York Times*, 19 October 1932.
78. *Commercial Appeal*, 24 October 1932; *New York Times*, 19 October 1932. The best source for information about this network of women is Susan Ware, *Beyond Suffrage: Women in the New Deal* (Cambridge, MA: Harvard University Press, 1981).
79. *New York Times*, 1 January 1933.
80. *Commercial Appeal*, 24 October 1932.
81. Fain took her seat as a delegate from Norfolk in 1924, along with Helen Timmons Henderson of Buchanan County. She served three terms and did not seek reelection in 1929. After running unsuccessfully for Congress, Fain moved to Washington, D.C., and worked in the New Deal. She helped found the U.S. Information Service and served as its first director. Encyclopedia of Virginia, www.encyclopediavirginia.org.
82. Estimates of tour mileage varied widely, from the 4,500 miles reported by the *Commercial Appeal* on the eve of the tour to 25,000 miles noted in the *Memphis Press-Scimitar*, 24 October 1932 and 21 February 1935, respectively. Many secondary sources mention the larger number. One example: Claudia M. Oakes, *Women in Aviation 1930–1939* (Washington, D.C.: Smithsonian Institution Press, 1985), 40. Phoebe wrote that she "flew over 20,000 miles often landing in cow pastures," but she may have been including her second campaign tour in 1936, *The Omlie Story*. Some later press clippings have her serving as Roosevelt's "personal pilot."
83. *Memphis Press-Scimitar*, 7 November 1932.
84. Scharlau, *Phoebe*, 84.
85. *New York Times*, 1 January 1933; Dewson wrote a similar sentiment in a letter to Phoebe, noting that "both Republican women aviatrixes came to grief." I could find no information about women fliers for Hoover. Letter, Molly Dewson to Phoebe Omlie, 22 November 1932, Molly Dewson Papers, Correspondence, Box 16, Franklin D. Roosevelt Presidential Library, Hyde Park, New York (hereinafter FDRL).
86. Letter, Sue Shelton White to Molly Dewson, 24 June 1933, Dewson Papers, FRDL.

Phoebe later wrote, "1932 campaigning for Roosevelt by air and we go broke." Annotated outline, *The Omlie Story.*

87. Ware, *Beyond Suffrage*, 45–48.

88. Letter, Molly Dewson to Phoebe Omlie, 22 November 1932, Dewson Papers FDRL.

89. Clipping from *Memphis Press-Scimitar*, n.d., Dewson Papers, FDRL.

90. Phoebe noted, "Trip to Warm Springs to ask President R. for a job. I go to Washington and have a long wait for the job, living in a hall bedroom." Annotated outline, *The Omlie Story.*

91. The Women's Air Reserve was a group of female fliers organized along military lines, whose purpose was to fly rescue missions in times of disasters. Letter, Phoebe Omlie to Pancho Barnes, 23 November 1932, copy supplied to author by Harry Friedman. WAR described in a letter from Phoebe to Eleanor Roosevelt, 5 February 1934, in which she asked the first lady to accept a position on WAR's advisory committee. ER declined. Letter and enclosure in Eleanor Roosevelt, White House Correspondence, 1933–1945, Box 599, FDRL. See also Lauren Kessler, *The Happy Bottom Riding Club: The Life and Times of Pancho Barnes* (New York: Random House, 2000), 100.

92. *Memphis Evening Appeal*, 2 February 1933.

93. Letter, Lavinia Engle to Molly Dewson, 9 June 1933, Dewson Papers, FDRL.

94. Lavinia Engle went on to say, "Recalling that she [Amelia] refused to sign a statement that she was a Democrat and expected to vote for Roosevelt or make a speech during the campaign I think that is rather hard to swallow." Letter, Lavinia Engle to Molly Dewson, 22 May 1933, Dewson Papers, FDRL.

95. Letter, Lavinia Engle to Molly Dewson, 9 June 1933, Dewson Papers, FDRL. Phoebe apparently felt that Crump had aided her bid for an aviation post, or at least she had the courtesy to thank him for his efforts on her behalf. Letter, Phoebe Omlie to "Honorable Ed. Crump," 14 March 1935, Crump Papers, Memphis Public Library.

96. Letter, Sue Shelton White to Molly Dewson, 27 September 1933, Dewson Papers, FDRL.

97. Molly Dewson, "Fifteen Women Democratic Leaders Submitted at the President's Request as the Most Valuable to Reward with Important Positions Listed According to Desirability of Appointment," with cover letter to "Dear Franklin," 21 October 1933, Dewson Papers, FDRL.

98. Komons, *Bonfires to Beacons*, 228–230. Phoebe had apparently predicted this result in a letter quoted by Scharlau: "I guess the senator's son-in-law will get the position I wanted." Scharlau, *Phoebe*, 88.

99. Note to "Eleanor" from Molly, "One ray of light. Mr Vidal saw Phoebe Omlie today— thanks to you. He was not definite but that is not significant." Molly Dewson to Eleanor Roosevelt, 30 October 1933, Official File, 300, Dewson Folder, Box 44, FDRL.

100. Job description in Department of Commerce press release, 2 September 1936, Personnel File, Omlie Collection.

Chapter 5

1. *Washington Post*, 23 November 1933. Her appointment was temporary until 16 January 1934 when it was made permanent; her pay was $5,600 per year. Certificate

of oath of office and letters reflecting temporary and permanent appointments in Personnel File, Omlie Collection.

2. D.S.O. is Distinguished Service Order, a British military decoration. Stern, "Aviation's Nursemaid," 19.

3. NACA was created by PL 271, 63rd Congress, signed 3 March 1915 by President Wilson. Deborah G. Douglas, "Three-Miles-a-Minute," in *Innovation and the Development of Flight*, ed. Roger D. Launius (College Station: Texas A&M University Press, 1999), 154–156.

4. Douglas, "Three-Miles-a-Minute," 157–158.

5. "Appointments Under Section 10, Rule II," Fifty-first annual report of the United States Civil Service Commission for the fiscal year ended June 30, 1934, Serial Set Vo. No. 9980, Session Vol. No. 68.

6. Stern, "Aviation's Nursemaid," 5.

7. Following a restructuring in 1934, the branch was renamed the Bureau of Air Commerce and the director of aeronautics became the director of air commerce. See *FAA Historical Chronology, 1926–1996*, available online at htttp://www.faa.gov/about/media/b-chron.pdf.

8. The Federal Airways System was created under the Air Commerce Act of 1926; Letter, Rex Martin, Assistant Director of Aeronautics, Department of Commerce, to G. W. Lewis, Director of Aeronautical Research for NACA, 14 December 1933, requesting Phoebe's services, National Advisory Committee for Aeronautics (NACA) file, 50–8, National Archives.

9. Letters between Phoebe Omlie and Washington-based personnel in NACA file.

10. This work was continued and extended under the Public Works Administration. See Phoebe Fairgrave Omlie, "Aviation Under the New Deal," *Democratic Digest*, April 1935, 9–10; Komons, *Bonfires to Beacons*, 236–244.

11. Letter, Phoebe to John F. Victory, Secretary to the NACA, 19 December 1933; she delivered a similar message in letter, Phoebe Omlie to Dr. George Lewis, Director of Aeronautical Research, NACA, 31 December 1933, NACA file.

12. *Democratic Digest*, April 1935, 8.

13. Letter, J. F. Victory, Secretary of NACA, to Phoebe Omlie, 18 May 1934, NACA file.

14. Letters, Phoebe Omlie to John Victory and Phoebe Omlie to George Lewis, 19 December 1933 through 18 June 1935, NACA file. After eleven months development by the bureau, a blind landing system (that is, landing by instruments only) was adopted as the standard in September 1934. See *FAA Historical Chronology, 1926–1996*.

15. *Memphis Press-Scimitar*, 12 June 1934.

16. Letter, Joseph Ames, chairman of NACA to Herbert D. Brown, government efficiency expert in the Hoover administration, 23 April 1932, spelling out the differing functions of NACA and the Aeronautics Branch, quoted by Alex Roland, *SP 4103 Model Research*, Vol. 1, ch. 6, note 34, http://history.nasa.gov/SP-4103. Amendment in *Congressional Record*, 80 (16 June 1934): 12203; cited in Tom D. Crouch, "An Airplane for Everyman," 171, 185.

17. Eugene L. Vidal, "Low-Priced Airplane," *Aviation*, February 1934, 40–41; Corn, *Winged Gospel*, 99–100.

18. Vidal, "Low-Priced Airplane," 40–41.
19. Crouch, "An Airplane for Everyman," 172.
20. "This Light Plane Business," *Aviation*, December 1935, 25; cited in Crouch, "An Airplane for Everyman," 173. See also Corn, *Winged Gospel*, 99; Courtney, "Wings of the New Deal," 49.
21. Komons, *Bonfires to Beacons*, 247.
22. Corn, *Winged Gospel*, 99.
23. Crouch, "An Airplane for Everyman," 173.
24. *Memphis Press-Scimitar*, 12 June 1934.
25. *Los Angeles Times*, 11 July 1934.
26. Undated clipping, *Washington Times-Herald*, Omlie Collection.
27. *Minneapolis Tribune*, 5 August 1934.
28. "Memorandum for Mrs. Omlie," from G. W. Lewis, Director of Aeronautical Research, NACA, 12 February 1934. A memorandum from the NACA, 7 February 1934, listed the "General program of tests to be made on experimental airplane built by Fred E. Weick and associates" including wind tunnel tests: tests for lift and drag: angles of yaw; control handling; performance tests of speed, climb, and glide; tests of stability and handling. This memo was attached to Phoebe's orders to work with both agencies, NACA file.
29. Tricycle landing gear later became standard on most of the world's aircraft. Much of the discussion that follows comes from Phoebe Omlie's essay, "How and Why I Happened to Lead the Fight for the Return of the Tri-Cycle Landing Gear for the Airplane," Omlie Collection.
30. Phoebe described her model as "more streamlined and comfortable looking than the flying model." It now hangs in the Pink Palace Museum in Memphis; "How and Why," Omlie Collection.
31. "How and Why," Omlie Collection.
32. *New York Times*, 27 May 1934.
33. Ibid., 19 October 1934.
34. Ibid., 28 August 1934; Crouch, "An Airplane for Everyman," 178–179.
35. *New York Times*, 19 October 1934.
36. Her pilot log book, dated 18 November 1930 to 15 May 1936, lists 1 hour and 5 minutes in Hammond NS73. Log book in Omlie Collection.
37. "How and Why," Omlie Collection.
38. Gore Vidal wrote about this incident in several pieces, including, "Love of Flying," *New York Review of Books*, 17 January 1985; *Point to Point Navigation* (New York: Random House, 2006), 165; and *Palimpsest: A Memoir* (New York: Random House, 1995), 13. *Pathe* newsreel film of Gore Vidal flying the Hammond is available for viewing on YouTube.
39. Smithsonian National Air and Space Museum, "Stearman-Hammond Y," http://www.nasm.si.edu/research/aero/aircraft/stear-ham.htm.
40. Mary Margaret McBride, *Washington News*, 25 May 1934.
41. *Washington Herald*, 25 November 1933. Corn dubbed this way of thinking "aerial domesticity," an emphasis on traditional womanly roles when speaking of women in the

air age, which on some level aided in domesticating the image of flying in the popular imagination. Corn, *Winged Gospel*, 81.

42. The races that year were controlled by the men-only Professional Racing Pilots' Chapter of the National Aviation Authority, which governed civil aviation. Richey's friend, Frances Marsalis, was killed in an accident at the National Women's Air Meet when her biplane crashed after being caught in the backwash of five other planes in a pylon race. *Pittsburgh Post-Gazette*, 4 August 1934; Planck, *Women with Wings*, 89.

43. Quoted in *Charleston Daily Mail*, 27 January 1935.

44. Ibid.

45. Not until 1973 did a U.S. airline hire another woman pilot. Susan Ware, *Still Missing: Amelia Earhart and the Search for Modern Feminism* (New York: W. W. Norton & Company, 1993), 76–78; Corn, *Winged Gospel*, 80; Butler, *East to the Dawn*, 313–315.

46. Helen Welshimer, *Ironwood Michigan Daily Globe*, 12 December 1935.

47. Journal cited in "Memorandum to Mrs. Franklin D. Roosevelt," 10 October 1934, in Eleanor Roosevelt, White House Correspondence, 1933–45, Box 271, FDRL.

48. Letter, Phoebe Omlie to Louise Thaden, 31 July 1973, Omlie Collection.

49. Phoebe strongly resented the Ninety-Nines' later claiming credit for the defeat of the proposed limits on women's licenses. In numerous letters, she reiterated that she broke with the organization in "1934 when they flatly refused to help in fighting the Bureau of Air Commerce whose chief of regulations was trying to limit the hours and times a woman could fly." See letters, particularly those to Louise Thaden in Omlie Collection. The Ninety-Nines continue to claim credit for getting the first female medical examiner appointed to the Department of Commerce and fighting the menstrual issue on multiple Web sites today.

50. Kessler, *The Happy Bottom Riding Club*, 103–104; Barbara Hunter Schultz, *Pancho: The Biography of Florence Lowe Barnes* (Lancaster, CA: Little Buttes Publishing Co., 1996), 118, 122.

51. "Memorandum to Mrs. Franklin D. Roosevelt," FDRL.

52. Letter, Phoebe Omlie to Louise Thaden, 31 July 1973, Omlie Collection.

53. Phoebe was ordered to interview physicians in connection with "the medical research program of the Bureau of Air Commerce" in letter, J. F. Victory to Phoebe Omlie, 22 September 1934, NACA file.

54. Letter, Phoebe Omlie to Louise Thaden, 20 July 1973. Louise's letter to Phoebe, 28 July 1973, indicates her role in the matter. She wrote that she didn't know about Phoebe's role, and had always thought that "AE and I were responsible for squelching it. Gene Vidal had told AE what that dumb medical guy was considering; she called me; we took ourselves to DCA and talked with him; then the two of us kept a 'research log' for 6 months or so together with several others we enlisted . . . not too long thereafter the thing died." Letter, Phoebe to Louise Thaden, 31 July 1973, Omlie Collection. Researchers continue to study the issue, however. A 2001 study tested twenty-four female pilots during their menstrual cycles as they performed a seventy-five-minute simulator flight. The researchers found "no significant differences in overall flight performance between the menstrual and luteal phases." Martin S. Mumenthaler et al., "Relationship between variations in estradiol and progesterone levels across the

menstrual cycle and human performance," in *Psycho-pharmacology* 155, no. 2 (May 2001).

55. There is little evidence of these. One article says she seldom saw her husband "except week-ends" and this is the Mary Margaret McBride article that describes her in cloyingly domestic terms. McBride, *Washington News*, 25 May 1934. An occasional clipping from Memphis mentions her being home for a visit; Flora Orr, writing in *Holland's, The Magazine of the South*, September 1935, noted Vernon was in Washington with Phoebe for the Christmas holidays. Gene Scharlau asserts that during these years Vernon "and Phoebe saw each other often, either by his coming to Washington or her flying down to Memphis." Scharlau, *Phoebe*, 95.

56. Quoted by Mary Margaret McBride, *Washington News*, 25 May 1934. Given the dearth of evidence, it is impossible to accurately characterize their relationship beyond this. Only one letter between the Omlies survives, Vernon to Phoebe, 18 July 1936 (probably his final letter). Addressed to Dearest Phoebe, the letter is chatty about business and friends, and signed with "Loads of love, honey." Letter, Vernon to Phoebe, 18 July 1936, Omlie Collection.

57. *Memphis Evening Appeal*, 12 April 1933.

58. Joseph Boltner, *Faulkner: A Biography* (Jackson: University Press of Mississippi, 2005), 60–67.

59. Boltner, *Faulkner*, 141.

60. The circus also sometimes featured a jumper named J. M. "Navy" Sowell. Boltner, *Faulkner*, 330–353; see also Dean Faulkner Wells, "The Man Who Walked in the Sky," *Parade*, 25 October 1981, 27.

61. Boltner, *Faulkner*, 338.

62. William Faulkner, *Pylon* (New York: Random House, 1935; Vintage Books Edition, 1987). *The Tarnished Angels*, a 1958 film starring Rock Hudson, Robert Stack, Dorothy Malone, and Jack Carson, was based on the novel *Pylon*.

63. Faulkner, *Pylon*, 42.

64. Ibid., 41.

65. Ibid., 197–200.

66. Letter, Phoebe Omlie to Roger Q. Williams, 8 February 1973, Omlie Collection.

67. Vernon quoted by Phoebe in letter to author Carvel Collins, an authority on William Faulkner's work, who had written to ask how true the characters were in *Pylon*. She did not comment in this letter upon Faulkner's portrayal of Laverne. Letter, Phoebe Omlie to Carvel Collins, 6 June 1971, Omlie Collection.

68. *Commercial Appeal*, 11 November 1935; David Dawson, "The Flying Omlies: A Barnstorming Legacy," *Memphis*, December 1980, 44–49; Boltner, *Faulkner*, 353–356.

69. Appropriations for the air-marking program reached $1,122,388. *New York Times*, 16 August 1936.

70. For one example, see *Washington Post*, 5 October 1935.

71. United States Department of Commerce, Aeronautics Branch, *Annual Report of the Director of Aeronautics to the Secretary of Commerce for the Fiscal Year Ended June 20, 1929* (Washington, D.C.: U.S. Government Printing Office, 1928), 35–36. See also Annual Reports from 1927, 19 and 1929, 58–59.

72. Earhart, *The Fun of It*, 91.

73. Phoebe describes this meeting and their joint efforts to lobby the new auditor for the WPA, Corrington Gill, by inviting him to her "country-place on the South River" to meet with aviation people. She also wrangled an invitation to the National Air Races for Gill. This lobbying was apparently successful in securing the funds for the air-marking program. See essay, "Air Marking," Omlie Collection.

74. Memo, Eugene Vidal to John S. Wynne, 25 March 1936, Omlie Collection.

75. Memo, Phoebe Omlie to Robert Lees, WPA, undated, Omlie Collection.

76. "Three Women Mark the Airways," *Democratic Digest*, November 1935, 12–13. After Harkness left the program to get married, Phoebe immediately hired Helen Richey, who had recently resigned from Central Airlines. After Dewey Noyes was killed in a plane crash, Phoebe hired Blanche Noyes to join the team. Noyes joined 13 August 1936 when the project was essentially completed and Phoebe was ready to resign. *Washington Daily News*, 13 August 1936.

77. Thaden notes she occasionally got the use of a bureau plane but they were in such disrepair that she had a series of near-disasters flying them. She relates, for example, a Stinson in which she made five forced landings in one afternoon, a Monocoupe whose windshield blew in and hit her in the face, a Curtiss-Wright Sedan whose landing gear collapsed, and another borrowed plane that blew a valve over San Francisco Bay. Thaden, *High, Wide and Frightened*, 100–104. Phoebe also had only ground transportation authorization. Letter, J. F. Victory to Phoebe Omlie, 25 November 1935, NACA file.

78. *Nashville Banner*, 1 November 1935; "Air Marking," Omlie Collection; for a detailed report on the air-marking program, see Louise Thaden, "Five Women Tackle the Nation," *N.A.A.* [National Aeronautical Association] magazine, August 1936, 14–16, 24. See also Helen Welshimer, "The Women Who Mark the Air Lanes," *EveryWeek*, 18 July 1937, 15.

79. *Newsweek*, 22 August 1936, 25.

80. *Time*, 24 August 1936, 48; *New York Times*, 16 August 1936. See also six-month report, Phoebe Omlie to J. F. Victory, 1 April 1936, NACA file.

81. *Commercial Appeal*, 9 March 1935.

82. *Washington Daily News*, 1 January 1935.

83. The National Air Races were held in Los Angeles 4–7 September 1936. Cleveland, the traditional site of the Air Races, was undergoing an airport expansion.

84. Don Dwiggins, *They Flew the Bendix Race: The History of the Competition for the Bendix Trophy* (Philadelphia: J. B. Lippincott, 1985), 60.

85. Thaden, *High, Wide and Frightened*, 109.

86. When Phoebe was home in June, they planned the fishing trip to begin with his arrival in Washington on August 11. *Memphis Press-Scimitar*, 7 August 1936; *New York Times*, 7 August 1936.

87. She wrote him again a month later to say that she had learned that the City of Memphis could request her "services in an advisory capacity on their airport work from September first until after the election" and thereby avoid her having to resign. Crump declined, saying he couldn't "figure out anything for you." She resigned

September 15. Letters, Phoebe Omlie to E. H. Crump, 27 May 1936 and 1 July 1936;
E. H. Crump to Phoebe Omlie, 8 July 1936, Crump Papers.

88. Letters to and from Molly Dewson in 1936 indicate that in the event of a reorganization in the new FDR administration and/or the expected resignation of Eugene Vidal, Phoebe should be considered for assistant secretary of commerce (the position she had tried to secure in 1933). Letters and memos in Democratic National Committee, Women's Division, folder 151, Correspondence TN Omlie 1936–1937, FDRL.

89. "How and Why," Omlie Collection.

Chapter 6

1. *New York Times*, 7 August 1936.
2. Story here recapped from numerous newspaper articles published after the crash, including those in the *New York Times*, *Washington Daily News*, *Time* (17 August 1936), *Commercial Appeal*, *Memphis Press-Scimitar*, *Syracuse (NY) Herald*, and the *Edwardsville (IL) Intelligencer.*
3. Phoebe filed a death claim against Chicago & Southern Air Lines that was settled for $5,000 a year later. *Commercial Appeal*, 15 July 1937.
4. *Memphis Press-Scimitar*, 6 August 1936; *Commercial Appeal*, 7 August 1936.
5. Foreword, *The Omlie Story.*
6. *Memphis Press-Scimitar*, 7 August 1936.
7. Longtime friend and associate, W. Percy McDonald donated a portion of his family's plot to the Omlies; Phoebe was later buried beside her husband in another McDonald plot. Crawford McDonald, interview with author, October 2006, Memphis.
8. *Memphis Press-Scimitar*, 10 August 1936; *Commercial Appeal*, 10 August 1936.
9. Dedication and Foreword, *The Omlie Story.*
10. John Faulkner had obtained his pilot's license shortly after his brothers Dean and Bill, though he did not join the Flying Faulkners. As manager of Mid-South Airways, he continued to offer flying lessons, charter work, and run the agency for Waco airplanes until his brother Bill bought a farm called Greenfield in 1938 and wanted John to run it for him. John Faulkner, *My Brother Bill: An Affectionate Reminiscence* (London: Trident Press, 1963), 176; see also Boltner, *Faulkner*, 353, 392. Copy of stock certificate, issued to Maud Falkner, 15 September 1936, Omlie Collection. After Faulkner left, Harry T. Wilson, who had worked for Omlie for many years, took over management of the company. See Lydia Spencer and Cathy Marcinko, "Father of Mid-South Aviation" *Old Shelby County Magazine*, No. 32, 2001, 5.
11. Letter, Phoebe Omlie to Louise Thaden, 12 August 1974, Omlie Collection.
12. Thaden, *High, Wide and Frightened*, 117.
13. Ibid., 119–121.
14. *Washington Post*, 1 September 1936.
15. Letter, Phoebe Omlie to George Lewis, 26 August 1936, Personnel File, Omlie Collection.
16. Letter, J. F. Victory to Phoebe Omlie, 28 August 1936, Personnel File, Omlie Collection.

17. Because of her unfamiliarity with the program, Blanche confronted some serious problems working with the WPA. In early 1937, Phoebe was obliged to return to Washington to try to save the program. She later convinced President Roosevelt to support legislation to make air marking a permanent part of the CAA. Letter, Phoebe Omlie to Louise Thaden, 31 August 1974, Omlie Collection.

18. By the end of the war, only about 3,500 of the original markers remained and Noyes's postwar responsibility (she was now employed by the CAA) was to raise money to reconstruct the markings. However, with the advent of technological developments like radio navigational beacons, air marking became much less important and eventually evolved into airport marking, painting large numbers and letters on runways. Noyes remained with the program until she retired as chief of air marking in 1972. Today, Ninety-Nines continue the tradition of airport marking. *Jefferson City (Missouri) Daily Capitol News*, 30 July 1938; Jenny T. Beatty and Ellen Nobles-Harris, "99s Then and Now: Airmarking," *International Women Pilots Magazine*, May/June 2003, 6.

19. Phoebe and Stella were close personal friends. In an article discussing the lack of domestic skills of both women—"Mrs. Omlie pays virtually no attention to her home" and "Miss Aiken [*sic*] admits that she can't boil water"—they discussed frequently dining together. Emma Perley Lincoln, *Washington Post*, 24 August 1935.

20. Susan Ware, *Partner and I: Molly Dewson, Feminism and New Deal Politics* (New Haven, CT: Yale University Press, 1987), 307.

21. "Taking to the Air," *Democratic Digest*, December 1936, 17; *Memphis Press-Scimitar*, 2 November 1936; *New York Times*, 5 September 1936.

22. *St. Paul Pioneer Press*, 3 October 1936.

23. "Taking to the Air," *Democratic Digest*, December 1936, 17.

24. *St. Paul Pioneer Press*, 3 October 1936.

25. Phoebe Omlie report to Max Cook, "Aviation Training Prospectus," Omlie Collection.

26. This ensured Blanche Noyes a permanent position in the CAA; the agreement also led to the federal Civilian Pilot Training Program modeled on the Tennessee example. Letter, Phoebe Omlie to H. Glenn Buffington, 16 October 1973; letter, Phoebe Omlie to Louise Thaden, 31 August 1974, Omlie Collection. A similar letter is referenced in Ann L. Cooper, *How High She Flies* (Arlington Heights, IL: Aviatrix Publishing, 1999), 67.

27. Exchange of letters between Molly Dewson and J. M. Johnson, Assistant Secretary of Commerce, 17 December 1936 to 23 December 1936 respectively, Democratic National Committee-Women's Division, Correspondence, Tennessee, Omlie, Mrs. Phoebe, 1936–1937, Box 151, FDRL.

28. Letter, Phoebe Omlie to Molly Dewson, 23 December 1936, FDRL.

29. Letter, Phoebe Omlie to Molly Dewson, 31 December 1936, FDRL.

30. Letter, Molly Dewson to Eleanor Roosevelt, 14 January 1937, FDRL.

31. Telegram and follow-up note in FDRL.

32. Letter, Molly Dewson to Eleanor Roosevelt, 7 April 1937, Eleanor Roosevelt Papers, Section 213, FDRL.

33. Letter, Eleanor Roosevelt to Molly Dewson, 21 April 1937, Eleanor Roosevelt, White House Correspondence, Box 1537–1539, FDRL.

34. Photo of Amelia and Phoebe in Miami before her last flight published in the *Memphis Press-Scimitar*, 11 June 1937; copy of the photo in the Omlie Collection. See Carol Ankney article in *Sturgis (Michigan) Daily Journal*, 2 July 1970; see also letters to Glenn Buffington, 28 December 1974, and to Louise Thaden, 31 August 1974, in which she describes her visit with Amelia in Karl Voelters's hangar at Miami and the photograph taken at the time, Omlie Collection. Phoebe also describes this meeting in a letter to Mardo Crane, 28 March 1974, Omlie file, Ninety-Nines Museum.

35. Tennessee General Assembly, House Bill No. 1709, Chapter No. 305, *Public Acts, 1937*, 1190–1203.

36. *Facts on Aviation for the Future Flyers of Tennessee*, booklet published by the Tennessee Bureau of Aeronautics, 1941; Curriculum for Memphis City Schools ground school, 1938; Exhibit "B," Personnel File, Omlie Collection.

37. The cost of learning to fly in 1938 as revealed in Phoebe Omlie's report: 15 hours of dual instruction at $7 per hour and 35 hours of solo guidance at $5 per hour. Total cost: $280.

38. *Nashville Tennessean*, 11 December 1938.

39. Roosevelt Letter to the National Aviation Forum, 24 January 1939, available at *The American Presidency Project*, www.Presidency.ucsb.edu.

40. Dominick A. Pisano, *To Fill the Skies with Pilots: The Civilian Pilot Training Program, 1939–1946* (Washington, D.C.: Smithsonian Institution Press, 2001), 58–59.

41. The CPTP is often referred to by historians as "the brainchild of Robert H. Hinckley." However, Hinckley acknowledged that he modeled the national program after Tennessee's in a speech at Nashville, 19 May 1942. Once the federal government launched its program, Tennessee abandoned its own program. By that time, TCPTP had given free ground school courses to more than 4,000 people and turned out 150 private pilots. See Pisano, *To Fill the Skies with Pilots*, 3, 10; Janene Leonhirth, "They also flew: Women Aviators in Tennessee, 1922–1950" (MA thesis, Middle Tennessee State University, 1990), 20. Hinckley speech cited in Personnel File, Exhibit "B," Omlie Collection.

42. "Civilian Pilot Training Program," National Museum of the United States Air Force, www.nationalmuseum.af.mil/factsheets. See also Pisano, *To Fill the Skies with Pilots*, 50–57, 76.

43. Roosevelt Executive Order #8974, issued 12 December 1941, shifted all pilot training to military purposes and converted the CPTP to the War Training Service. John R. M. Wilson, *Turbulence Aloft: The Civil Aeronautics Administration Amid Wars and Rumors of War, 1938–1953* (Washington, D.C.: U.S. Department of Transportation, Federal Aviation Administration, 1979), 102.

44. Letter, Robert Hinckley to Eleanor Roosevelt, quoted in Planck, *Women with Wings*, 150.

45. The three-member Air Safety Board was part of the CAA but operated independently. It was assigned to investigate accidents, determine their probable cause, and make recommendations for accident prevention. *FAA Historical Chronology, 1926–1996*.

46. Exchanges, dated 31 October 1939 to 4 April 1939, Presidential Personal Files, Box 3969, FDRL.
47. Exhibit "B," Personnel File, Omlie Collection.
48. Letters in White House Correspondence, Eleanor Roosevelt, Box 1564–1565, FDRL.
49. Letter, Phoebe Omlie to Eleanor Roosevelt, 15 January 1941; Letter, Eleanor Roosevelt to Jesse Jones, 23 January 1941, White House Correspondence, Eleanor Roosevelt, Box 1607, FDRL.
50. *Memphis Press-Scimitar*, 5 February 1941.
51. Letter, Phoebe Omlie to Louise Thaden, 6 December 1973, Omlie Collection.
52. *New York Times*, 9 March 1941; *Miami Herald*, 11 January 1946.
53. "Phoebe Omlie Hops Off for Defense," *Democratic Digest*, March 1941, 16.
54. *New York Times*, 9 March 1941; Exhibit "A" Personnel File, Omlie Collection.
55. *Commercial Appeal*, 28 May 1941. The Civil Pilot Training Act of 1939 contained a provision introduced by Rep. Everett Dirksen stipulating that "none of the benefits of training or programs shall be denied on account of race, creed or color." As a result, the CPTP offered instruction for African American students in five black colleges, training approximately 2,000 black pilots during the war. Pisano, *To Fill the Skies with Pilots*, 49.
56. *Jackson (Tennessee) Sun*, 1 December 1942.
57. *Washington Daily News*, 6 April 1943.
58. In November 1942, a couple months after the instructor school began in Nashville, the first class of fifty women entered training for the WAFs. *New York Times*, 18 November 1942.
59. Percy McDonald, "Aviation in Tennessee," address delivered 10 August 1944, Nashville, Personnel File, Omlie Collection. Janene Leonhirth, "Tennessee's Experiment: Women as Military Flight Instructors," *Tennessee Historical Quarterly* 51 (Fall 1992): 170–178.
60. Tennessee Aeronautics Commission, Minutes, 27 November 1942, p. 7, TAC Box 1, Folder 4, Tennessee State Archives, Nashville.
61. Col. Herbert S. Fox, "Women Take Wings," *Charm* magazine, May 1943, 57.
62. Letter, Robert Hinckley to W. Percy McDonald, 30 June 1942, quoted in Leonhirth, "They also flew," 63.
63. Letter of invitation, W. Percy McDonald, "Re: Free Flying Instructors Course for Women Pilots," 1 September 1942, Omlie Collection.
64. Jane Eads, *Asheville (North Carolina) Citizen-Times*, 13 December 1942.
65. Gene Slack, "Tennessee's Airwomen," *Flying* magazine, May 1943, 128.
66. Ibid.
67. Slack, "Tennessee's Airwomen," 46–47, 128–130; Jane Eads, *Asheville (North Carolina) Citizen-Times*, 13 December 1942.
68. Quoted by Eads, *Asheville Citizen-Times*.
69. Gene Slack, "Tennessee's Airwomen," 128.
70. An overseas cap, or garrison cap, is a foldable cap with straight sides, part of the uniform issued to military personnel.
71. TAC Minutes, 27 November 1942, 7.

72. Slack, "Tennessee's Airwomen," 128; Dorothy Swain Lewis, interview with author, 21 October 2000; Emma Jean Whittington Hall, interview with author, 9 July 2001, North Little Rock.

73. *Commercial Appeal*, 13 June 1943; Cooper, *How High She Flies*, 71.

74. Dorothy Lewis interview.

75. *Nashville Tennessean*, 11 September 1942; Emma Hall interview.

76. *Nashville Tennessean*, 30 September 1942.

77. Slack, "Tennessee's Airwomen," 130.

78. *Washington Daily News*, 6 April 1943.

79. *Atlanta Journal*, 30 May 1943.

80. *Memphis Press-Scimitar*, 31 December 1942.

81. Leonhirth, "Tennessee's Experiment," 175.

82. *Nashville Tennessean*, 4 February 1943.

83. *Washington Daily News*, 6 April 1943; Cooper, *How High She Flies*, 75.

84. *Nashville Tennessean*, 4 February 1943.

85. *Memphis Press-Scimitar*, 3 March 1943.

86. Leonhirth, "Tennessee's Experiment," 177.

87. *New York Times*, 23 March 1943, 7 June 1943.

88. Leonhirth, "Tennessee's Experiment," 177.

89. Wilson, *Turbulence Aloft*, 98–105.

90. *New York Times*, 26 September 1943, 27 April 1944, 11 June 1944. In the summer of 1944, its five-year mandate having expired, the War Training Service was closed.

91. Phoebe was demoted from a CAF-12 to a CAF-11. Personnel File, Omlie Collection.

92. Exhibit "A", Personnel File, Omlie Collection; Wilson, *Turbulence Aloft*, 247–248.

93. Wilson, *Turbulence Aloft*, 134–150.

94. Exhibit "A"; Wilson, *Turbulence Aloft*, 165.

95. Wilson, *Turbulence Aloft*, 135.

96. Ibid., 267–268.

97. The initial LWOP was from 26 May 1947 to 25 November 1947; extensions from 26 November 1947 to 24 February 1948 and 25 February 1948 to 3 May 1948. Personnel File, Omlie Collection.

98. Memo, Omlie Collection.

99. *Memphis Press-Scimitar*, 23 August 1947.

100. Letter, Phoebe Omlie to Louise Thaden, 6 December 1973, mentions an episode when a ruptured ovarian abscess required hospitalization in 1938, Omlie Collection.

101. *Memphis Press-Scimitar*, 12 September 1947, *Washington Times-Herald*, 24 February 1948. Janette Rex, also known as Mrs. Ralph K. Rex and "Peggy" Rex, was the woman who hosted the breakfast for the women pilots at the end of the 1929 Women's Derby in Cleveland and suggested the idea that became the Ninety-Nines.

102. Taylor first worked with Phoebe on the manuscript in 1942; an undated later version, labeled 3rd draft, also found in Omlie Collection.

103. She listed only the American Legion Auxiliary. Personnel File, Omlie Collection.

104. Exhibit "A," Personnel File, Omlie Collection.

105. Wilson, *Turbulence Aloft*, 271–272.

106. Personnel File, Omlie Collection; June 1951, *FAA Historical Chronology, 1926–1996*.
107. *New York Times*, 25 August 1950.
108. After months of protesting, the CAA called an all-day board hearing on 30 May 1952, at which the pilots protested that the change would be confusing and dangerous. They asked that the adoption be reopened, contending that in the face of political pressure, the CAA and the CAB (Civil Aeronautics Board) "the only Government agencies to whom civil aviation can turn for help in such matters—had sold civil aviation 'down the river.'" A week later, the CAA reversed their decision, saying they were convinced that the conversion would be "an unnecessary burden and would introduce some hazard into private and commercial air operations." Two years and three months later, on 1 October 1954, aviation in the United States officially switched from the statute mile to the nautical mile. In an apparent compromise, non-airline craft, including private pilots, would be free to choose between the two measurements. *New York Times*, 31 May 1952, 5 June 1952, 1 October 1954.
109. Personnel File, Omlie Collection.
110. *New York Times*, 31 March 1952; longer AP story in *Commercial Appeal*, 30 March 1952.

Chapter 7

1. *Memphis Press-Scimitar*, 11 April 1952.
2. Scharlau, *Phoebe*, 128.
3. *Memphis Press-Scimitar*, 7 October 1952.
4. Scharlau, *Phoebe*, 128.
5. The property was purchased from Dr. and Mrs. Kotz Allen for $22,000 cash and a mortgage of $47,625. Warranty Deed recorded in Land Deed Book A30, p. 11, Office of Chancery Clerk, Panola County, Sardis, Mississippi.
6. A handmade rug with wings and the words *Rancho Fairom* is in the collection of the Memphis Pink Palace museum.
7. Scharlau indicates Phoebe bought 10,000 head of cattle and that she invested a total of $80,000 in the property. These cannot be verified. Scharlau, *Phoebe*, 129.
8. The new owner assumed Phoebe's mortgage. Trade of property listed in Deed Book A32, p. 407, Office of Chancery Clerk, Panolo County, Sardis, and in Book 13, p. 400, Office of Chancery Clerk, Quitman County, Marks, Mississippi.
9. Property contents listed in loan application to the Bank of Lambert, 5 October 1957, reflect modest furnishings and kitchen equipment. Deed of Trust recorded in Book 78, pp. 558–560, Office of Chancery Clerk, Quitman County, Marks, Mississippi.
10. *Laurel (Mississippi) Leader-Call*, 15 November 1958.
11. Letter, Phoebe Omlie to Pancho Barnes, 29 December 1968; "Short resume," Personnel File, Omlie Collection.
12. Quit Claim Deed recorded Book 16, pp. 118–119, Office of Chancery Clerk, Quitman County, Marks, Mississippi.
13. *Memphis Press-Scimitar*, 16 May 1962; Omlie speech, "Let's Call a Spade a Shovel," in *Congressional Record*, 87th Congress, 2nd Session, 12 June 1962, Appendix A 4325–4327.

14. Ibid.

15. Her dream in retrospect seems remarkably prescient. Federal Express (FedEx), head-quartered at Memphis International Airport, began overnight delivery service in 1973. Since 1993, Memphis International has had the largest cargo operation of any airport in the world. *Memphis Press-Scimitar*, 14 February 1962.

16. E-mail exchange with Pat Thaden Webb, 28 November 2007, 14 May 2010, 9 June 2010.

17. What follows is the result of information extracted from news clippings and letters found in the Glenn Buffington Collection at the Ninety-Nines Museum (Buffington was a journalist who wrote frequently about women in aviation, and who during the 1960s and 1970s endeavored to contact Phoebe about various pieces he was writing), from letters found in the Omlie Collection, and the summary by Scharlau in *Phoebe*.

18. "Between You and Me by Mary E.," *St. Paul Pioneer Press*, 10 July 1967.

19. Ibid., 24 July 1967.

20. Amendment text found in *The Silent Majority Speaks Out*, Omlie Collection.

21. *St. Paul Pioneer Press*, 24 July 1967.

22. Letter, Phoebe Omlie to Everett Dirksen, 27 May 1967, and Dirksen reply, 13 June 1967, originals in Dirksen Center, Pekin, Illinois, reproduced in Scharlau, *Phoebe*, 139–140.

23. "Federal Education Programs," *Congress and the Nation*, Vol. II, 1965–1968 (Washington, D.C.: Congressional Quarterly, 1969), 709–713.

24. "About the Author," *The Silent Majority Speaks Out*, Omlie Collection.

25. One example is letter, Phoebe Omlie to Mrs. Martha Mitchell (wife of the attorney general), 26 April 1971, Omlie Collection.

26. Letter, Phoebe Omlie to Donald F. Graff, 19 November 1969 and Phoebe Omlie to Don Phillips, 1 November 1969, Omlie Collection.

27. Letter, Phoebe Omlie to Glenn Buffington, 24 February 1968; Letter, Lillian Fields to Glenn Buffington, 8 September 1968, Buffington Collection.

28. Scharlau, *Phoebe*, 137–138.

29. Letter, Percy McDonald to Glenn Buffington, 2 May 1969, Buffington Collection.

30. Phoebe worked from March until May for Ruth Hoffner in Chicago. Copy of ad and records of employment in Omlie Collection.

31. Letter, Phoebe Omlie to Glenn Buffington, 4 February 1970, Buffington Collection.

32. Letter, Glenn Buffington to Glenn Messer, 17 February 1970, Buffington Collection.

33. *Memphis Press-Scimitar*, 14 January 1970.

34. Letter, Phoebe Omlie to Louise Thaden, 9 February 1970, Omlie Collection.

35. Letter, Phoebe Omlie to Glenn Buffington, 4 February 1970, Buffington Collection.

36. Foreword, *The Silent Majority Speaks Out*, unpublished manuscript in Omlie Collection.

37. Introductory, *The Silent Majority Speaks Out*.

38. Ibid., 7.

39. Ibid., 28.

40. *The Silent Majority Speaks Out*, appendix.

41. "Rough estimates of cost of production" for *The Silent Majority Speaks Out*.

42. Example, Phoebe Omlie to Alan McConnell & Son, Inc., 10 March 1973; others in Omlie Collection.
43. Letter, Donald Graff to Phoebe Omlie, 19 November 1969, Omlie Collection.
44. See "To Publish and Distribute the Book *The Silent Majority Speaks Out*," Omlie Collection.
45. Phoebe often saved carbon copies of her letters clipped to their responses, Omlie Collection.
46. Letter, Phoebe Omlie to Louise Thaden, 26 May 1972, Omlie Collection.
47. Letter, Philip Wendell to Phoebe Omlie, 4 October 1970, Omlie Collection.
48. Letter, Philip Wendell to Glenn Buffington, 23 November 1970, Buffington Collection.
49. Wendell died in 1972. In a letter to his widow, Phoebe complained that when she and Phil disagreed, "he always checked with someone else, but I lived it." Letter, Phoebe Omlie to Margaret Wendell, 18 May 1972.
50. Letter, Robert McComb to Bobbi Trout, 17 February 1979, Buffington Collection.
51. Letter, Phoebe Omlie to Pancho Barnes, Christmas 1972, William E. Barnes Collection (private collection shared by Barbara Schultz).
52. Receipts in Omlie Collection.
53. Letter, Louise Thaden to Phoebe Omlie, 2 September 1970, Omlie Collection.
54. Text of the Liberty Amendment, first proposed in the immediate postwar period, is on the Web site www.libertyamendment.com.
55. Letter, Phoebe Omlie to Louise Thaden, 20 January 1974, Omlie Collection.
56. Letter, Phoebe Omlie to Louise Thaden, 8 September 1973. See also letter to Indiana speaker Kermit O. Burrows, 18 May 1974; letter to White House protesting a government employee campaigning for the ERA in violation of the Hatch Act, 12 June 1974. All letters in Omlie Collection.
57. Letter, Phoebe Omlie to Margaret Wendell, 18 May 1972; Letter, Phoebe Omlie to Karl Voelter, 29 December 1970, Omlie Collection.
58. See literature and letters in Omlie Collection.
59. Letter, Phoebe Omlie to Louise Thaden, 31 August 1974, Omlie Collection.
60. Her monthly income was $184 ($93 from Social Security and $91 from a veterans' widows pension) or $2,208 a year. Minimum wage in 1975 was $2.10 an hour, or roughly $4,350 per year.
61. One example was an exchange with Faulkner author Carvel Collins in 1971 asking him to try to recover a box of files and photographs she left with a friend in Memphis since deceased. He managed to recover some of the files, but no photographs were among them. Letters between Phoebe Omlie and Carvel Collins, 13 April 1971, 26 May 1971, Omlie Collection.
62. Many letters on this issue are in the Omlie Collection.
63. Letters, Phoebe Omlie to Glenn Buffington, 19 January 1975 and 3 February 1975, Buffington Collection.
64. Letter, Louise Thaden to Glenn Buffington, 1 February 1975, private collection shared by Pat Thaden Webb.
65. Memo, Dr. Jean Woerner, "to whom it may concern regarding Mrs. Phoebe J. Omlie," 29 May 1975, Omlie Collection.

66. Letter, Phoebe Omlie to Mr. and Mrs. John Bieschke, 23 November 1974, Omlie Collection.
67. Copy of her Christmas letter, 29 December 1974, Omlie Collection.
68. Letter, Phoebe Omlie to Pancho Barnes, 1 January 1975 and 22 January 1975, William E. Barnes Collection.
69. Della May Hartley-Frazier, interview with author, 12 December 2007.
70. Letter, Jeanira Ratcliffe to Phoebe Omlie and Della May Frazier, 3 June 1975, Omlie Collection.
71. Phoebe's niece, Deloris Navrkal, recalled a "shouting match" between Phoebe and her brother at the funeral of Andrew Fairgrave, their father, in March 1956, which apparently was the last time the brother and sister ever spoke to each other. Author telephone interview with Navrkal, 5 November 2007. Power of Attorney drafted 18 June 1975; Last Will and Testament signed and notarized 25 June 1975, copies of both in Omlie Collection.
72. Agreement, 23 June 1975, Omlie Collection.
73. Memo, Dr. Woerner, "to whom it may concern," Omlie Collection.
74. Application to Pine Needle Court 31 May 1975 reflects her income, Omlie Collection; Hartley-Frazier interview with author, 12 December 2007.
75. Letter, Louise Thaden to Glenn Buffington, 6 July 1975, private collection shared by Pat Thaden Webb.
76. Indiana Death Certificate, 17 July 1975.
77. The Memphis chapter of the Ninety-Nines assumed the cost for the minister and for her grave marker, according to Fern Mann, then treasurer of the chapter. Phoebe's bankbook, bills, and invoices for the funeral arrangements in Omlie Collection.
78. Hartley-Frazier interview.
79. Author of this piece is identified by Scharlau as Margaret Moore Post. Scharlau, *Phoebe*, 114; obituary in *Indianapolis News*, 23 July 1975.

Epilogue

1. *Memphis Press-Scimitar*, 30 September 1975.
2. Following an interview with the author in 2004, James Kacarides shared copies of all correspondence concerning the airport and tower naming activities, herein referred to as Kacarides Collection, in author's possession.
3. Baker allegedly convinced the city of Millington to donate the property for the airport. See letters to the editor, *Memphis Press-Scimitar*, 3 April 1970, 10 April 1970.
4. Letter, James Kacarides to Airport Authority, 13 April 1970; *Memphis Press-Scimitar*, 5 May 1981.
5. Letter, W. M. Fletcher for the Airport Authority to James Kacarides, 16 February 1981, Kacarides Collection. This small room, containing clippings and trophies, has since been edited down to a poorly lit window hidden behind the stairs.
6. *Memphis Press-Scimitar*, 28 October 1980. Rumors of alcoholism wafted around Phoebe from time to time. Her erstwhile biographer, Gene Scharlau, tried her best to track them down through interviews with Phoebe's friends and colleagues. Friend

Elaine McClure believed Phoebe had started drinking "Coca-cola highballs" to ease the pain from her various ankle injuries. McClure discounted the rumors of alcoholism, saying that Phoebe "didn't have enough money to drink on," since she could only afford one meal a day. Scharlau contacted Dr. Jean Woerner, who signed Phoebe's death certificate, about the issue. Woerner replied that Phoebe had died of lung cancer, and "acute alcoholism had nothing whatsoever to do with her demise." Scharlau interview with Elaine McClure, 1982, IWASM; Copy of death certificate with attached letter from Dr. Woerner in Ninety-Nines Museum.

7. Letter, James Kacarides to the editor, *Memphis Press-Scimitar*, 1 November 1980.

8. Ibid., 9 December 1980.

9. Letter, Carolyn Sullivan to the editor, *Memphis Press-Scimitar*, 16 December 1980.

10. *Commercial Appeal*, 19 December 1980.

11. Letter, Jack K. Barker of the FAA to Thomas L. Campbell, secretary Memphis-Shelby County Airport Authority, 10 February 1981, Kacarides Collection.

12. Letter, James Kacarides to W. M. Fletcher, 20 February 1981, Kacarides Collection.

13. *Memphis Press-Scimitar*, 5 May 1981; copies of letters in Kacarides Collection.

14. John M. Fowler, General Counsel for the U.S. Department of Transportation to Rep. James J. Howard, Chairman Committee on Public Works and Transportation, U.S. House of Representatives, 8 March 1982, Kacarides Collection.

15. *Memphis Press-Scimitar*, 8 June 1982.

16. S.896 introduction with accompanying remarks in *Congressional Record*, 7 April 1981, S3542–3543; *Memphis Press-Scimitar*, 8 April 1981, 8 June 1982.

17. U.S. senator Howard Baker, "Washington News Update," July 1982, Kacarides Collection.

18. Letter, James Kacarides to Rep. Harold Ford, 9 May 1981, Kacarides Collection.

19. Letter, W. M. Fletcher to James Kacarides, 9 August 1982, Kacarides Collection.

20. *Memphis Press-Scimitar*, 31 August 1982.

21. Letter, James Kacarides to W. M. Fletcher, 10 November 1982, Kacarides Collection.

22. FAA southern region administrator Doug Murphy Sr.; FAA leadership developer Bob McMullen, and FAA southern region communications and public affairs manager Kathleen Bergen, conference call with author, 1 July 2010.

23. Thanks to the efforts of George T. Wilson and Pat Thaden Webb, who nominated her; the sponsorship of Wilson Air in Memphis; and Bob Minter, founder and chairman of the Tennessee Aviation Hall of Fame, Sevierville, Tennessee.

24. Letter, James T. Kacarides to the editor, *Memphis Press-Scimitar*, 1 November 1980.

Afterword

1. Following the wishes expressed in Phoebe's will, found among her papers, the sorted materials were returned to Memphis. The papers, scrapbooks, and photographs are archived in the Memphis Room of the Memphis Public Library. The three-dimensional objects now belong to the Memphis Pink Palace Museum. Items I acquired in my research have also been placed in these two repositories. Phoebe's scattered possessions, to the extent to which we could collect them, are now home in Memphis.

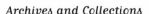

Bibliography

Archives and Collections

Benson Ford Research Center, Dearborn
Franklin D. Roosevelt Presidential Library, Hyde Park
Memphis and Shelby County Airport Authority
Memphis Public Library and Information Center
Minneapolis Public Library
Minnesota Historical Society
National Archives
Ninety-Nines Museum of Women Pilots, Oklahoma City
Pink Palace Museum, Memphis
Quad Cities Airport Archives, Davenport
Southern Museum of Flight, Birmingham
Tennessee State Library and Archives, Nashville
Western Reserve Historical Society, Cleveland

Private Collections

William E. Barnes Collection
James T. Kacarides Collection
Louise Thaden Collection

Interviews

Glenn Messer and Elaine McClure, interviews by Gene Scharlau, 1982,
International Women's Air and Space Museum
Interviews by author:
>Emma Jean Whittington Hall
>Della May Hartley-Frazier
>Deloris Navrkal
>Dorothy Swain Lewis
>Pat Thaden Webb

Secondary Sources

"Air-Rail Line Spans America in 48 Hours." *Modern Mechanics*, November 1929, 27,
165–168.
Allard, Noel E., and Gerald N. Sandvick. *Minnesota Aviation History 1857–1945*.
Chaska, MN: MAHB Publishing, 1993.
Barry, John M. *Rising Tide: The Great Mississippi Flood of 1927 and How It Changed
America*. New York: Simon & Schuster, 1997.
Beatty, Jenny T., and Ellen Nobles-Harris. "99s Then and Now: Airmarking."
International Women Pilots Magazine, May/June 2003, 6.
Blair, Margaret Whitman. *The Roaring 20: The First Cross-Country Air Race for
Women*. Washington, D.C.: National Geographic, 2006.
Bobbitt, Charles. "The North Memphis Driving Park, 1901–1905: The Passing of an
Era." *West Tennessee Historical Society Papers* (1972): 40–55.
Blotner, Joseph. *Faulkner: A Biography*. Jackson: University Press of Mississippi, 2005.
Brooks-Pazmany, Kathleen. *United States Women in Aviation 1919–1929*.
Washington, D.C.: Smithsonian Institution Press, 1991.
Buffington, H. Glenn. "The First Women's Air Derby." *American Aviation Historical
Society Journal* (Fall 1964): 222–224.
———. "Phoebe Fairgrove [*sic*] Omlie: USA's First Woman Transport Pilot."
American Aviation Historical Society Journal (Fall 1968): 186–188.
Butler, Susan. *East to the Dawn: The Life of Amelia Earhart*. Reading, MA: Addison-
Wesley, 1997.
Caldwell, Cy. "The World's Greatest Show." *Aero Digest* (October 1929): 61, 284–286.
Callen, Charles Land. "There's No Stopping a Woman with Courage Like This."
American Magazine, August 1929, 28–29, 141–144.
Christy, Joe. *American Aviation*, 2nd ed. Blue Ridge Summit, PA: TAB Books, 1994.
Congressional Quarterly. *Congress and the Nation, Vol. II, 1965–1968*. Washington,
D.C.: Congressional Quarterly Press, 1969.
Cooper, Ann L. *How High She Flies*. Arlington Heights, IL: Aviatrix Publishing,
1999.
Coppock, Helen R., and Charles W. Crawford, eds. *Paul R. Coppock's Mid South*,
Vol. 2, 1971–1975. Memphis: The Paul R. Coppock Publication Trust, 1993.

———. *Paul R. Coppock's Mid South*, Vol. 3, 1976–1978. Memphis: The Paul R. Coppock Publication Trust, 1993.

Coppock, Paul R. *Memphis Sketches*. Memphis: Friends of Memphis and Shelby County Libraries, 1976.

Corn, Joseph J. *The Winged Gospel: America's Romance with Aviation, 1900–1950*. Oxford: Oxford University Press, 1983.

Courtney, W. B. "Wings of the New Deal." *Democratic Digest*, April 1935, 9–10.

Crouch, Tom D. *Wings: A History of Aviation from Kites to the Space Age*. New York: W. W. Norton & Co., 2003.

Dawson, David. "The Flying Omlies: A Barnstorming Legacy." *Memphis*, December 1980, 43–49.

Dick, Ron, and Dan Patterson. *Aviation Century: The Early Years*. Erin, Ontario: Boston Mills Press, 2003.

———. *Aviation Century: The Golden Age*. Erin, Ontario: Boston Mills Press, 2004.

Dowdy, G. Wayne. *Mr. Crump Don't Like It: Machine Politics in Memphis*. Jackson: University Press of Mississippi, 2006.

Dwiggins, Don. *The Air Devils: The Story of Balloonists, Barnstormers, and Stunt Pilots*. Philadelphia: J. B. Lippincott Company, 1966.

Earhart, Amelia. *The Fun of It*. Chicago: Chicago Academy Publishers, 1992 [reprint of 1932].

Faulkner, John. *My Brother Bill: An Affectionate Reminiscence*. London: Trident Press, 1963.

Faulkner, William. *Pylon*. New York: Random House, 1935.

Finger, Michael. "Flying a Steady Course." *Taking Flight* (a supplement to *Memphis* magazine), 2005, 8–13.

Forden, Lesley. *The Ford Air Tours, 1925–1931*. New Brighton, MN: Aviation Foundation of America, 2003.

"For More Flying." *99er*, March 1934, 4, 9.

Fox, Col. Herbert S. "Women Take Wings." *Charm*, May 1943, 57.

Fulbright, Jim. *Aviation in Tennessee*. Goodlettsville, TN: Mid-South Publications, 1998.

Gaudiani, Claire. *The Greater Good*. New York: Times Books, 2003.

"Grandstand Observations," *Aero Digest*, October 1931, 36–40.

Grant, R. G. *Flight: The Complete History*. Washington, D.C.: Smithsonian National Air and Space Museum, 2007.

Greenwood, Jim and Maxine. *Stunt Flying in the Movies*. Blue Ridge Summit, PA: Tab Books, 1982.

Gunston, Bill. *Aviation: The First 100 Years*. Hauppauge, NY: Barron's, 2002.

Hollander, Lu, Gene Nora Jessen, and Verna West. *The Ninety-Nines: Yesterday, Today, Tomorrow*. Paducah, KY: Turner Publishing Company, 1996.

Jessen, Gene Nora. *The Powder Puff Derby of 1929*. Naperville, IL: Sourcebooks, 2002.

Johns, Russell C. "Observations at the National Air Races and Exposition." *Aero Digest*, September 1929, 55–56, 120.

Kessler, Lauren. *The Happy Bottom Riding Club: The Life and Times of Pancho Barnes.* New York: Random House, 2000.

Keyhoe, Donald E. "Seeing America with Lindbergh." *National Geographic*, January 1928, 1–46.

Komons, Nick A. *Bonfires to Beacons: Federal Civil Aviation Policy Under the Air Commerce Act, 1926–1938.* Washington, D.C.: Smithsonian Institution Press, 1989.

Larson, John W. "'He Was Mechanic Arts': Mechanic Arts High School: The Dietrich Lange Years, 1916–1939." *Ramsey County History* 41, no. 2 (Summer 2006): 4–17.

Launius, Roger D., ed. *Innovation and the Development of Flight.* College Station: Texas A&M University Press, 1999.

Leonhirth, Janene. "Tennessee's Experiment: Women as Military Flight Instructors." *Tennessee Historical Quarterly* (Fall 1992): 170–178.

———. *They also flew: Women Aviators in Tennessee, 1922–1950.* M.A. thesis, Middle Tennessee State University, 1990.

Matowitz, Jr., Thomas G. *Cleveland's National Air Races.* Charleston, SC: Arcadia Publishing, 2005.

Moolman, Valerie. *Women Aloft.* Alexandria, VA: Time-Life Books, 1981.

Mumenthaler, Martin S., et al. "Relationship between variations in estradiol and progresterone levels across the menstrual cycle and human performance." *Psycho-pharmacology* 155, no. 2 (May 2001): online.

"The National Air Races and Aeronautical Exposition." *Aero Digest*, September 1929, 55–56, 120.

Nevill, John T. "The National Air Races, Day by Day and in Summary." *Aviation*, 7 September 1929, 524–526.

Norris, John. "Park Field—World War I Pilot Training School." *West Tennessee Historical Society Papers* (1977): 59–76.

Oakes, Claudia M. *Women in Aviation 1930–1939.* Washington, D.C.: Smithsonian Institution Press, 1985.

Omlie, Phoebe Fairgrave. "Aviation Under the New Deal." *Democratic Digest*, April 1935, 9–10.

———. "Women in the Air Races." *Aero Digest*, October 1930, 40–42.

Orr, Flora G. "Phoebe Fairgrave Omlie: Special Assistant to Air Intelligence, N.A.C.A." *Holland's: The Magazine of the South*, September 1935, 32–33.

Percy, Walker A. *Lanterns on the Levee.* New York: Alfred A. Knopf, 1941.

"Phoebe Omlie Hops Off for Defense." *Democratic Digest*, March 1941, 16, 30.

Pisano, Dominick A. *To Fill the Skies with Pilots: The Civilian Pilot Training Program, 1939–1946.* Washington, D.C.: Smithsonian Institution Press, 2001.

———, ed. *The Airplane in American Culture.* Ann Arbor: University of Michigan Press, 2003.

———, "The Greatest Show Not on Earth: The Confrontations Between Utility and Entertainment in Aviation." In *The Airplane in American Culture.* Edited by Dominick Pisano. Ann Arbor: University of Michigan Press, 2003, 39–74.

Planck, Charles E. *Women with Wings.* New York: Harper & Brothers, 1942.

Powell, Herbert F. "The 1929 National Air Races Gets Underway." *Aviation,* 31 August 1929, 464–466.

Poynter, Dan. *The Parachute Manual: A Technical Treatise on Aerodynamic Decelerators.* Santa Barbara, CA: Para Publishing, 1984.

Rich, Doris L. *The Magnificent Moisants: Champions of Early Flight.* Washington, D.C.: Smithsonian Institution Press, 1998.

Scharlau, Gene Slack. *Phoebe: A Biography.* Unpublished manuscript.

Schultz, Barbara Hunter. *Pancho: The Biography of Florence Lowe Barnes.* Lancaster, CA: Little Buttes Publishing Co., 1996.

Slack, Gene. "Tennessee's Airwomen." *Flying,* May 1943, 46–47, 128–130.

Smith, Elinor. *Aviatrix.* New York: Harcourt Brace Jovanovich, 1981.

Spencer, Lydia, and Cathy Marcinko. "Father of Mid-South Aviation." *Old Shelby County Magazine,* 2001, 5.

Stern, Max. "Aviation's Nursemaid." *Today,* 23 February 1935, 5, 19.

"Taking to the Air." *Democratic Digest,* December 1936, 17, 26.

Thaden, Louise McPhetridge. *High, Wide and Frightened.* Fayetteville: University of Arkansas Press, 2004 [reprint of 1938].

———. "Five Women Tackle the Nation." *National Aeronautical Association* magazine, August 1936, 14–16, 24.

———. "The Women's Air Derby." *Aero Digest,* October 1929, 62, 299.

"This Light Plane Business." *Aviation,* December 1935, 25–27.

"Three Women Mark the Airways." *Democratic Digest,* November 1935, 12–13.

Tilly, Betty B. "Memphis and the Mississippi Valley Flood of 1927." *West Tennessee Historical Society Papers* (1970): 41–56.

Underwood, John W. *Of Monocoupes and Men: The Don Luscombe, Clayton Folkerts Story.* Glendale, CA: Heritage Press, 1973.

Van West, Carroll, ed. *Tennessee Encyclopedia of History and Culture.* Nashville: Rutledge Hill Press, 1998.

Vidal, Eugene L. "Low-Priced Airplane." *Aviation,* February 1934, 40–41.

Vidal, Gore. "Love of Flying." *New York Review of Books,* 17 January 1985, online.

———. *Palimpsest: A Memoir.* New York: Random House, 1995.

———. *Point to Point Navigation.* New York: Random House, 2006.

Ware, Susan. *Beyond Suffrage: Women in the New Deal.* Cambridge, MA: Harvard University Press, 1981.

———. *Partner and I: Molly Dewson, Feminism and New Deal Politics.* New Haven, CT: Yale University Press, 1987.

———. *Still Missing: Amelia Earhart and the Search for Modern Feminism.* New York: W. W. Norton & Company, 1993.

Wells, Dean Faulkner. "The Man Who Walked in the Sky." *Parade,* 25 October 1981, 27.

Welshimer, Helen. "The Women Who Mark the Air Lanes." *Every Week,* 18 July 1937, 15.

Williams, Edwin M. "How Phoebe Omlie Won the 1931 Air Derby." *Southern Aviation,* April 1932, 15–16.

———. "The Thrilling Experiences of a Pioneer Woman Flyer." *Southern Aviation,*
    July 1932, 14–16.
Wilson, John R. M. *Turbulence Aloft: The Civil Aeronautics Administration Amid
    Wars and Rumors of War, 1938–1953.* Washington, D.C.: U.S. Department of
    Transportation, Federal Aviation Administration, 1979.
Wohl, Robert. *A Passion for Wings: Aviation and the Western Imagination, 1908–
    1918.* New Haven, CT: Yale University Press, 1994.
———. *The Spectacle of Flight: Aviation and the Western Imagination, 1920–1950.*
    New Haven, CT: Yale University Press, 2005.
Wynne, H. Hugh. *The Motion Picture Stunt Pilots and Hollywood's Classic Aviation
    Movies.* Missoula, MT: Pictorial Histories Publishing Company, 1987.
Yellin, Emily. *A History of the Mid-South Fair.* Memphis: Guild Bindery Press, 1995.

Newspapers

Atlanta Constitution
Atlanta Journal
Asheville (North Carolina) Citizen-Times
Cairo (Illinois) Bulletin
Charleston Daily Mail
Chicago Daily Tribune
Cleveland Plain Dealer
Dallas Morning News
Des Moines (Iowa) Daily News
Des Moines (Iowa) Evening Tribune
Des Moines (Iowa) Register
Des Moines (Iowa) Sunday Capitol
Detroit News
Fairfield (Iowa) Daily Ledger-Journal
Fort Wayne (Indiana) Daily News
Fort Wayne (Indiana) Journal-Gazette
Ironwood (Michigan) Daily Globe
Jackson (Tennessee) Sun
Jefferson City (Missouri) Capitol News
Kokomo (Indiana) Daily Tribune
Lancaster (Ohio) Daily Watch
Laurel (Mississippi) Leader-Call
Los Angeles Times
Memphis Commercial Appeal
Memphis Evening Appeal
Memphis News-Scimitar
Memphis Press-Scimitar
Mexico (Missouri) Intelligencer
Milwaukee Sentinel

Minneapolis Morning Tribune
Moline (Illinois) Dispatch
Nashville Tennessean
New York Evening Sun
New York Times
Ogden City (Utah) Standard Examiner
Olean (New York) Evening Times
Oneonta (New York) Daily Star
Pittsburgh Post-Gazette
San Antonio (Texas) Express
St. Paul (Minnesota) Daily News
St. Paul (Minnesota) Dispatch
St. Paul (Minnesota) Pioneer Press
Sturgis (Michigan) Daily Journal
Tulsa Tribune
Washington News
Washington Post
Washington Times Herald
Waterloo (Iowa) Times-Tribune

Index